D0188316

Unconditional

A GUIDE TO LOVING AND SUPPORTING YOUR LGBTQ CHILD

BY

TELAINA ERIKSEN

Cover Design: Roberto Nunez
Theme and Layout: Ronchon Villaester

For permission requests, please contact the publisher at:
Mango Publishing Group
2850 Douglas Road, 3rd Floor
Coral Gables, FL 33134 USA
info@mango.bz

For special orders, quantity sales, course adoptions and
corporate sales, please email the publisher at sales@
mango.bz. For trade and wholesale sales, please contact
Ingram Publisher Services at customer.service@
ingramcontent.com or +1.800.509.4887.

Unconditional: A Guide to Loving and Supporting Your
LGBTQ Child

Library of Congress Cataloging-in-Publication has been
applied for.

ISBN: (paperback) 978-1-63353-515-2
        (ebook) 978-1-63353-516-9

Printed in the United States of America

Table of Contents

For my sister Tara and my daughter Casandra

Note

Since I began writing this book, the United States has elected Donald Trump president. Vice President-elect Mike Pence has encouraged a federal constitutional amendment banning same-gender marriage and signed a bill to jail gays in Indiana who sought marriage licenses. He wanted to divert funds from HIV prevention to conversion therapy. He opposed the repeal of Don't Ask, Don't Tell and complained about the passage of the Matthew Shepard hate crimes bill. The Southern Poverty Law Center has tracked 867 cases of hateful intimidation/harassment just in the ten days following the 2016 election, including attacks on LGBTQ people. What had been a challenging but optimistic time for LGBTQ people and their rights has become a potential future of rights and protections being stripped from our loved ones, as well as a deepening concern for our children's physical safety. I don't know what the future holds, but I do know your LGBTQ child will need your love and support more than ever in these coming years.

Foreword

If you're wanting honest-to-goodness practical advice from a parent who had to figure out how to raise and support a lesbian, gay, bisexual, transgender, queer or questioning (LGBTQ) child, then you've found it here. This book discusses all the stages of parenting an LGBTQ child from toddlerhood to adulthood, how to understand sexual orientation versus gender identity from what to do before the "coming out" to dating and marriage, and all directly from the experience and perspective of a real-life parent.

For me to fully endorse this book, I first need to explain a little about me. I've been a licensed clinical psychologist since 2008 and have worked primarily in university counseling centers and community mental health clinics in Southern California. I've provided individual, couples, family, and group therapy while specializing in youth, women's issues, people of color issues, and LGBTQ issues. And much of my passion comes from my own personal experience as an LGBTQ community advocate. I came out as bisexual in 1999, and went on to co-found three bisexual organizations in Los Angeles (Fluid UCLA, amBi - LA's bisexual social community, and the Los Angeles Bisexual Task Force), publish multiple works, attend the landmark 2013 Bisexual Community Roundtable at the White House, serve as a board member for numerous LGBTQ organizations, and teach LGBTQ-affirmative psychotherapy classes at Antioch University Los Angeles, AULA. So you could say that being an LGBTQ advocate is my second career.

In my almost two decades as a clinician and community leader, I've gotten acquainted with hundreds of clients and community members who are LGBTQ and coming out to themselves and their families. I've heard a wide range of personal stories, from the very hopeful to the very tragic. I've seen 13 year olds end up homeless and addicted to drugs because parents kicked them out for being LGBTQ. I've seen young transgender women of color becoming sex workers on the streets just to survive. And I've mourned the suicides of young bisexual adults and elders in my community. On the flip side, I've also worked with bright transgender college students who transitioned during college, kept their friends, and graduated with good grades. I've seen LGBTQ people go on to become successful doctors, lawyers, teachers, artists, and therapists. I've attended beautiful same-sex weddings of friends who had parents proudly walking them down the aisle.

What makes the difference between these sad and happy stories? It starts with the parenting. Parenting based on unconditional love, which means unconditionally loving your child *no matter what*. No matter if your child cuts off their hair or takes on a different religion than you. You don't necessarily have to throw them a party for it, but you still need to care for them and support them just as you would your other children. I've seen a lot of people save their unconditional love for romantic partners but parent their children based on conditional love. They've got it backwards. Romantic partners should *earn* your love and commitment based on agreed upon conditions. On the other hand, your children need you to stand by them no matter what. Food, shelter, safety, affection, and a feeling of belonging should never be conditional. And that's the difference between a tragedy and a success story.

And Telaina Eriksen has got it right. I got connected to Telaina through a mutual friend, Seth Fischer, MFA, freelance writer and fellow bisexual advocate. Seth and Telaina were grad school buddies at AULA, and Seth fully vouched for her, calling her the "bee's knees." AULA connects the three of us, and since social justice is a core part of AULA's mission, I know that anyone who chooses to go there would be passionate about social issues. She also coincidentally has a tremendous amount of lived experience, having three close family members who are LGBTQ. And Telaina's instincts are on-point because her parenting tips are what I would recommend as a clinician since they're based on warmth, communication, and unconditional love. Somehow she has figured it out as a mom, sister, aunt, and friend. She is also savvy on social media, which is highly timely today for millennials. And her non-sugar-coated wisdom makes her work accessible and relatable. Perhaps it's easier to take advice from another parent who had to figure it out "from scratch." Then Telaina's your person.

How should you use this book? Use it to educate yourself on basic terms, to understand what your child might be going through, to gain awareness of your emotions and your blind spots, and to learn tools for handling adversity. The book starts out with the fundamentals of "coming out" and mourning your own loss, which is where you might be right now. Chapter 2 discusses LGBTQ history and very hot topics like science and religion. Read about preteens, teens, and bullying in Chapters 3 and 4. Chapter 5 is all about how YOU, the parent, can get help for yourself. She also includes information on bisexual and transgender identities, which often get left out. She discusses how to be an ally, extracurriculars, college, and dating in the latter half of the book. And each chapter includes a handy dos and don'ts list, narratives from LGBTQ people, and recommended articles, books, and videos.

This book was enjoyable, informative, and easy to consume. I learned a lot even as an experienced therapist and advocate, and I very much look forward to using it with my clients and friends. It truly reminds me why parenting is the most difficult and insomnia-inducing job in the world, but also why it could be the most deeply rewarding and ultimately the most beneficial for society: it's about teaching people how to love. I hope you learn how to love more deeply through this book.

Take good care,

Dr. Mimi

Mimi Hoang, Ph.D.
www.drmimihoang.com

December 2016
Los Angeles, CA

Chapter 1

COMING OUT

Chances are if you're reading this book, your child has told you that they are not heterosexual, or they might be questioning their gender or their identity in some way. Or perhaps you suspect your child might be queer, and may not know how or whether you should talk to them about their gender and/or sexual orientation. The good news is, you are living in a better time to parent your LGBTQ child than at any previous time in history. People can legally marry their same-sex partners. LGBTQ people can openly serve in our country's military. In many municipalities throughout the United States, LGBTQ people can no longer be fired from their jobs just because of their gender identity or sexual orientation. LGBTQ people are in the media (Anderson Cooper, Don Lemon, Rachel Maddow) and there are positive role models of LGBTQ people in movies, television (Ellen Degeneres, LaVerne Cox, Neil Patrick Harris, Alan Cumming, and a host of others), sports (John Amaechi, Orlando Cruz, Brittney Griner), politics (Jared Polis, Mike Takano, Kate Brown), business (Tim Cook, Megan Smith), and literature (Alice Walker, David Sedaris, Rita Mae Brown, Gore Vidal). And I'm writing this book in 2016, an Olympic year, and the number of out USA Olympic athletes with inspirational stories is truly amazing.[1]

Many teens are coming out earlier and earlier, feeling safe at their middle or high schools and with their families and their friend group. Older kids (and their parents!) have access to the Internet, with its wealth of information, support, resources, and community. (Almost three-quarters of LGBTQ teens say they are more honest about themselves online than they are in the real world.)

But. But. According to research and youth surveys,[2] 40 percent of LGBTQ youth say they live in communities that are not accepting of LGBTQ people. LGBTQ youth are *still* twice as likely to be physically assaulted at school (kicked, shoved, or hit). Twenty-six percent of LGBTQ youth say their biggest problems are not being accepted by their family, being bullied at school, and fear of coming out. Ninety-two percent of LGBTQ teens say that they hear negative messages about LGBTQ people at school, on the Internet, and among their friends. In the United States, 1.6 million youth experience homelessness each year. Of that number, 40 percent of those youth identify as LGBTQ.[3]

According to *A Healthy Chicago for LGBT Youth*,[4] LGBTQ youth were more likely to report depression and depressive symptoms, suicide attempts, and self-injury. They were more likely to be underweight and vomit to lose weight. They were more likely to report risky sex behaviors, to not have had proper HIV education, and were more likely to become pregnant (I know this seems strange, but LGBTQ youth are less likely to use a birth control method if they engage in heterosexual sex). LGBTQ youth were also more likely than their heterosexual cisgender (those who identity with the gender in which they were born) counterparts to use tobacco, alcohol, and marijuana. They were also more likely to experience sexual violence and victimization. The paper's abstract concludes, "Due to the presence of these disparities at such a young age, they are likely to influence the health and well-being of LGBTQ Chicagoans throughout their lifespans." I'm not a social science researcher, but I think one could easily imagine that the data in Chicago probably is a fair reflection of the rest of the United States.

That's a lot to take in. Parenting, an enterprise already fraught with worry (breast-feeding, formula feeding, co-sleeping, sleep-training, *oh my God is it normal for them to have a fever this high with an ear infection?*, disposable diapers, cloth diapers, money concerns, education choices, extracurricular choices, friend drama, and always, no matter what the age, AM I SCREWING UP MY KID?) becomes doubly if not triply more fraught as your child's risk of mental, emotional, and physical peril increase, simply because they were born "different."

The good news is, parents can do a lot. They can't do everything. We still live in a very homophobic and intolerant world, but we can do a lot. I hope this book is a resource in helping you and your child make it through this challenging time.

The Many Different Reactions to Coming Out

Sometimes in novels, TV shows or movies, an LGBTQ child comes out to a distant parent. The distant parent stands in shock. Depending on the narrative, the distant parent hugs their child and says they love them anyway (ouch) or hits them (oh God). These are the two stories that play out the most frequently in popular culture. And like most over-used tropes, they are damaging in their simplicity, reducing real life to two not-so-good extremes. I'm not saying neither one of these things ever happen, but in addition to these two stereotypes, there are a lot of other parental reactions. Those reactions, and the consequences of those reactions, need to be discussed in a realistic (non-romanticized / non-Hollywood) way.

In many cases, your child has been thinking about coming out to you for a lot longer than you have been expecting them to come out. One of the clichés that surrounds being the parent of a gay child is that before your child comes out to you, "you must have known on some level." When my daughter Casandra came out to my husband and me shortly before her 13th birthday, I did not even suspect that she was attracted to girls. My sister is a lesbian and many of my close friends are gay. Because of my relationships with them, very early in my life I realized that sexual orientation is just one small aspect of any human being. My cluelessness about my daughter's sexual orientation wasn't denial. Like many parents of adolescents, I just didn't know what was going on in her head. Whatever stereotypes there are about gayness, my daughter doesn't fit them (some kids do and some kids don't). Casandra played with dolls. She loved *Blues Clues*. Her favorite Disney movie was *Mulan*. Casandra liked her long hair braided. She didn't care if she wore a dress or sweatpants (now jeans and a t-shirt are her favorites). She was (and is!) my beloved little girl—not my beloved-little-girl-who-might-be-gay.

The trouble with finding support (or sharing with other parents) when your child comes out is that you might inadvertently out your child to others before they are ready. Your LGBTQ child may also have already heard horrible messages about gay people from our culture and society—even from friends, the media, or perhaps from their religious community. To add further complexity to this delicate situation, your child has probably planned this talk with you for days, weeks, maybe even months or years. They've been looking for the right opportunity to discuss this and you may have been oblivious. You've been stressed about work, worried about what's for dinner, and trying to remember what time you're supposed to pick them and/or their siblings up from basketball practice. So you might very well be driving them home from soccer practice or school and your preteen or teen might turn to you and say, "Mom... I think I might be gay," or "Dad, I've been questioning my gender." And yes, you could have had your suspicions. Or you could have known for sure. Or you could have not had a clue. All of these are possibilities. None of them mean you are a bad parent. And it will still be different because it will be the first time they've vocalized this and entrusted you with this important aspect of who they are, regardless if they are nine or nineteen.

Dead silence to the coming out pronouncement is probably your child's greatest fear next to a screaming match. Even if you are totally baffled and blindsided, try to say something nonjudgmental like, "Can you tell me a little bit more about this?" or, "Okay, let's talk." Don't let this be a one-time conversation. Bring it up again when you feel more prepared and have had a chance to think about what your child has shared with you. Affirm your child with love--tell them you love them and want good things for them, regardless of their gender or the gender of their future spouse. When my daughter Casandra came out, she was young and didn't know all the words surrounding gender and sexuality. She was still working through what she felt. My husband and I told her we didn't care whether her future partner was a man or a woman. What we cared about was whether he or she loved Casandra and treated her well. I told Casandra I wanted her to have what her dad and I have—a long, good marriage full of ups and downs and personal growth and couple growth (and secretly I was also thinking grandchildren... but no pressure, Casandra!).

This may be not politically correct to say, but it *is* okay to mourn. You and your child have lost something. You've lost belonging to a social norm, and with it the rights and privileges of "normal." It really upset me at first that I would never see my daughter get married in a Catholic church. My husband and I were both raised Catholic, and our children even attended a Catholic school for a time. I watched that dream die and I had to be okay with it. I knew that sending a message of unconditional love to my daughter was even more important than that particular (and unfortunately deeply homophobic) way of expressing my religious faith. I was very worried (and still am) about Casandra's physical, psychological, and emotional safety. But just remember that with everything that is "taken away" with an LGBTQ identity, other things are given. Casandra (who is now 20) and I are close, and part of the reason for that is because we have had to face "not normal" together. Your child will see the world in a different way because they are in a minority. So yes, mourn, but then remember that the loss of normalcy offers up other gifts to you and to your child, including the loss of the sometimes toxic heteronormative (the assumption that everyone is straight and a family consists of a mother and father, etc.) expectations of our society, expectations such as how someone of a certain gender should dress or act: "the woman" being expected to do the bulk of household chores, boys not crying, etc.

Whenever anything happens that might cause our child pain or put them at risk or in harm's way, we tend to blame ourselves as parents. We will cover this in the next chapter, but recent studies have shown that being gay probably has to do with genetic protectors called epi-marks[5] and that being transgender is probably the brain structure with which a child is born. It's not something you or they can control, any more than you could have controlled their eye color or their height.

When you are responding in that series of conversations to your child coming out, please try to be as gentle as you can. Remember how much your parents' opinions and reactions mean(t) to you, especially in those younger, vulnerable years. Words that would be fine to a friend, sibling, or co-worker may be taken in a different way by your child, who will be reading every bit of your body language for clues to what you are thinking. And don't trick yourself into thinking they can't read you well. They've spent their whole lives with you. They probably know what you're going to say and do before you do. Parents can inflict a lot of damage on their LGBTQ children, or they can do a lot of good. Good is a lot easier and better for your kid, as well as for our aching, conflicted world.

Try to avoid saying, "Are you sure?" in response to whatever they are telling you. If they are talking about this, they are pretty sure. And even if they aren't sure, they don't want to be asked this question as a first response to their initiating this discussion. That doesn't mean if you say, "are you sure" or if you've already said, "are you sure?" you've scarred your child for life. Just keep the lines of communication open, and ask them what they've been thinking and what they are feeling.

If you suspect your child might be LGBTQ but they have not said anything to you yet, it is hard to know what "the right thing" to do is. Asking someone if they are gay should not be seen as a negative question, but unfortunately, sometimes shame is attached to that word, especially in the heteronormative culture in middle and high schools. Your child might have already been teased at school for being gay and they may not have told you. Male students at my son's high school frequently call the male swimmers and water polo players gay "because they wear Speedos" for practice and competition. (This reminds me of a saying that went through my high school in the 80s about guys getting pierced ears—"right's gay but left is okay.") Yes, just by putting on a Speedo or piercing your right ear, it changes your sexual preference/identity *just like that.*

But to have your parents question your identity in these younger years may be taken the wrong way; through no fault of yours, this may be seen as interrogation from a preteen or teen perspective. You know your own child best, so if you think you can ask that question and not over-question or inadvertently hurt your child, then ask. But if you're not sure, just give them space. Create opportunities to talk positively about LGBTQ people. This should be easy to do between the news, social media, and daily events. Tell stories about your friends and/or family who are LGBTQ. Talk about their challenges as well as their daily lives. Leave some quiet space in your own life (I know how challenging this is) to allow opportunity for your child to start a conversation with you if they want or need to. When they feel the time is right, your child will come to you.

We've Come a Long Way

In the struggle for the LGBTQ community to get the rights that they and their allies have fought so hard for, it has been necessary to show stories and messages that allow straight people to see and understand how discrimination affects an LGBTQ's person everyday life. For instance, the right to marry brings many everyday things that make LGBTQ people's lives easier—the default right of inheritance, the default right of making medical decisions if their spouse is incapacitated and doesn't have a power of attorney, visitation rights in intensive care, taxes, and even little things like some car companies letting your spouse drive your rental car too with no additional cost or paperwork.

The good thing is this has been very effective and these narratives are true. The downside is that easily digested stories don't always reflect the nuances and difficulties of real life. Sometimes when someone says they are bisexual, it is a "stage" on the way to realizing and/or accepting they might be gay. Sometimes it means they will be bisexual for the rest of their lives. Someone can be both transgender and gay. People can be "gay" and non-binary gender, or prefer not to identify with either gender. People can be bisexual and "choose" their partner, regardless of their partner's gender, just because they really love that particular person. I personally think that the Kinsey Scale, while old and often used in unhelpful ways ("oh? You're a four? You're *mostly* gay"), still does offer a useful way to look at sexual orientation. Some teens do get confused (questioning) because they have experienced attraction to both boys and girls. The Kinsey Scale, when not used to gather ammunition to label people, shows that all of our sexuality exists on a spectrum, and it can reassure a teen that they are not the only person on the planet who has had these seemingly conflicting thoughts. According to the Kinsey Institute website,[6] "The Kinsey Scale does not address all possible sexual identities. The Klein Sexual Orientation Grid and the Storms Scale have stepped in to further define sexual expression. The Klein Sexual Orientation Grid, developed by Fritz Klein, features seven variables and three situations in time: past, present, and ideal. The Storms Scale, developed by Michael D. Storms, plots eroticism on an X and Y axis. This allows for a much greater range of descriptions. Kinsey, Storm, and Klein are three of more than 200 scales to measure and describe sexual orientation." As Patrick Richards Fink says on his Huffington Post blog,[7] "It (The Kinsey Scale) was a valuable and useful thing when it first came out, because it was one of the first attempts to show that there are plenty of ways to be human other than strict heterosexuality." My friend who is a therapist and social worker says, "Sometimes when people are confused about their sexual orientation, I ask them about who they think about when they masturbate. That gives a clue." Another friend, who identifies as lesbian, told me, "I've enjoyed sex with men before, but I've never fallen in love with a man. Only women." Casandra jokes that she is 97 percent gay, but Misha Collins (who plays Castiel on the TV Show *Supernatural*) is her three percent straight. Identities can change, and as much as we love a neat and tidy story, there aren't too many of those in parenting, or across the scope of a single lived life.

Some LGBTQ History

To understand a little of what your child is going to face in the United Sates as someone with a nontraditional sexual orientation or gender identity, you have to understand that until 1973, the American Psychiatric Association classified homosexuality as a mental illness.[8] Gay men and lesbian women were condemned by pretty much all major religions, and many religions and sects keep up that condemnation today. The act of homosexual sex, even in your own home, was punishable by fines, 20 years in prison, or even a life sentence, depending on what state you lived in. (Except for Illinois—little known bastion of gay rights in the United States, who repealed their sodomy laws in 1962.) Despite the Supreme Court decision (Lawrence v. Texas) which struck down sodomy laws almost 14 years ago, sodomy laws are still on the books in 12 states, and in four of those states, sodomy is only legal if you aren't gay.

But we've come a long way, and as a parent of a gay child, I am forever grateful to the people who fought so hard and so long so that not only can she one day get married to her future partner (if she so chooses), but they fought for her physical, mental, and emotional safety as well.

One of the key turning points in gay rights was the Stonewall Uprising, which began on June 28, 1969. According to the PBS special *American Experience: Stonewall Uprising*[9] in the early morning, police raided the Stonewall Inn, a popular gay bar in the Greenwich Village section of New York City. These raids were not unusual in the late 1960s. (This is why June is traditionally Pride month, to honor the Stonewall riots.) New York City had the largest gay population in the United States at that time, and aggressively upheld its anti-sodomy laws. Vice squads regularly raided gay bars and baths, and they solicited and entrapped the gay men there. These vice squads arrested on average over 100 men a week. "It was a nightmare for the lesbian or gay man who was arrested and caught up in the juggernaut but it was also a nightmare for the lesbians or gay men who lived in the closet," Yale Law School professor William Eskridge says in *American Experience: Stonewall Uprising*. "This produced an enormous amount of anger within the lesbian and gay community in New York City. Eventually something was bound to blow."

The Stonewall Inn was "a dive." According to the pbs.org website describing the film, Stonewall was "operated by the Mafia, the bar served watered-down drinks without a liquor license." But it was one of the few places in New York City (and really the entire United States) where LGBTQ people could just go and hang out and be their authentic selves. Many of the people who went to Stonewall were among the most marginalized of the LGBTQ community, the "outcasts" at the time—drag queens, transgender individuals, etc.

Previous vice squad raids of Stonewall had all followed the same pattern. The police came in and arrested people; the bar closed and then reopened in a couple of hours. But on that night, the people in the bar resisted arrest, and the police quickly realized they were vastly outnumbered. An LBGTQ crowd filled the street outside of the bar and threw things at the police, shouting things like "gay power." The spontaneous uprising continued for six days.[10]

This happened when I was just over a year old. This tremendous battle for acceptance, equality, and basic human rights has been fought, inch by inch, in less than 50 years.

On June 24, 2016, President Obama designated the Stonewall Inn as a national monument.[11] "I'm designating the Stonewall National Monument as the newest addition to America's National Park System. Stonewall will be our first national monument to tell the story of the struggle for LGBTQ rights. I believe our national parks should reflect the full story of our country, the richness and diversity and uniquely American spirit that has always defined us. That we are stronger together. That out of many, we are one," the president said.

Your child could be coming out in a better world, certainly. But, without these and many other LGBTQ heroes, it would be much worse. With your love, guidance, and support, your child will take their place in this welcoming community full of diversity.

Do's and Don'ts

1) DO—make this more than one conversation. Even if you are feeling uncomfortable, you are the adult, and you need to be there for your child.

2) DO—affirm with love. Even if you have never said or done a single homophobic thing in your life, there is still a part of your child that is worried you will think less of them. If you have made jokes about "the gays" even just in fun, your child might be worried whether you will still love them. Eliminate this fear. They are still that great kid that you've been parenting all along. Let them know that.

3) DO—seek resources together. Go the library or order some books and movies online. Find age-appropriate materials and take turns reading them, or watch a documentary or movie together.

4) DO—be human. You're not perfect and neither is your kid. As long as you are making a real effort with love and respect, your child will see that, and that love and respect will get you through many a parental misstep. (And I've found that if you show your kid love and respect, a good 80 or 90 percent of the time, they will show that love and respect right back to you.)

5) DO—keep an open mind. Depending on your life circumstances, a lot is being asked of you right now. If you've been raised in a strict Christian household and you believe every word of the

Bible is word-for-word straight from God's mouth, I'm asking you to think about if it is your job to judge your child. Can you just love your kid and let your child be responsible for their own faith and beliefs? They already know what you feel and believe. Trust in that.

6) DO—talk about what age-appropriate expectations you have now. If your son is 15, has just come out as gay to you, and his friend Ryan has been spending hours up in his room with him or having sleepovers, you need to have a conversation. Maybe several conversations.

7) DON'T—"Are you sure?" your child. I don't know where we got this strange idea in America that something that is true one day will be true the next. As an example, I hated asparagus as a child. Hated it. We grew a bountiful supply in the backyard growing up, and I couldn't stand it. Now asparagus is one of my favorite foods. I love it. Your daughter may tell you she is bisexual. She may end up with a man as a partner. She may end up with a woman. These are both "true" options and possibilities. Which leads me to...

8) DON'T—judge, lecture, or assume. These can be some of our favorite things to do as parents. Listen. Ask for more information if you're not sure. Don't interrogate your child, but it's fine to say things like, "I'm not sure quite what you mean. Tell me a little more." Or, "Is there anything else you want or need to tell me?" and even, "Okay, how can I support you right now?"

9) DON'T—scream, yell, or criticize their timing. If they are coming out at a certain time, it happened for a reason. Stay calm. Use all of your mad adulting skills. Remember, they are doing the best they can right now. Just like you.

10) DON'T—take it personally. This isn't about you. It's about them. And it's going to be okay.

In Their Own Words

Tara Morse (my sister), Colorado

I was scared of my mother. My coming out was textbook how to do everything wrong. My mother, mentally ill and abusive, took it as an affirmation that she had in fact given birth to a distasteful monster, and she threatened to kill me and my girlfriend. She would appear at my softball games going to great lengths to say shitty stuff. "Your hair is so short I don't want to look at you." But sitting with rational people in the stands, they would think she was a caring parenting parent, cheering her manly daughter on. She liked the high of people applauding my great plays, and then after the game she would say, "gay slut" under her breath. A lot of it was what would people think of HER, that she gave birth to a freak? Parents' biggest mistake is making it about them, their own shit and beliefs, and not really hearing or acknowledging the huge step their child has taken. There's a moment there you can never get back. That moment is when acceptance and love is everything. Some parents can pull it off and some parents cannot. When coming out, some of the consequences could include being put out and disowned and even threatened with death (as I was). One of the pitchers on our softball team, only a sophomore in college, drove her Tercel into an oak tree after trying to come out to her parents, who were ministers.

I never really had to tell most people I was gay. It's obvious by my appearance. With no hips, large muscles, and short hair, an immediate (and correct) assumption is made. But never did I feel like I was a guy trapped in a woman's body. I've always been happy being a lesbian. Now that I'm older, I realized that my "different" manly body has served me well despite having taken a beating.

It was hard back in the 80s, living rurally, to find books and information. Thankfully there was a small bookstore in Ann Arbor; tucked away in the back behind every new age book on crystals was a shelf with sex manuals and Rita Mae Brown novels, Holly Near albums, and the comedy albums of Lea Delaria (sorry *Orange is the New Black* fans, she's been around forever).

Being okay with it personally and being free as a person is what coming out is about. Families can leave huge scars and do irreparable damage. Hopefully your family grows along with you. Your family accepting you goes a long way in your accepting yourself.

Michael Whelan, Colorado

I don't really have a "coming out to my parents" story, because I was never really "in." In kindergarten I joined the girls in chasing the boy I had a crush on, on the playground. I played with Barbies. I wanted to have long hair. My non-binary gender identity didn't leave much room for speculation, nor did the fact that I didn't try to hide it. I still didn't understand that there was something "wrong" with me.

From ages eight to fifteen my mother took me to see over a dozen therapists. But they always turned us away when they realized she just wanted them to change me.

My parents made everything into an opportunity to change me. They took away my dolls so I started to hide them like the forbidden contraband they were. They buzzed my head, wouldn't allow me to have hair longer than an inch until I was in my late teens. They always tried to pressure me into liking girls.

"She's pretty, isn't she?"

"I saw the way you were looking at her, you should go ask her out." I was nine.

They wouldn't let me have friends who were boys over, just girls. It became clear to me by the time I was fourteen that they were hoping for something to happen—like it would change me.

I think a lot of parents would be horrified if their 14-year-old son got a girl pregnant, but not mine. They would have been relieved—like it was the goal the whole time.

My mother went to a PFLAG meeting one time, but she never told me. I guess she was scared I would have thought she finally approved. I found out later, and it was whispered to me by someone else, like a dirty secret.

My dad didn't fully come around until I was in my thirties. My mom never will. Which is weird to me, because they knew who I was since I was a toddler. I never had to come out, because I was obvious and oblivious to it being something to be ashamed of. I'm grateful I never thought of being gay as something "wrong" because my parents would have only been too happy to set me "right."

When I was thirty years old my dad came out to visit me and my husband. It was the first time he had visited me—ever. He wanted to apologize and he did. I had already forgiven him years ago, for me, not for him. And now it was for him. He told me he didn't know how to handle "my problems."

I'm not a parent, though I hope to be one day, but isn't this parenting in a nutshell? Not having a clue. I think as long as you love and accept and try—you're good. But my dad back then, he didn't even try. And so many of my LGBTQ friends, their parents didn't try. People would say things like, "Your mom/dad is doing the best she/he can," but that isn't accurate. Doing the best you can requires effort.

Charlie Bondhus, New Jersey

I came out as bisexual in the late 90s. Or more accurately, I was outed by my brother—nine years older—when he found gay porn under my bed. Being the generally terrible person that he is, my brother stomped out to the yard where I was mowing the lawn, handed me the magazine (*Blue Collar Tales—Erotic Fiction*. It wasn't even real porn!), and said "Thanks for breaking my heart." I was the queer one, but it seemed my brother had claimed the role of Madame Butterfly.

When he told our parents, it set off a weird, painful weekend in which everybody kept breaking into cancer diagnosis-level tears. My sister-in-law's sister—who would later go on to marry a wealthy Boston Republican—was also visiting, so there were all these absurd attempts to conceal from her what was going on. I remember the four of us screaming and crying in the living room while she and my sister-in-law were out shopping. When we heard their car pull into the driveway, everybody started shushing everybody else. When they walked in, we were figuring out dinner plans.

Things got still more interesting the next day, when my heterosexual Catholic family decided to educate me on gay sex. My brother—who's basically a nastier version of Alex P. Keaton—trotted out the "AIDS is god's punishment" line, which had been a cliché since at least Jesse Helms. My parents provided some much-needed comic relief when my mother, in impeccable Faye Dunaway, shrieked "Do you know what gay men do? They put their weenies (yes, she said "weenies") up each others' butts!" True to form, my dad was less fiery but more awkward, staring at the floor and mumbling "So the idea of... rectal sex... appeals to you?"

At the end of the weekend, my sister-in-law's sister departed, politely feigning total ignorance of the blood tragedy that had been unfolding around her for three days, and my exhausted parents asked me if I wanted to see a psychologist. At first I thought it was because they were afraid I'd been traumatized by hearing my Dad say "rectal sex," but then I realized it was because they were, like so many other parents of LGBTQ kids, hoping a shrink would fix me. I said yes, not because I felt like I needed to figure out my sexuality, but because I knew I needed to talk to somebody who would help me deal with my family.

Since my parents were concerned that a psychologist might somehow let slip my full name and professed sexual orientation while he was in line at the deli, they made sure to get a guy whose practice was over an hour away from where we lived. They also paid him cash, since if there was a paper trail, it could come back later and damage my political career (a path I had not once expressed interest in, but hey, you never know).

The psychologist was fine. To my parents' chagrin, he supported my expressing my sexual identity. It was nice to be validated by an authority figure, but he wasn't telling me anything I didn't already know.

Despite all this, I still retreated into the closet for a few years, having convinced myself that, as much as I liked dick, I would ultimately marry a woman and be happy with that. Naturally I kept sleeping with men, but that seemed irrelevant. Like many men, I never had much trouble separating love from sex.

It took me until sophomore year of college to finally admit I was not straight, not bi, but gay. I was watching *Edge of Seventeen*, a cheesy coming-of-age flick set in the mid-'80s where a twink sings along to "Hey Mickey You're So Fine" and still manages to shock everyone when he comes out as gay. About 30 minutes in, the "Hey Mickey" twink goes to a hotel with one of his coworkers and the two share a hot, shirtless kiss before the scene fades to white. That kiss was the sexiest thing I'd ever seen. The moment I realized that, it was—"Whoa. I'm gay." No doubt.

I managed to keep it from my parents for a while, but from time to time they hinted that they knew. The kitschiest moment was when I was getting ready to meet a guy I was secretly dating and nonchalantly said, "I'm going to see Adam" and my Mom sadly said, "I wish it was Eve." All the skirting and veiling ended junior year of college, when Mom found in my room a business card for an LGBTQ youth center. There were more traumatic/humorous attempts to straighten me out, including a trip to a priest and my mother pointedly commenting on every attractive woman we passed. (She gave that up when I lisped, "Oh yes; she's SOOOO statuesque!")

It took them the rest of my college years, but they finally came around. In their way. Dad shocked me by telling me that he'd respect any boyfriend/husband I ever had as a son-in-law. Mom scandalized some of the women at church by saying she felt there was "nothing wrong" with gay men becoming priests. My (now ex) husband came to all our family gatherings and was treated well; ditto for my current partner. And even at the worst moments, I never had to worry about being disowned. It was hard, but I know I had it easier than some queer kids.

But here's the thing; on the one hand, I respect my parents' working through their limitations to reach a place of decency. But that's just it. It's decency. They don't deserve medals for learning to treat me and the person I love with the same outward respect as they treat my brother and his wife with. However, holding onto my resentment is far more damaging to me than it is to them, so I try not to do that either.

Writing as an almost 35-year-old, I think my parents and I have come to recognize that our lives and values are quite different, and it helps to keep the peace if we pretend that we fully respect each other. There is, for a variety of reasons, a considerable gulf between us—three days visiting with my parents is my max—and it's hard for me to look at their in my opinion very limited lives without feeling critical. Likewise, things they've said and the general vibe they give off tells me that they don't "get" my life and, as a result, find it suspect. I don't doubt they would turn me straight in a heartbeat if they found that proverbial magic wand. But again, that's more a function of their limitations than it is outright selfishness; they likely genuinely think that my life would be better if I was more like them.

My current therapist tells me that one of the best markers of mental health is not letting your parents' anxieties become your own. It's also important to individuate from your family. I've made a lot of progress in both areas, and even though my parents can't exactly get behind my life, I can be thankful they at least no longer try to stand in my way.

Resources

Straight Parents, Gay Children: Keeping Families Together by Robert A. Bernstein

Always My Child: A Parent's Guide to Understanding Your Gay, Lesbian, Bisexual, Transgendered, or Questioning Son or Daughter by Kevin Jennings

American Experience: Stonewall Uprising DVD—a ninety-minute history of the Stonewall uprising

Milk—Sean Penn stars as the gay-rights activist and martyr in this biopic

Notes from a Unicorn by Seth Fischer

Chapter 2

UNDERSTANDING THE HISTORY AND SCIENCE OF GENDER AND SEXUALITY

I have talked to some very confused parents, both in real life and online, about why their child is gay. Though we are living a decade+ into the 21st century, myths and stereotypes about LGBTQ people abound. And these myths have been around for a while; for instance, my grandmother told my mother the reason my sister was gay was because she had been breastfed for too long.

These anxiety-ridden parents, who I really do believe love their children and want what's best for them, are trying to understand why this has "happened" to them and to their child. In extreme cases, parents may resort to harmful conversion/reparative therapies. These therapies and camps boast that they can "turn" people straight through prayer and/or psychological "treatment" of some type. These therapies are never the answer and have been condemned by medical and mental health authorities for decades. Adolescents are particularly vulnerable to these therapies, and children who have been subjected to conversion therapies are at increased risk of anxiety, depression, substance abuse, homelessness (they would rather run away than be subjected to more conversion therapy), and suicide.[12]

Some of the parents who email me are supportive of their child, but their spouse may not be. Many times, these parents come from a deep religious tradition and they are honestly worried about their child's soul and whether their child will end up in heaven in the afterlife. Some of these emails I don't respond to—I don't see the point. If someone's belief system is so entrenched that they take every single word of the Bible as literal and holy, I don't think my lapsed Catholic's vision of the afterlife is going to be useful to them. But one email I received a couple of years ago said, "You and your daughter are going to hell." I hit reply and responded that if my daughter was going to hell just for being who she is, then I wanted to be there, too. The man responded with something like, "eternal suffering and damnation, away from the light of God for you both." I again responded that if God wanted no part of my daughter, I wanted no part of Him. (And isn't it interesting how we use such gendered words to describe a being that is supposed to be beyond time and space?)

I was a devout churchgoer, going once a week at minimum, and many times twice a week. I miss my Catholic faith. I miss knowing exactly what liturgical time of year it is. I miss singing in the choir. I miss the Eucharist. I miss the incense on Holy Days. I miss the community of people at my former church. But I also could not sit through one more homily from a certain priest about how if a person acted on their homosexual urges they weren't welcome in the Catholic Church. I couldn't read what Pope Benedict said about LGBTQ people without feeling over and over again like I had been stabbed in the stomach, knowing so many good, kind, and loving LGBTQ people—including my own sister and daughter. (The former Pope Benedict opposed same-gender marriage, wanted to ban even celibate gay priests, and repeatedly said things along the lines that gays were distorted and not natural creation.) And I was really angry at the hypocrisy of a Church that could cover up the rape of innocents for years but felt free to condemn my daughter for the very basic human need of wanting to meet a nice person and have a relationship with them.

This is a parenting book—not a theological one. So if your concern truly is for your child's eternal soul, I would start doing some research. I would talk to leaders of all different faiths. I would read books and articles and talk to other parents of LGBTQ children. I've included resources at the back of this chapter to help explore this question of faith and queerness. But the bottom line, the tough love version of this is, *you have to leave your child's relationship with God to them.* They've lived in your house. They've absorbed your teachings, values, and morals for years. It is not your place to judge them. Leave the judging to God and continue to do what is expected of you—loving and supporting your child. If you are a Christian who believes the Bible, Jesus does not once mention or condemn homosexuality. But the word "love" occurs over 200 times in the New Testament.

Sometimes a parent *says* the reason for not accepting their child's queerness is fear for their child's eternal soul. But what they really fear is that their child's queerness will humiliate them in front of their church family. They believe their LGBTQ child will reflect badly on their parenting. These parents either believe they have done something wrong to cause their child to "become" LGBTQ, or they fear their peers will believe they have done something wrong, and they will lose their friends and their standing in their church and/or community.

This visceral feeling of connection to our children— our pride when they do well and are well thought of, and our shame when they fail and we place the blame on ourselves and what we have done and haven't done—is completely normal. I believe every parent has felt some version of this in some circumstance. But it is important to recognize the feeling, feel it, and then realize (this is an ongoing realization in my case) that it isn't about me—it's about them. Our kids have quite enough of their own stuff to deal with without us forcing them to take on our issues as well. (Or as my sister Tonya used to say, "I don't have issues; I have whole subscriptions.")

I do feel for these parents. The United States is a very strange place. Women can show cleavage in low-cut dresses, and their full breasts in R-rated movies, but a woman who is breastfeeding in public should "cover herself." We are supposedly a "god-fearing" people, but our church and temple pews are pretty empty. We are supposedly a nation of forgiving Christians, but gun violence was on the rise in 2015. It can get pretty confusing living in our society, and the urge to protect our children from these extremes and raise them with the right values to contribute to the world is to be commended.

Unfortunately, we seem to have come to the point in the United States where we can't even agree on facts. I'm not sure how that happened, but we're in an age where someone will present a fact, well-documented and well-supported, and some other person will respond, "I don't believe that. It's not true." And that is it. The fact is discarded and is refused entry into someone's belief system, even for consideration. Maybe it's because we have more information at our literal fingertips than ever before. Maybe it is information overload. But here are some history and facts about how and why people are LGBTQ. If you find yourself resisting some of this history or science, ask yourself why.

There Have Been LGBTQ People Throughout History

There is a funny scene in a Thanksgiving episode of *Saturday Night Live* where a family (with all different political beliefs) sits down at the dinner table and the only thing they can agree on is Adele's song "Hello." One of the family members says something to the effect of, "There weren't any of those transgender folks back in my day." I've also heard statements like this in real life—that the United States is going downhill because many of us are reconsidering the societal construct of gender and sexual orientation.

Egyptologists discovered two men buried in a tomb (dated approximately 2400 BC) buried in the same position a husband

and wife would be buried in. Some researchers thought this meant they were brothers, or twins, but both men were very high-ranking in the society (you had to have serious dough and stature to rate a tomb), and the hieroglyphics for their professions indicated that they were manicurists, probably some of the few people who could actually touch the Pharaoh. Other hieroglyphics indicate that their names, Niankhkhnum and Khnumhotep, were joined together as one name, which was an indication of marriage.[13]

Homosexuality and bisexuality have been practiced in almost every world culture that has been researched by historians. In some times and places, homosexuality and bisexuality were fully accepted and commonplace. In other times and geographies, it was extremely prohibited and taboo.[14] Perhaps most known and most referred to is the very licentious sex lives of the ancient Greeks and Romans, but there is also historical evidence in early societies that gay people existed within even our most nomadic and ancient tribes, and far from being ostracized, they were gratefully given orphan children of their relatives and the tribe to raise.

A Hindu medical text dated around 400 BC talks about homosexuality, transgender, and intersex people.[15]

In Native American cultures, there were "two-spirit" people. These people wore the clothing and did the work of both genders. Native people believe in the existence of male-females, and female-males. Some sort of two-spirit or cross-gender people have been documented in over 155 tribes in pre-European North American. Two-spirit people were often considered special in tribes because of their unique attributes, and were the tribe's visionaries, healers, medicine people, and the nannies of orphans.[16]

A pope in the 15th century legalized sodomy in the summer months.[17]

A Virginia court in 1629 recorded the first gender ambiguity among American colonists. Thomas(ine) Hall was declared both a man and a woman so that colonists wouldn't be confused. Hall was ordered by the governor to wear both men's and women's clothing (together) each day.[18]

This is by no means even close to an exhaustive list. I'm just giving you a few examples of LGBTQ history. It is, in all seriousness, the history of the world itself.

The Science Behind "Baby, I was Born this Way."

This section will cover the science behind the LGB in LGBTQ. I will talk more about gender in the upcoming non-binary and transgender chapter.

Sometimes people are reluctant to talk about the science behind sexual orientation because they fear a dark future where gayness is "cured" by gene selection, or perhaps they think scientists are searching for a cure, or that a scientific explanation means that being gay is "not normal," a message gay people already hear quite enough. I certainly understand all these concerns, because there have been too many times in human history where there have been ethnic or religious cleansings. Societies have always preferred a certain set of traits, and the desire is strong to select for those traits, whatever they may be. So this is not just a LGBTQ concern, it is a concern of any person who has any characteristic that doesn't conform to whatever the impossible standards are of a given society. My take on the scientific research is that it is actually very reassuring to many LGBTQ people and their families. Our society is still so homophobic and unforgiving that it is a relief to just be able to know, "I was born this way. This is who I am."

The hereditary (a set of characteristics passed through families) link of LGB has been established for decades now, but scientists knew it was not a strictly genetic link, because there are identical twins who have different sexual orientations. Scientists from the National Institute for Mathematical and Biological Synthesis theorize that homosexuality seems to have an epigenetic, not a genetic link. LGB is linked to epi-marks—conduits of information that control the expression of certain genes. These epi-marks usually disappear between generations. In LGB people, the epi-marks don't disappear. Instead, they pass from father-to-daughter or mother-to-son, William Rice, a biologist at the University of California at Santa Barbara and lead author of the study, said. [19]

"There is compelling evidence that epi-marks contribute to both the similarity and dissimilarity of family members, and can therefore feasibly contribute to the observed familial inheritance of homosexuality and its low concordance between [identical] twins," Rice said in a 2012 US World and News Report article.

Rice's theory makes total sense; if homosexuality was just a genetic trait, scientists would expect the trait to become rarer, because homosexuals would probably not reproduce. But epi-marks helped the parents of the LGB children when they themselves were in the womb. Epi-marks protected the fathers of LGB children from underexposure to testosterone, and protected the mothers of LGB children from overexposure to testosterone while they were developing embryos and fetuses themselves. Rice also said that homosexual behavior is common in the animal kingdom and has been observed in black swans, penguins, sheep, and other animals.

But epi-marks aren't the whole story. Sex hormones in prenatal life also play a role. Girls born with congenital adrenal hyperplasia, which results in increased levels of male sex hormones, often report same-gender attraction as teenagers and young adults.[20] There are also cases of genetic males who, through accidents, or having been born without a penis, were subjected to sex change and raised as girls.[21] As teenagers and young adults, these men are typically attracted to girls and women. The fact that you cannot make a straight genetic male sexually attracted to another male by raising him as a female makes any "choice" or social theory of sexual orientation seem pretty unlikely.

A 2015 article in the Guardian[22] said that brain scans of gay and heterosexual people show their brains also appear to be organized in different ways. Gay men appear on average to have more female typical organization in brain pattern responses, and lesbian women are somewhat more male typical in their responses. Scans also show differences in cognition between gays and straights. Not bad or worse, just different. But these scans might also help explain why so many LGB people are talented business people, athletes, and original artists. Differences in cognition may mean differences in psychology, personality, and relationships, and difference can also mean creativity and original problem-solving, which are real assets in any society. I like to think that though things are hard for our children, they may have also received gifts along with their challenges.

Another important note from *The Guardian* article: It's good to remember that sexual orientation is not a behavior, nor is it the sex acts someone may enjoy. People have had sex with people of the same or different genders without labeling themselves, and the sex acts might still feel good or be enjoyable. Sexual orientation is a "pattern of desire," it's who you fall in love with, who you want to spend time with. It's not just who you want to have sex with.

Do's and Don'ts

1) DO—question your religious beliefs. If we are made in God's image, then God is pretty curious. Questions are not sacrilegious. They are at the heart of a loving, informed, and mature faith.

2) DON'T—make your child go to a place of worship if there is an anti-LGBTQ message or condemnation of LGBTQ people there.

3) DO—think about finding an affirming place of worship. You can visit gaychurch.org or similar sites to help find LGBTQ-positive places of worship throughout the world.

4) DO—realize that your child being LGBTQ is natural, and they can no more help it or change than they can change the shape of their hands or the color of their eyes.

In Their Own Words

Josephine, parent, Montana

My son came out to me at age fourteen while being a little sneaky and getting busted.

It was a summer morning, and he had been at his friend's house for two days. He texted me, "Can I sleep over one more night?" This was a new friend, and I hadn't met the parents yet, and even though my son had been trustworthy in choosing great friends thus far, I wanted him to come home and check in. Plus, I wasn't sure this other family was that cool with suddenly adopting a new child. So I replied, "No, two days is enough in a row, you have been at your dad's for a week, it's my birthday, and I want to see your face." A few minutes later, I get a text from his dad: "Do you know this new friend? I saw some texts between them, and I think I saw them calling each other bb." "Hm. Will ask," I replied. Welcome to modern co-parenting.

When my son came home, I didn't delay. "Do you have a crush on this boy?" I peered at him jovially. "Yes," he replied, beaming. "We are dating." As a queer parent, I felt an amazing new sense of kinship with my child, and I knew this was a special, unforgettable memory being formed. His admission was adorable, but he was also BUSTED. He knew I would probably say no to sleepovers if there was any kissing involved. I wasn't sure at first how to respond. Would getting grounded scar him if it was part of his coming out story? My head was whirling with parental duties and raw emotion. I decided to go with supporting him first. Squealing like I just saw 400

cute puppies, I said, "OMG THAT'S SOOOO cuuuuute!!"
My son rolled his eyes, which also glinted with joy. Then
I said, "Were you even planning to come out to me?" And
he said, "Well, I thought it would be really funny to get in
an actual closet and then jump out and scare you and say
"I'M GAY!!" That is my son. Classic him. We laughed.

Next, we talked about the other boy. I asked if his
parents knew he was gay, and I told my son that was
pretty sneaky sleeping over for a couple days. I assured
him that they could still spend time together, but there
were going to have to be some boundaries. Concerned the
other boy might come from a conservative family, I was
nervous for him, but I wanted to talk to the other parents,
or at least the other boy, if I could. I asked my son if he
could ask his boyfriend to talk to his parents so that we
could work out curfews and rules. I added, "Don't pressure
him. If he doesn't want to come out, we'll figure out what
to do." My son started texting away.

The other boy told his parents immediately, and my
son gave me the mother's phone number.

When he gave me her name, I realized that I did know
the parents. I was even friends with the mom on Facebook.
I relaxed a little and called her. I was still nervous, because
we live in a small college town, where even well-meaning
liberal people don't quite understand the life of LGBTQ. I
braced myself for weirdness.

But it wasn't weird. She and I were both tickled by
their attempt to be sneaky. We agreed a summer curfew
of midnight was comfortable for each of us. And then she
told me that even though she is married to a man, she is
bisexual herself! I was the one who'd made assumptions
based on appearances! So I came out to her as well. Even

better, she has an older daughter. She offered parenting guidance about teen romance, and I resonated with her style. For her, these teen years are about modeling healthy relationships and setting boundaries, and otherwise allowing them to make choices on their way to becoming adults. My relief turned to gratitude, and happiness as I realized our kids are in a whole different world than the one I knew when I was 12, when I first started to realize I was not straight.

I checked with my son's dad. He was all right with the curfew plan, but asked a common question that hetero adults ask about LGBTQ youth, "Do you think it's just a phase?" I replied, "It doesn't matter if it is a phase, we still need to treat him like his identity is real." He agreed. He has always been accepting of my sexuality, but to see him commit to treating our son supportively was nothing short of beautiful.

Since then, the kids have been pretty good with the curfew. Their big thing is to make crazy flavors of homemade ice cream at his house, or wander around the neighborhood, or hang out with friends in our tiny downtown, getting slices of pizza or sitting by the river. The other boy has popped into my house for glasses of water, and we have awkwardly begun to get to know each other. My son says many of his friends are queer, or genderqueer, or some form of LGBTQ. I have talked to my own queer friends, some of whom are in their 20s, and even they say how lucky my son is compared to as recently as seven years ago. For now, he is in a nurturing environment in which to explore his sexuality with healthy boundaries, adult guidance, and peer support. Amazing.

Sadly, I know an ugly reality does exist. We are in a rural state. Hate is real. We are not always safe. There is a fine line between being careful while still not closeted. I have experienced discrimination at work, socially, and around our city. I have crossed streets with transgender friends while giant pickup trucks rev their engines like they want to mow us down. I have been scared to hold my partner's hand when we don't fit the expected gender combo and have held hands anyway. I have seen friends be discriminated against in stores because they weren't as straight-passing as I am.

But I am glad for now that instead of contending with that ugly world, my son is experiencing puppy love, like all the straight kids get to do. I hope all the support helps him become strong in his identity, so that when the world pushes back, he is ready.

Resources

Gay & Lesbian History for Kids: The Century Long Struggle for LGBT Rights, with 21 Activities by Jerome Pohlen

The Right Side of History: 100 Years of LGBTQ Activism by Adrian Brooks and Jonathan Katz

For The Bible Tells Me So—a documentary that walks viewers through the historical context of many Biblical passages.

https://www.youtube.com/watch?v=DSXJzybEeJM—a scene from the TV series *The West Wing* explaining all the ways we don't follow Leviticus

Kidnapped for Christ Filmmaker Kate Logan, an evangelical Christian, set out to make a heartwarming film about Escuela Caribe, a Christian reform school in the Dominican Republic. She thought she would find troubled teens dealing with "their issues" through prayer, song, group therapy, etc. Instead, she encountered an infestation of mental, physical, and possibly even sexual abuse.

Chapter 3

SURVIVING AND THRIVING IN THE PRETEEN AND TEEN YEARS

A s I write this book, my children are 20 years old (Casandra) and 16 years old (Matthew). I distinctly remember one day when Casandra was four and Matthew was a little over one (they are technically three years and nine months apart in age). At the time, I was doing some public relations and marketing consulting work for an educational software company. I had a deadline, and Casandra and Matthew were busily tearing apart our tiny living room. (Our house at the time was a total of about 1,000 square feet.) Matthew loved to dump all of his giant Duplos out of their containers over and over again and say "uh-oh!" each time he did it. Casandra was going through a mermaid phase and had wrapped a blanket around her legs, immobilizing them, and she was trying to crawl everywhere with her "fin." I looked at the chaos that surrounded me and thought to myself, "Wow, parents with kids in school just *have it made.*"

As with most things I'm wrong about, the passing of time makes it ever more clear (daily) that I quite underestimated what it took to get a child through 13 years of institutional education. If you are a parent of a teen, you know what I'm talking about. If you're a parent of a preteen, you probably know what I'm talking about, but just as a warning, it's going to get worse in high school.

Welcome to High School... Again

Adolescence is just a mess, both for parents and our kids. Then you add the pressure cooker of today's average middle or high school and things can get even messier. Our local high school is just a few blocks from Michigan State University, a large Research I-designated, Big Ten University. This means that a lot of students who go to the high school have at least one parent who has a PhD, and possibly two who have a PhD. Then there are the parents who don't have a PhD, but they may want their kid to be smarter than that other kid whose parents do have PhDs. *Everyone* wants to feel their child is advanced (I include myself in this. I am not free from sin on this topic). It can become a ludicrous contest—whose child can take the most AP classes, and who can get not only a 4.0 GPA but a 4.1 or higher, depending on how many AP classes they can stack their schedule with.

And then there are the sports! Student-athletes are now expected to train year-round in their sport or sports. Three full weeks before school starts in August, all the fall sports begin their two-a-day practices. Football, volleyball, water polo, swimming, tennis, and golf all practice for two hours in the morning and another two hours in the afternoon, sometimes with strength training/conditioning between.

Or maybe your child goes to a school with the opposite problem. Maybe no one is invested academically and there aren't a lot of good role models for success in grades or sports. Maybe the school your teen attends had to cut extracurricular activities just to make ends meet, and your child is spending too much time indoors on social media and/or video games. Regardless, high school looks very different now than it did 30 years ago.

Whatever you and your child's experiences have been with their schooling, this is a time of life when their bodies are changing (or not changing, which is also stressful), and our society wants to determine a large amount of their future using standardized tests; there's homework, friend-drama, maybe even a peer they are interested in romantically; then there's competition, parental expectations, perhaps learning to drive, maybe an after-school job, chores, and on top of all of this, they are LGBTQ.

Parents, if you drink, you have my permission to go pour yourself a cocktail.

I have seen (and you probably have too) parents so over-involved in their child's sports, music, and/or academics you can scarcely believe it. I'm not just talking about the notorious "helicopter parent" (who I think is exaggerated by the media. Seriously, how many parents have the kind of money to take time off work to go with their kids to job interviews or buy houses where they are going to college?), I'm talking about parents who have become so invested in their child's high school career that they forget it's *their child's* high school experience. One mom I know said her daughter's name 27 times (!!!) in our 20 minute conversation. (I counted.) "Brenda said..." "Brenda can't stand it when..." "Brenda is just like me when...." "Brenda won't be able to..." "You do know that the college scouts came to look at Brenda?" "Brenda doesn't get the recognition she deserves..." "Those girls are jealous of Brenda because she's so much better at _____ than they are." I wanted to slip her the number of my therapist. I wondered about the last thing she had experienced as herself, and not as "Brenda's mom." Did she even have her own identity anymore? Or was she solely living through her child? What is she going to do when Brenda goes off to college? Or gets a job in another state? Or gets married?

As much as her daughter may enjoy being the center of everything to her mother, you can also bet Brenda is also absolutely terrified. When you are built up that much by a parent(s), even a little failure can seem like a big fall. It is easy (so easy) to let our egos get wrapped up in our parenting. But it is very important, even more so with an LGBTQ child, that we recognize this and overcome our egos and hang onto our unconditional regard and love for them. When we only take pride in our children for their accomplishments, and let them know our disappointment when they fail, we are operating on the pride/shame axis as parents that Eric Parens talks about in his book *Surgically Shaping Children: Technology, Ethics, and the Pursuit of Normality*.[23] Children learn quickly to feel proud when they achieve or when they are "normal," and shame when they fail or "aren't good enough." This can evolve into an external locus of control where the child constantly seeks external validation and the approval of authority to complete goals, rather than an internal locus of control, where the child and adult can self-regulate and monitor without the constant need for external validation. An external locus of control also results in fragility, where every time a child fails, they can feel as though they themselves are failures, rather than just processing their failure as something to learn from.[24]

Alice Dreger writes in *The Pacific Standard* in her article, "What's Wrong With Trying to Engineer Your Child's Sexual Orientation?"[25] (the answer is *a lot*, in case you were wondering) about a father who is overwhelmed and wants to abort upon finding out the baby has a cleft lip. "My friend and I both were thinking: Come on! If you can't handle this, what are you going to do when your kid smokes a little dope? What are you going to do if she ends up pregnant at 16? What are you going to do if she's terrible at math or suffers from a lot of acne? ... The problem with such a parent is that he is planning to live his entire existence with his child on the shame-pride axis,[26] where everything his child does is rated according to whether it makes her father proud or ashamed... You can't seriously expect your whole parenting experience to consist of softball trophies and bumper stickers that brag about your Honor Roll child. It is not your child's job in life to make you proud. It is your job to make your children proud of you as their parent."

Don't raise your child to be just someone you can brag about. Though we use crazy words like "investing" in our children, they are *not* a product. Raise a child who can be a positive, functional person who feels good about themselves. This is even more important because someone in the world will always be telling them they aren't "normal" because they are LGBTQ.

There is nothing wrong with achievement. It's great. Just try to make sure your kids are achieving because they want to—not just because they think they have no choice. Sometimes LGBTQ children will internalize shame about being LGBTQ and try to overachieve to compensate or prove their worth. But our children don't exist on the planet to please us or achieve for us. They didn't ask to be born.

Give to Your Child Because You Want to

I know a parent who is constantly arguing with her young-adult daughter. They both have had difficult lives, but the mom will constantly list everything she has done for her daughter—as if she's Santa Claus keeping a naughty and nice list. "I gave her money for college. I drove her to Ohio when she wanted to see her cousins. I paid her speeding ticket when she shouldn't have been speeding." These are admirable things this mom did, but the fact that she recites them back to her daughter is harming their relationship. Her daughter has begun to think that whatever her mom does for her will be thrown back in her face the next time they argue or the next time she displeases her mom.

Try to give to your child with open hands and an open heart. That doesn't mean never telling your child no about something! What it does mean is that what you *give* your child you are giving of your own free will and choice, and not expecting them to be perfectly obedient or bend to your will because you bought them something or took them to their piano lessons for 12 years. If you can't afford that time or the money for things your teen wants, don't buy/do it. If you don't *want* to buy (or do) for your teen whatever they're requesting, don't. But if you can afford that item and *want* to buy it, by all means buy it! Just don't bring it up again six months later when she is asking to borrow money or when you're having a fight about who she is romantically involved with. Your relationship with your child is never going to be perfectly reciprocal. If you have certain expectations for your child in terms of thanking and generosity, spell these out. For instance, one teen I know was given a very nice car by his grandmother when she bought a new vehicle. The parents sat down with the teen and talked about not only conditions for his ownership of the car, how he would pay for his insurance, license plate and registration annually, but also how to thank his Gram for her generosity. They didn't just expect their 16-year-old son to know exactly what to do to thank Gram. He had thanked her profusely over the phone, but then his parents offered a few options to further show his appreciation. (In some families this may not have been necessary, but the dynamics in this family definitely indicated Gram didn't want money for the car, but would love to be thanked in some other way. You know the dynamics of your extended family, so I'm sure you know what I'm talking about. In some families, Gram would have "sold" him the car, and he would have made $50 payments each month for years, etc. In other families, Gram would have been mortified to be thanked beyond a thank-you on the phone. Every family is different.) These parents asked their teen if he would like to take Gram out to lunch in his new car on a Saturday? Gram also loved going to the theater—would he like to take her to a play or show she might like to see? The teen chose to write Gram a note, and this line of thinking also made him remember that she loved hydrangeas, so he bought her another hydrangea for her yard and treated her to lunch to thank her for the reliable car that he can hopefully use through his high school and college years and maybe even beyond.

Some kids may not need this level of coaching. But some may. Do not assume your child is a bad person because they forget to make a nice gesture or thank someone. Help them see what expectations might be in conjunction with things they are experiencing or have been given. One of the things I hear from other parents is how ungrateful their child is. If I gently ask whether the expectations for gratitude have been spelled out, they look at me as if I have three heads. Being self-centered is the very definition of being a teenager. Teens need to be guided through the transition of, "you are a young adult now, and these things are expected of you." (If your mother makes an extra trip to the school for you, be sure to thank her.) Those lessons we taught them as preschoolers may still need to be reinforced depending on what is going on in their young lives.

Comparing the Inside of Our Families to Everyone Else's Highlight Reel

We will talk more about your child's use of social media in the next chapter, but right now we're going to talk about *our* use of social media. According to a 2015 Pew Study,[27] 75 percent of parents use social media, citing it as important for parenting information and social support. But social media can also cause depressive symptoms,[28] especially if we compare ourselves to one another too much. And unfortunately, in the case of Facebook, parents love to post pictures of their child with the state championship trophy or a picture of their kid's 4.0 grade card. And it's *great* if you are one of those parents doing that. But if you are happy your kid got a B on that U.S. History test, keep reading.

The trouble with social media is, we compare our daily lives with the "highlight reel"[29] everyone else is presenting. I do this too—I will almost always post when a journal or a website publishes one of my essays or poems, but I rarely post when I get a rejection. It's not a bad thing to celebrate our kids, our marriages, or our successes at work. But what could happen if we're struggling with our parenting, or if our kid is having a hard time at school or with friends, is that we might start comparing our kid to this supposedly perfect kid online. The fact that there is no perfect kid doesn't occur to us. All we see is that so-and-so was on the homecoming court and they have a 4.0 GPA *and* they have already been signed for a college basketball scholarship. We don't see their DUI from last month. We don't see that maybe they are scared to be anything less than perfect because their parents might not love them. We don't see that in ten years they may not have any internal resources to combat a problem, because their parents have spent their lifetime telling them things weren't their fault and that they were the best, better and more special than anyone else! Sometimes parents don't post the bad (or just real) stuff on social media for privacy—let's face it, Facebook probably isn't the place to open up about your kid's DUI. But we assume there's not another side of the story there, and I'm telling you right now, there always is.

There are so many fun things about social media! Keeping in touch with cousins, news, funny memes, cat pictures(!)—I'm just saying we need to be aware, mindful if you will, of our thoughts and reactions to what other parents post. Chances are if something is really bothering us on social media, it's probably because it's triggering something, an insecurity or issue that we might have to work on or be aware of.

Navigating Public Spaces

Amidst all this competition, achievement, and learning to become a functional young adult in the middle and high school years, there are some other things, which depending on your child, the area in which you live, their peers, and their age, can be very challenging for your LGBTQ child. I want to be clear on something here—it would be great if we lived in a world where each LGBTQ child could be out in all circumstances and lovingly supported and guided to the resources that they might need in any community. (And oh, also have those resources actually *exist* in every community.) But we are still a long way from that day, and I think that a child's safety and emotional well-being is *always* more important than representing Pride—especially at these ages. As adults, LGBTQ people can make choices to be out even though they might be fired, or to stand up to a physical bully, who might be carrying a concealed weapon. These are adult choices that adults make, with at least some inkling of the consequences. When a child is younger, their impulse may very well to be out in every circumstance. This touches my heart, but we don't want anything to happen to our dear ones. They need time to grow and mature, and they need time and safety in which to do that. Hiding is never good, but if a child chooses to be out to their family and not their friends, that is okay. If a child chooses to be out to their family and close friends, but not the whole school community, that is fine too. If a child feels well-supported enough to be out at home and school, but not with Uncle Blake who constantly makes homophobic jokes, that too is okay. But if a child knows they may face being assaulted or emotional abuse by peers just for being out at this age, I'm sorry. It's not worth it. The most important goal during these years is for your child to survive and hopefully with your caring attention, thrive.

If you child is non-binary or transgender, public bathroom use at their school and in other public spaces can be a nightmare. According to the Lambda Legal website, 53 percent of transgender people have been "harassed or disrespected in a place of public accommodation." *The law is on their side.* Yes, places like North Carolina are making a point to be hateful and discriminatory, but I don't think these so-called "bathroom laws" will stand for long, as they are fundamentally unconstitutional. (HB2 in North Carolina is already being challenged in Carcano v. McCrory.) And just imagine if everyone was stopped at the door of public restrooms and asked to show proof of their gender. I'm 48 years old and have had two big babies, and I'm in the midst of perimenopause. There would be times when I probably would pee on my interrogator's feet if they asked me to drop my pants.

Lambda Legal says on their website,[30] "The bottom line is that you should be allowed to use the restroom or locker room that matches your gender identity, regardless of whether you're making a gender transition or appear gender-nonconforming. There is no rule that you must look a certain way to use a certain restroom. That's "gender policing" and it's harmful to anyone dressed or groomed in a way that doesn't conform to someone else's idea of gender. If your child is stopped or harassed, make sure they're safe and then report the incident to police, school administrators or other authorities. They do have the law on their side: Courts have increasingly found that discrimination against transgender people is sex discrimination, so it's not acceptable to institute different kinds of bathroom rules for transgender and non-transgender people." (See also the Lambda Legal fact sheet under "Resources" at the end of this chapter.)

Have your child use the buddy system whenever they can if they are in place and you don't know if they will be safe. If you are traveling as a family, and you have a parent or sibling of the same gender identity, send them into the bathroom with your LGBTQ child. If your child is a teen or preteen and traveling with family friends, talk to the other parent(s) beforehand if you believe public restroom use might be an issue at concerts, sports arenas, rest areas, etc. If your teen or preteen is traveling with friends and one of the friends has the same gender identity, send the friend in with your teen. Be cautious. Just because they have not been harassed at that place previously, it does not mean they will not be harassed there in the future. Family or unisex bathrooms can also be a choice, but these are not always available and sometimes waiting in line for one of these bathrooms is very awkward for teens and opens them up to comments like, "Where's your family?" etc.

The Law is on Your Child's Side

Laws exist at many levels to stop discrimination against LGBTQ people.[31] First and foremost is the United States' Constitution and each state's constitution as well. The United States' Constitution guarantees *all* people "equal protection of the laws." State constitutions generally reiterate this right. Translated, this means that public schools and public spaces can't single out LGBTQ people for different (negative) treatment. Courts have affirmed again and again that public schools must offer protection from bullying and harassment to LGBTQ youth, just as they would any other student at the school. (Read Lambda's "Legal Victories for Youth" in this chapter's resources for more details.) Lambda Legal's website also states, "Discrimination based on perceived sexual orientation or gender identity violates your constitutional rights, as may discrimination based on your friendship, family relationship or other association with LGBTQ people."

Title IX, a federal law passed in 1972, prohibits discrimination based on gender, and this law helps students at schools that receive federal funds. Courts have ruled that gender discrimination outlined in Title IX includes both sexual harassment and discrimination against students who don't adhere to gender stereotypes. LGBTQ students who have been harassed have been supported by Title IX in many court cases.

In addition to Title IX, some states have passed additional laws to protect LGBTQ youth. These laws specifically prevent harassment based on sexual orientation and gender expression and identity. California, Iowa, Maryland, New Jersey, New York, and Vermont (and hopefully more states soon) offer specific protections to LGBTQ youth and require local schools to have anti-harassment policies regarding LGBTQ issues.

Other laws in other states may look different and may not mention LGBTQ students, but they still may offer some protection against harassment and abuse. Even if your state legislature does not have laws on the books about LGBTQ discrimination, sometimes your school district, city or township might. More and more communities—from small cities (like our home, East Lansing, Michigan, the first city in the United States to offer anti-discriminatory policies to its LGBTQ citizens) to large cities like Dallas, Miami, Nashville, and Philadelphia—have enacted laws protecting their LGBTQ people from harassment.

Proms and Dances

Lambda Legal also has tips and advice on proms and dances.[32] Many schools still have rules prohibiting students from bringing their same-gender date to their school dance or prom, but these rules are against the law. Federal courts as early as 1980 have upheld the right of LGBTQ people to bring their same-gender dates to proms and dances. Supreme Courts and federal courts have ruled that any law banning same gender couples from attending proms and dances "violates students' rights to free expression and association, which are guaranteed by the First Amendment of the United States Constitution." A federal court again upheld this right to equal treatment in 2008. The federal court ordered Scottsboro High School in Alabama to let two female students attend the prom together and overturned the school board's efforts to prohibit them from attending the celebration.

The Right to Freedom of Expression at School

LGBTQ students also have the right to express themselves and should not be discriminated against for voicing their support of LGBTQ equality at school. They should be able to wear T-shirts and distribute literature expressing LGBTQ concerns and statements, and they should be able to hang posters, make announcements, and hold meetings for LGBTQ-related groups and activities on their school grounds. Students also have the right to write columns or articles in their student newspapers about LGBTQ concerns. These rights have all been tested and upheld by various courts across the United States. [33]

Contact Lambda Legal or the ACLU

Parents, if your child is facing discrimination, consult a local attorney or call Lambda Legal at 1-866-542-8336, or go to www.lambdalegal.org/help. (They are also a great organization to remember in your charitable donations. They do a lot of good.) You can also contact the American Civil Liberties Union. (Another great organization to think about in your non-profit giving.) These two organizations will have more precise information about the laws in your area and how those laws have been enforced. (See more about this in the following chapter on bullying.) Private schools are also a different matter, with different rules and laws then discussed here. If you have questions about what sorts of protections exist for the private school your child attends, check out "Private Schools" at Lambda's website.

Safe Sex

Maybe you're like me and thought, "Gee, I have a gay kid. I don't need to have the sex talk with them!" After a little reading and some reflection, I realized that I still had to talk about safe sex with my teenager. Lesbians *can* get STDs, transmitted through bodily fluids, blood, and sharing toys. And lesbians may also engage in heterosexual sex at some point in their lives, if they meet a man they like. So they need information about condoms and birth control as well. If you child is bisexual, safe sex information is equally crucial. Providing factual information about disease and pregnancy prevention to your LGBTQ teen is non-negotiable. You cannot assume that your middle or high school will "take care of it."

It is crucial to have the age-appropriate safe sex talk (and maybe buy some books) for your LGBTQ child, even if they say they have no interest in sex for now. They need all the information—about STDs, HIV, and pregnancy risk. All of it. We don't know what circumstances they may run into as a young adult, and we need to prepare them to make smart choices even in an unlikely scenario.

I know how awkward this can be, and if you're like me, you may not *know* all the information your child might need. I gave Casandra some books because I figured they would cover things a lot more in depth and more knowledgeably than I could. I also gave her the pregnancy/STD talk and extolled the virtues of condoms. If you feel really awkward, it is fine to start the conversation via email or text with a couple of links to articles.

It is good and right to frame the safe sex talk within the moral and religious values you want to pass onto your child. I know parents who tell their children "anything between two consenting adults is fine," and I know parents who tell their children "Sex should wait until marriage." Regardless of where you fall on this parental spectrum, they need safe sex information. Ignorance does not prevent pregnancy, STDs, or HIV, and history has shown us repeatedly that parents telling teenagers not to have sex does not always prevent them from doing so. You can say, "I hope you don't have sex until you are older and in love (or married, or 18, or graduated from college), but I want to give you this information so you are prepared."

The safe sex talk shouldn't be just one talk. It should be a dialogue. Let your child know that however they want to communicate about any questions they have is fine. Email and texting *do* count as a dialogue. (Plus it gives parents a chance to look things up they don't know!)

Drugs and Alcohol

One of the bad things about having a teenager is that you remember all the stuff you did as a teenager that you didn't tell your parents about. I was overall "a good kid." I got decent grades and enjoyed my extracurriculars of band, softball, track, and volleyball, but this didn't stop me from underage drinking, or sharing the occasional joint with friends. I would also tell my mother I was _____ (fill in the blank with: at the movies, studying at a friend's, at the laundromat, etc.), and be in a different place altogether, and those places sometimes did involve alcohol. (This is now a bit harder with the Internet and cellphones, which make it easy for Mom and/or Dad to check if there really is a showing of that movie you said you were going to.) While my forays into underage drinking never resulted in any catastrophes, now, over 30 years later, I still cringe thinking about what could have happened, and who I might have harmed, the few times I drove home tipsy.

Our LGBTQ children are twice as likely to experiment with drugs and alcohol. [34] There are many theories about why this is—stress from marginalization, unfriendly communities and schools, unsupportive parents or family members. Most kids, over three-quarters, will have experimented with alcohol, marijuana, prescription drugs or other drugs, before they graduate from high school. [35]

With this experimentation comes risk—to their developing brains, to car or pedestrian accidents, to driving while impaired (or riding with someone who is impaired), to the drugs not being "what their friend said," to making poor choices (like unprotected sex) while impaired.

If you suspect that your teen is using drugs or alcohol, the first thing to do is ask them. Drugfree.org has some great tips on how to ask and also the signs to look for if your teen is using drugs or alcohol. Some of the behaviors—tiredness, moodiness, trouble at school, a car accident, can also be completely normal teenage stuff, so don't panic when you look over the list.

One of the easiest things to do is to stop problems before they start. One concrete thing you can do in your own house is to keep close track of your prescription medications, including the number of pills in the bottle. It is good to keep all prescription medications somewhere they don't cause temptation for your teen. Change the place where you keep your medications frequently. My son Matthew had his wisdom teeth out last summer and received a small script for pain to help him sleep for a few days afterward. We kept those pills right on the kitchen counter, and he would take one before he headed up to bed.

If you keep alcohol around the house, you might want to lock the bottles up during your kids' teen years, or at least when you know teens are going to be around and you aren't going to be there to supervise. My friend told me a funny story about a dad who kept his vodka in the freezer for an occasional drink and one day he opened the freezer to pour himself a drink and his "vodka" had frozen. His teens had been slowly drinking the vodka while he was gone and replacing it with water. It is hard not to laugh at this, especially if we were prone to messing around ourselves as teens, but this is also something we need to take seriously, since our LGBTQ children are also at higher risk of chronic substance abuse.[36]

If your teen is driving, tell them you need to borrow their car without any warning. I'm a big believer in trusting your kids, but it also can't hurt for them to know they can't store drugs or alcohol in their car because you may "need" to use their car at random times. In the "Only Part of Who They Are" section of this book, I talk about having your house be the hangout house. The nice thing about having your kids' friends over is you can randomly walk into wherever they are gathered and see what they are doing. If they know you will walk down to the basement to throw a load of laundry in, or walk into the family room to get a spare blanket while they are watching Netflix or playing video games, they are probably not going to break out the MJ right then and there. Another concrete thing to do is to keep your kids busy—more about this later in the book. Those hours after school are dangerous when most teens are unsupervised. It is especially easy to get into trouble if they don't have a structured activity during those hours. Being involved in a sport, music, dance, art, or a faith or community activity also ups their chances of having peers who give the good kind of peer pressure and who don't use alcohol or drugs (or only do so occasionally). Do not kid yourself that drug and alcohol use is not prevalent at your kid's school.

Another concrete thing to do is to tell your child that they can call you at any time—if they're uncomfortable at a party that you didn't know they were even attending, or if they drank and are considering driving home. Make them a promise you will not yell and scream at them. You will go get them, wherever they are, and you will discuss what happened the next day away from the heat of the moment. This doesn't mean there won't be consequences for poor choices, but it does mean that you won't be so unreasonably angry that they fear being honest with you. You have every right to be angry with your child when they make a poor choice, especially if it concerns their personal safety *and* breaking the law. But you need to exhibit self-control and be reasonable. If you are not, they may not call you when they are in trouble because they fear your anger and disapproval.

The biggest risk factor in kids using drugs and alcohol as teens (or earlier) is family history. This is also the hardest thing for you to do anything about. You can't help it if there is a history of this in your family. This isn't a bad thing to communicate to your teen, either. If they know that their grandfather has attended AA meetings for 27 years, they may think twice before drinking that shot at a party.

If you are vigilant looking for warning signs—keeping the lines of communication open, keeping track of the substances you have around your house, keeping them busy in the after-school hours, and in general being a bit nosey (but not too nosey), hopefully they will get through these adolescent years safely. If your child *has* experimented with drugs or alcohol, it is not the end of the world. There are many, many people who did experiment and who are now productive members of society. But the more experimentation, the greater risk of them developing an addiction. Try to find a balance of understanding and communicate your concerns for their safety and for their future.

Drugfree offers a helpline at 1-855-DRUGFREE. If you live in an area with an LGBT Center (more about this in the following chapters), they may also have resources for LGBTQ teens who may be abusing substances.

Do's and Don'ts

1) DON'T—let your child use the problems they encounter as an LGBTQ person as an excuse not to achieve their goals. Yes, the journey to their goals will be more difficult sometimes because they are LGBTQ, but there are many successful people in all walks of life who are LGBTQ. No excuses.

2) DO—enlist adult allies. Prejudice and homophobia are real. Adults at your child's school have a responsibility to protect students from anti-gay and anti-trans discrimination. Allies like other parents and teachers can talk to your students' principal or other administrator, reminding them that many laws require the school to take action when LGBTQ students encounter discrimination. Adult allies can also help ensure the safety of LGBTQ students at proms, dances, and other school events by being vigilant to what is happening around them.

3) DO—encourage your school board and administrations to pass antidiscrimination rules and policies that specifically deal with LGBTQ issues like gender expression and sexual orientation.

4) DO—talk to your child before any big event (overnight travel with their sports team, dances, prom, sleepovers, etc.) See what their questions and concerns are. If they feel uncomfortable talking about it face-to-face, send them a text

or email which they can respond to in their own time without pressure.

5) DO—examine your ego regularly during their teen years. I have to interact regularly with a mom who triggers me badly competition-wise. She seems to feel that it is necessary to put my teen down so her teen can be "better." I have to talk myself through these triggers regularly.

"Why are you angry?"

"Because she said something mean about my kid."

"Why does that matter to you?"

"Because she shouldn't do that."

"Is it true?"

"No. My child is healthy, overall happy, and working toward their goals."

"So why are you angry?"

"I'm afraid my kid isn't good enough."

"Good enough for what?"

"Well, when you put it like that..."

Sometimes it takes some journaling, some self-talk, and sometimes some talk therapy to see why we have certain expectations for our children. Expectations are great. I do believe our kids (to some degree) become what we expect them to become, but our expectations also have to line up with what they expect for themselves. It can't just be a rat race with other parents so you and/or your kid can be "the best."

6) DO—problem solve with your kid. If there is an upcoming sleepover and your child wants to change in the bathroom, strategize the best way to do this. Ask them who they think are their closest allies in their group of friends. Friends (and friends' parents) are powerful allies. If kids are surrounded with allies, what could be problematic situations like sleepovers and locker rooms and bathrooms will seem much easier to your LGBTQ child.

7) DO—use resources like Lambda's and the ACLU's web pages to help figure out what your child's rights are in a given situation.

8) DON'T—compare your family to other families. Especially on social media. Each family has their own set of joys and burdens. Even if you think those people are perfect, I guarantee you they are not.

9) DO—talk about safe sex and drugs and alcohol with your child. Pretending they may not encounter these choices in their school years is not in anyone's best interest.

In Their Own Words

Casandra Eriksen (my daughter), Michigan

Dear High School Self,

You are so quiet. You hardly open up to anyone ever. You are a one-woman army, against everyone else. If no one can get in your head, no one can hurt you. But they are in your head, aren't they? You've given them space in there, and they never pay their rent, so you get nothing. It's time to kick those motherfuckers out.

But it's hard to kick them out, isn't it? You see them every day. You wonder what they think about you, your fellow classmates, and your teachers. They get under your skin. Every word, every action, is overanalyzed. What was the underlying meaning? Future me can tell you, there was none. And if there was, it isn't worth your thinking space. Your thinking space should be your sacred space.

It's hard to kick them out, because they seem to be always right there. In class, in the lunchroom, in the hallway. Most of the time they ignore you, but there was that one day you dressed up a little nicer and were catcalled. Time to stick to T-shirts and jeans. T-shirts and jeans are comfortable, and baggy, and feel safe. No catcalling when you wear a T-shirt and jeans.

Most of the time they ignore you, but sometimes they don't. I know one day you were just getting books out of your locker, wearing jeans, but as one of the guys walked by he put a finger in between your legs, and his friends all laughed. I know you never told your parents because you didn't want there to be a parent meeting. Plus, you weren't even sure which guy it was.

I know you had to play your trumpet in front of your teacher, and in front of the class, even though you weren't that great. I know when you messed up your face grew hot, and you felt really embarrassed. I know you quit, and it felt like one of the best damn decisions you had ever made.

I know your swimming coach yelled at you one time, and you cried. I also know you broke your hand and didn't shed a single tear. I know you finished that water polo tournament with that broken hand.

I know there were some days you wanted to give up and not go to school anymore. I know you were tempted to walk to the library and stay there until the end of the school day some days. I know you never did. You went to every single fucking class.

I know that a lot of days during senior year you ate lunch alone because your close friends had all graduated. I also know you were really thankful that one stranger introduced herself and ate lunch with you several times, even though you had never talked before that.

I know that you enjoyed psychology so much you felt like you would read the textbook just for fun. I know you enjoyed your comparative religion class so much that it made your day a lot of days. Good news. You are now majoring in psychology and comparative religion and they are still both endlessly fascinating.

I know you loved your AP Literature class. You loved getting lost in the books, and you loved being able to write, to bring thoughts and feelings to life on paper. Good news, you now write articles for a news website, and your boss and editor are super cool. You are also writing small things for your mother's book, and you still write in your journal.

You still have the same friends you had in high school, and a few new friends. You are slowly but surely getting better at talking to humans. You never see the people that laughed at you anymore.

Your family members are still by your side, even after all of your crazy emotional breakdowns and breakthroughs. They all deserve fucking medals of honor.

You still have challenges but you have gotten stronger and smarter, and you have an amazing support system. You aren't as afraid of talking anymore. You take more risks, and even though things don't always work out, it is much better to take healthy risks than sit around and think about what might have been.

So I would say to anyone going through hell in middle school or high school, don't be afraid to speak up. Don't be afraid to approach new people and try new things. Don't be afraid to stop doing what makes you unhappy and go after what makes you happy.

It's important to do well in school, but don't stress out about your grades too much. Life has a way of working itself out. Don't worry too much if you don't know what career you want. You'll go where you need to go and do what you need to do. There is nothing wrong with making it up as you go along. You can change your mind as many times as you want.

Yes, people can be mean and cruel, but you shouldn't shut yourself out of the world just because a few people are mean. This just causes more loneliness and sadness. I learned that the hard way. My relationships are not perfect, but I have found that being more open and honest is the best way to go.

Your high school may feel like an ugly hell, but trust me, there are so many beautiful parts of the world. There are

people and books and parties and sunsets.
There is paddle boarding and looking out at
the ocean. There is biking and hiking and
discovering music that speaks to you. Yes,
there will always be ups and downs. You will
still have bad days, but somehow, at least
for me, bad days are more manageable than
they used to be. Leaving high school, there is
just so much more room. More room to mess
up. More room to cry. More room to laugh.
And more room to spread your wings. Don't
be afraid to fly.

Much love,
Present Moment Casandra

Imani Williams, Michigan/California

As parents, we have dreams for our kids. A lot of times
we write the script providing the narrative we hope to see
played out. For most, the ideal situation places kids in
heteronormative settings and situations that lead to the
set-up we envision. When we learn that it isn't going the
way we planned at all, we get in our feelings about it.

The "what ifs" take over. What if they pick the wrong
person to connect with? What if this impedes me from
having grandchildren? What if they're hurt and experience
violence at the hands of someone who hates gays?
What if I lose my child? The list of "what ifs" can go on
indefinitely. It's part of the grief and loss process.

You have a right as a parent to go through all of the
stages. It may feel like you'll never get past the denial

stage, but trust me, you will. Parents take the news differently depending on how the news reaches them. My ex-husband decided to "out" me in front of my dad as he was moving his things out. Trust me. That was not the way I wanted to tell my parents. My mother took her time, ten years in all, before she decided she'd rather have me in her life with a same-sex partner than not at all. If I had known that both my parents would soon be gone from this spiritual plane, I would have worked much harder on our relationships.

Finding community and my voice probably saved my life while my parents went through the various stages. During the waiting process, I joined LGBTQ groups (social media wasn't born yet), making it my business to find as many safe spaces as possible.

Resources

Lambda Legal's Equal Access to Public Restrooms Fact Sheet (pdf) http://www.lambdalegal.org/help or 1-866-542-8336

Lambda Legal Victories for Youth

ACLU LGBTQ Rights

What it's Like for Someone Who Looks Female to Use the Male Restroom by D. Michael Whelan (the effects of bathroom laws on someone who doesn't look stereotypically male)

The Available Parent: Radical Optimism for Raising Teens and Tweens by John Duffy

Masterminds and Wingmen by Rosalind Wiseman

Queen Bee Moms and Kingpin Dads by Rosalind Wiseman

Preventing Substance Abuse in LGBTQ Teens HRC/Drug Free (pdf)

The Talk by Alice Dreger

Author Alex Sanchez's list of recommended books for LGBT teens http://www.alexsanchez.com/gay_teen_books.htm

Chapter 4

BULLYING

From kindergarten to sixth grade, Casandra attended a Catholic school. My husband and I had a variety of reasons for choosing Catholic schools for our two children. Our Catholic faith was important to us; we lived at that time in a poor, rural school district with very few "extras;" we thought it would be nice for our children to talk about their faith and learn about their faith at school, and we thought the smaller class sizes and set-up of the Catholic school would work well for our family. We were both wrong and right.

I come from small, poor, rural schools myself. I graduated third in my class and expended little effort. I was ill-prepared for the amount of money parents had at this particular Catholic school, and I was definitely ill-prepared for Casandra "to compete" with children who had nannies (they hadn't gone to any common daycare, like Casandra and the rest of the masses...no way).

Casandra's classmates had had enrichment activities from the time they first opened their mouth to yawn, and they did things like "learn the cello through the Suzuki method." (Which is wonderful, don't get me wrong. I had just never even heard of it.) Since we were "let's have some boxed pasta and then take Casandra to a swimming lesson at the Y" people, I didn't quite know what to make of this new world.

Casandra had some great teachers and some good friends, but in fourth grade, her two closest friends left to go to public school. I thought the change to public school might be too much and too sudden for Casandra (by this time, we had moved into a better school district with more options), but also, the way East Lansing schools were set up, Casandra's two good friends were at a different elementary school than Casandra would go to if she were to leave the Catholic school. She still had one close friend, and she did okay in fourth grade. In fifth grade she had a very challenging teacher situation. Still, we clung to the Catholic school. At the end of fifth grade, Casandra's last close friend transferred to public school. This friend had a big family (11 siblings, if I remember correctly), and her parents could no longer afford the school tuition. But Casandra's class was so small (under 30 students), I thought Casandra would be accepted into another group of friends. I was wrong.

Casandra spent a miserable sixth grade year telling me her day had been "fine" when in reality, she was miserable and ostracized. Girls would hand out invitations to birthday parties and other events at the lunch table and she would be the only one who didn't get one. Girls asked her why she was so quiet. Girls asked her if she was stupid. Girls asked her if she was gay. Girls jockeying for a higher social position avoided her because she couldn't offer them any social benefit. A lot of the girls put on a good Christian act when teachers were around, but then at recess and at lunch, they would completely ignore my daughter or mock her. I still see some of these girls around our city, at home on breaks from college, or attending Michigan State University where I work. I will be honest with you, it is all I can do not to flip them off, with what the comedian Lewis Black calls "the double pump." I like to think of myself as a well-adjusted person, but when I think of the emotional and mental damage they did to my daughter, it is very, very difficult not to wish that they all suffer the same pain she did, multiplied by a considerable amount.

We switched Casandra to public school in seventh grade, and while things still were challenging, Casandra did find a place and a few good, very loyal friends (who she still sees on a regular basis). She found activities like swimming and water polo, which helped her cope with the mind-numbing boredom of her days, the catcalls in the hall, and the strange looks from other girls who straightened their hair every day, who ate only salads (with dressing on the side), and who were destined to go on to be the vice-presidents of their sororities. These heteronormative girls who seemed to embody how girls were supposed to be in the world were some of the meanest girls Casandra encountered.

In terms of LGBTQ student experiences, Casandra "got off easy" in middle and high school. At the very middle school Casandra attended, a young boy named Matt Epling committed suicide in 2002 after being hazed.

At www.mattepling.webs.com his family writes, "Matt
was a talented and giving young man who will be greatly
missed by his many friends and family members. His
creativity lives on through his writing, poetry, art, use of
drama and his quirky sense of humor. Matt was on both
the Citizenship and Honor Rolls at MacDonald Middle
School. He was voted by his eighth grade classmates to
have the best smile, the best personality, and most likely
to become an actor. He enjoyed the outdoors and spent
countless hours practicing stunts and tricks on his bike on
a ramp he built in front of his house. On Matt's last day of
Eighth grade he was assaulted by upperclassmen as part of
a high school 'Welcome to High School' Hazing. Although
this was an Assault and Battery, little was done at the time
to those who perpetrated the crime. Roughly forty days
later, the night before we were to go to the police to begin
formal charges, Matt ended his life. Perhaps because of
what happened and the corresponding threats he received,
he was afraid of retaliation, but we will never know... We
felt more time was spent to separate the two incidents
than to find out how connected they really were. Since
then we have met other families across America who have
faced the similar loss of a child, and we know we are not
alone. We lost our only son and the world lost a bright
star that faded far too soon. We have dedicated ourselves
to making sure that 'No child goes through what Matt did
and no family goes through what we have.'"

The East Lansing School District did respond to Matt's
death with a crackdown on hazing and bullying. And I'm
glad they did. Because Casandra started at MacDonald Middle
School just six years after Matt Epling was hazed.

This is one of our greatest fears as LGBTQ parents—that our children will attempt to take their own life or succeed in taking their own life. But even the lesser level of harassment and exclusion Casandra faced still affects her to this day. She still has trouble trusting and opening up to people. The effects of bullying go on and on, years after our children are no longer being bullied.

Why Does Bullying Still Happen?

Why, in today's day and age, does bullying still happen? People (not just kids) bully because of power. Sometimes these kids are well-connected socially, and use that social power to bully and harass others. Sometimes kids bully because they are isolated socially, and they will then bully because they themselves have been bullied or feel powerless in some way. According to the book *The New Bullying-How Social Media, Social Exclusion, Laws And Suicide Have Changed Our Definition Of Bullying, And What To Do About It*, half of all bullies are bullied at home by parents or siblings. Glenn Stutzky, clinical social work instructor at Michigan State University and bullying expert, said that bullying is "the most frequently occurring form of violence in American schools and it really is the engine driving the majority of school violence. It is a huge problem."[37] Kids who bully tend to have either less parental involvement at home and/or be experiencing some sort of difficulty at home. Bullying kids become frustrated easily, they have trouble following rules (though they may appear to be a "good kid" to parents, teachers, and administrators), and they view violence (verbal or physical) as a way to solve problems.

The stereotype is that the bully will be a large, physically menacing kid—this is not necessarily true. In Casandra's case, they were popular girls, or girls who wanted to be popular, following the popular lead. So bullies just need to have power in some other way—socially, academically, etc.[38] Contrary to stereotypes and conventional wisdom, *bullies are likely to be the well-liked kids in school.* Jill McDonald, an educator and national bullying expert, said in a 2005 *Detroit Free Press* article,[39] "That whole caste system, that social hierarchy—not only with students, but with teachers—determines who is treated better."

The targets of bullying are comprised of others who are perceived to be different in some way—overweight, underweight, shorter, new to the school, "behind" in puberty, "ahead" in puberty, those who dress differently, those who are perceived as being different (gay, bisexual, poor, trans, a different race or culture than is predominant in the school, not fitting into a clique or category), and those who are socially isolated or perceived as "annoying" to their peer group. But also at times the bullying target is well-liked, perhaps even popular. Sherri Gordon, in an article on verywell.com,[40] said that students who are bullied may get a lot of positive attention for sports, academics, art, music, or theater. These well-liked and/or high-achieving students may be a threat to the bully and their own position in the school hierarchy, so they become a target.

You can easily see the potential dangers for our LGBTQ children. In that same article, Gordon said, "Some of the most brutal bullying incidents have involved children who are bullied for their sexual orientation." Our kids might be poor, popular, dress differently, and be gay. They might be overweight or underweight, behind in puberty, great at music, and be bisexual. Their gender identity may not match gender stereotypes, and they might be new to the school.

The Gay, Lesbian and Straight Education Network (GLSEN) did an extensive school climate survey in 2013, conducting online interviews with almost 8,000 LGBTQ students in the 6th to 12th grades from all 50 states.[41]

- 55.5 percent of these students felt unsafe at school because of their sexual orientation.
- 37.8 percent felt unsafe because of their gender expression.
- Over 60 percent of LGBTQ students avoided school functions and extracurricular activities because they felt unsafe or uncomfortable.
- Almost three quarters of students had heard "gay" used in a negative way ("that's so gay"), frequently or often at school.
- 90.8 percent reported that they felt distressed because of this language.
- 64.5 percent had heard other homophobic remarks ("dyke," "faggot") frequently or often.
- 56.4 percent heard negative comments about gender expression—not being "feminine" or "masculine" enough.
- A third of those surveyed heard negative remarks about transgender people "tranny" "he/she" "shemale," etc.

- *Over half of students heard homophobic remarks and negative comments about gender expression from their teachers or other school staff.*
- Almost 60 percent of kids in the GSLEN survey did not report their harassment or assault to school staff, "most commonly because they doubted that effective intervention would occur or the situation would become worse if reported."
- 61.6 percent of the students who did report an incident said *that school staff did nothing in response.*[42]

LGBTQ students who had experienced discrimination and harassment had lower GPAs than their peers, lower self-esteem, and higher levels of depression, and they were twice as likely to state that they didn't plan to pursue post-secondary education.

Trans students are especially vulnerable. On a visit to Florida in October 2012, Vice President Joe Biden said that transgender discrimination is "the civil rights issue of our time."[43] Vice President Biden was absolutely correct, with transgender discrimination now apparent in public spaces, workplaces, colleges and universities, and yes, K-12 schools. Eight states, Washington D.C., and numerous municipalities have adopted laws and policies that state that trans people should not be discriminated against based on their gender identity and that they should be able to use the bathroom of their choosing. But some schools (and cities and states) are moving in the opposite direction of inclusion. Some states have introduced laws that would give cisgender students the right to sue trans students if they see them in the locker room or bathroom.

A Texas lawmaker wanted to set up a humiliating and discriminatory "crime stopper" phone line that would reward students with $2,000 if they reported trans students in the restroom that did not align with their biological sex. And some schools are taking a "neutral" approach (which in my opinion is almost as damaging as the schools who are actively discriminating). We will go further into the special issues trans students face in Chapter 6.

Bullying in Our Schools

Asked if bullying has gotten better or worse or stayed about the same, Stutzky said, "I get asked this question a lot and always struggle a bit. More bullying incidents are being reported—but that is in part because we have made it a more talkable subject and provided opportunities and encouragement to report it. However, with the advent of technology I would definitely say bullying has gotten worse—both in terms of frequency and impact. And I have a personal concern, having not come to a conclusion, wondering if, in fact, we are becoming less caring and meaner as a society. I hope not."

According to the Health Resources and Services Administration, about 20 percent of U.S. students have indicated in studies that they have been bullied.[44] (Note the much higher percentages and statistics for our LGBTQ children.) There has been a crackdown in recent years on physical bullying and assault, but verbal bullying continues in most schools daily. Teachers sometimes look on verbal abuse as personal conflict between students.

But bullying is not a personal conflict, it is rooted in power and control. Techniques for true peer conflict, like mediation (something many educators and counselors are well-versed in) depend on both participants having compassion and empathy for each other. This does not work in bullying situations, because if the bully had compassion and empathy, they wouldn't be bullying in the first place.

Most bullying happens out of teachers' sight, in hallways, cafeterias or on school buses, where teachers are outnumbered. Sometimes teachers don't recognize the indications of bullying. Take the example of the girls at Casandra's Catholic school, who would exclude her at the lunch table. The teachers probably didn't notice. A whisper of, "you're fat, you smell, you're a faggot, you're weird, go die" probably won't be heard in the noise of the hall, even with the most vigilant teacher listening.

But there are almost always witnesses to bullying—other students (and yes, sometimes even teachers) who watch and do nothing. These onlookers are one of the keys to preventing bullying. Another student simply going to stand next to the victim has been shown to be effective in diffusing aggression and abuse. The key is to teach the silent majority what to do or say to help victims. Bullying experts say there are three ways that bystanders can help stop the aggression.[45]

1) Direct intervention. A bystander tells the bully to stop.
2) A bystander takes the victim out of the situation and invites the student being bullied to come and walk or sit with them.

3) Showing verbal support after the incident, offering a smile, a brief talk, or hug.

Leadership camps and training for teens that focus on techniques such as these have been effective. Kids with good hearts look on, and they *want* to do something, but they don't know what to do, they don't feel it's their place to intervene, or they fear some sort of retaliation.

Not only do students need training, teachers do, too. Many school districts start anti-bullying programs, but few have the resources to fully implement them. Some schools may not even have psychologists and/or social workers; in the schools that do, these professionals are stretched very thin, sometimes with hundreds of students in their individual caseloads. Regular training for teachers, staff, and school professionals is a must, but too often it gets pushed aside until there is a crisis or suicide at the school. And even in the schools with intervention programs in place, those programs still need to be evaluated to make sure that the interventions are working.

"We've got to get involved much earlier, and the silent majority is the key. If we can engage them, give them the skills, they can tip the balance of power in many schools," Stutzky said. "Bullying is a form of abuse. I don't know how much progress we're going to make until we come to that understanding."[46]

Cyberbullying

According to a Pew Research study in 2007, students say they are still more likely to be bullied physically at school rather than online, but cyberbullying is a tremendous problem in today's school culture.[47] "About one third (32%) of all teenagers who use the Internet say they have been targets of a range of annoying and potentially menacing online activities—such as receiving threatening messages; having their private emails or text messages forwarded without consent; having an embarrassing picture posted without permission; or having rumors about them spread online."

In a focus group conducted by Pew for this project, a 16-year-old girl described how she and her classmates bullied a fellow student: "There's one MySpace from my school this year. There's this boy in my anatomy class who everybody hates. He's like the smart kid in class. Everybody's jealous. They all want to be smart. He always wants to work in our group and I hate it. And we started this thing, some girl in my class started this I Hate [Name] MySpace thing. So everybody in school goes on it to comment bad things about this boy."

There are some commonsense things students can do to prevent cyberbullying—they can protect their passwords, not lend their phones to others, and remember each time they are sharing something electronically, even with a single person, that that person has the ability to screenshot it and distribute it to whoever they would like. (The number one way students are cyberbullied is violation of privacy—a picture/snapchat/text etc. going somewhere it wasn't intended to go.) Students can remember to log out of public computers (like at their school or library), and when they are taking selfies, they can ask themselves, *Would I be comfortable with everyone in the world seeing this?* as a guide.[48] These are good precautions, but I must stress, if your child fails to do one of these things, it is still not their fault if they are bullied. We all trust people in our lives and sometimes we trust the wrong people. We cannot blame the victim in these circumstances, any more than we would blame a kid who was shoved or punched physically at school.

My Kid is Being Bullied—Help!

If your child has been threatened (either verbally or via technology) or assaulted by the bully, contact the police immediately. If the situation is less severe or less time sensitive, the first thing to do is to get a copy of the school's anti-bullying policy, which hopefully will be accessible online. Gather any evidence (this is especially important in cyberbullying), and go over what happened with your child, writing it all down so you have all the pertinent details, dates, and times. Be sure to tell your child that what happened wasn't their fault, and don't blame them if they handled the situation the "wrong" way. They were doing the best they could during a difficult experience. Just remember to verbally empathize with your child even if you are really, really angry inside (and then vent to your spouse or a friend later about what a nasty little piece of &*#!* the bully is).

Schedule a face-to-face meeting with your school's principal. Meeting with the principal could potentially be very emotional depending on what happened to your child, and it is good to have the notes you took during your conversation with your child to refer to. And if the school has paperwork to fill out, your notes will also help with that task. At the meeting, be calm. If the bully has violated the school's anti-bullying policy, indicate that. Take notes at this meeting as well. Write down the actions the principal says the school will take. If the principal will let you, use the voice recorder on your smart phone to record the conversation. After the meeting, write the principal a thank-you email or note. In the email or note, reiterate what your understanding of the outcome of the meeting was.[49] Keep all of your correspondence to the school, and all of the school's replies. You may need this record of events.

The next step is to follow up with your child to see if the harassment has stopped after the meeting. If it has not stopped, it may be necessary to give a notice of harassment to the principal, as well as the bully's parents. For a free notice of harassment template, go to http://www.documatica-forms.com/bullying.php. If the bullying *still* doesn't stop, you will need to file a complaint with your superintendent, your school board, and your local police as well. (You're going to have to become a bullying expert. I've put a ton of resources at the end of this chapter.) The very last step, outside of seeking legal recourse on your own, is to file a complaint with U.S. Department of Education and Civil Rights. This is only for serious and life-threatening complaints. Name-calling is horrible behavior and not desirable at all, but it would not be enough for a complaint of this nature. You can file an online complaint form here: https://wdcrobcolp01.ed.gov/CFAPPS/OCR/contactus.cfm or call 800-421-3481.

Stopping and Preventing Bullying

How do we, as parents, take on the system and the hierarchy that fosters bullying so the next LGBTQ students have a better school environment? The presence of a GSA (Gay-Straight Alliance) at a middle school or high school drops the instances of LGBTQ bullying substantially. The work that these clubs do at an individual school level cannot be overstated. LGBTQ students at schools with GSAs were less likely to hear "gay" used in a negative way and were less likely to hear homophobic remarks and/or negative remarks about gender expression. Schools with GSAs were more likely to report that school personnel intervened when hearing homophobic remarks. LGBTQ youth at schools with GSAs experienced lower levels of victimization related to their sexual orientation and gender identity and were less likely to feel unsafe because of their sexual orientation. [50] If your school does not have a Gay-Straight Alliance, help your child advocate for one. Contact sympathetic teachers and other allies who also might champion this cause.

Some schools have had success with restorative justice rather than retributive justice. Retributive justice is what our society is focused on—punishment for breaking rules. Restorative justice focuses on healing the harm caused by crime, bullying, etc. Nancy Schertzing, a restorative justice expert in East Lansing, Michigan, said that restorative justice differs from traditional discipline. "Often when you are speaking with an individual trying to avoid punishment, you are only getting part of the story. If you can bring the person who has been harmed, the person who harmed, their parents (or another adult ally), the story becomes more clear." Schertzing explained the process of restorative justice at the schools she has worked with. The students, their parents or adult allies, a trained restorative justice facilitator, and a teacher or an administrator meet in a facilitated discussion and talk about how to repair the damage from the occurrence. Both parties are allowed to ask questions and offer solutions for how to heal the harm as much as possible.

Schertzing said, "The trouble is when the school calls a parent and says, 'your child bullied another child,' the parent of that child shuts down. Most of the time they refuse to believe their child could do that, and they are no longer receptive to working with the school, so you don't have that ally at home to help with future behavior. Parents and guardians are much more receptive to being invited to a circle for a discussion about how to solve a problem rather than how to punish their child."

Schertzing also cautioned that the word bullying is thrown around a lot. "It's not that bullying isn't a real and serious issue, but sometimes every conflict is being labeled bullying, and the situation escalates from there." Schertzing said parents should first try to get more information before labeling a single instance "bullying."

According to the *Lansing City Pulse*,[51] when Schertzing coordinated the restorative justice program for the Lansing School District, the school district saved 1,838 days of suspension and prevented 15 expulsions and semester-end suspensions just in the 2006-2007 school year alone. Restorative justice can be a tool to break the cycle of violence, punishment, and resentment of the punishment (which sometimes then leads to more violence) in schools.

School-wide initiatives like "tickets" for random acts of kindness also help. A student group at East Lansing High School recently did sticky notes on lockers with compliments for every student and it was very well received.

Bullying must be addressed both individually and from an institutional standpoint to make real and substantial changes.

Do's and Don'ts

1) DO—be aware of the signs your child might be being bullied. If your child is depressed, they may not want to "bother" you, or they may not want you to worry about them. They may not think there is anything you can do. Look for: coming home with damaged or missing clothing or belongings, unexplained cuts and bruises, social isolation (does not hang out with friends, text or snapchat with friends on the weekends, etc.), seems afraid to go to school or ride the bus, or is "sick" a lot to avoid school, has lost interest in school work, appears sad, moody, depressed, complains of headaches or stomachaches, and seems anxious, or expresses anxiety. Rather than ask if they are being bullied, you can ask about teasing, or start a conversation about a news article about bullying. They may think they need to tough it out or handle whatever is happening on their own. Let them know they don't have to and that you are there for them.

2) DON'T—hesitate to change schools, home-school, or look into early-college programs if these are options for you. (Early colleges are relatively new programs that allow a student to go to a community college and earn their high school diploma and their associate's degree at the same time. This change of environment and focus is really good for some teens.)

3) DON'T—let your concerns be dismissed or diminished by school administration. (More on this in the advocacy chapter.) Administrators deal with parents constantly. Some take the tack of minimizing parents' concerns, and some also still feel kids should just suck it up and deal. It is *not* okay if your child is being physically or verbally harassed, or being cyberbullied. This is *not* something a kid should "just deal with."

4) DO—spend time as a family. If necessary, force your teen out of their room, away from their computer, phone, or gaming system and play a board game, watch a movie, go for a walk. Even if you are subjected to eye-rolling, it is important to engage and spend time with your teen, especially if they might be having a tough time at school. If they have a favorite cousin, or one of their siblings is at college or out on their own, consider a visit. A change of scenery and some positive interaction with people they love will help combat the negativity at school.

5) DO—advocate for a GSA if one doesn't exist at your school. Help your child find a teacher who would be willing to help with the club. If school administration is reluctant, show them the GLSEN climate survey as well as other literature that shows the positive impact of a GSA at the middle and high school levels.

6) DO—advocate for peer training, peer leadership training, and a restorative justice program at your school. Breaking the bystander and violence cycle is crucial to reducing bullying. Kids need to know

what to do if they encounter bullying. Advocate for training. You will be helping not only your own child, but all the LGBTQ children who go through the school in the coming years.

7) DON'T—dismiss your child's concerns. If it was something they were able to ignore or deal with themselves, they probably wouldn't have told you about it, or it probably wouldn't be interfering with their school work, etc.

8) DO—go over safe cyber behavior with your teen. Remind them about privacy controls, and that anything that they share electronically can stay on someone's phone or in cyberspace virtually forever.

9) DO—explore good content online and in books with your child. Unfortunately, LGBTQ children have been bullied for a long time now, but many have survived and gone on to lead wonderful personal and professional lives. Even if you don't think your child is being bullied, it may be good to emphasize that this time in their life will pass and that the world is much bigger than their school experiences.

10) DON'T—encourage physical retaliation.

In Their Own Words

Michael Whelan, Colorado

I hated middle school. I mean I absolutely hated it. Every day was all about survival. By first period I was teased and called at least five names, including but not limited to: princess, fairy, faggot, fudgepacker, and queer. By fourth period I had had something stolen and vandalized and been bookchecked three times. I typically was punched or flipped over by the end of lunch. By the end of the day, at least one teacher joined in when students taunted me. This wasn't an average day for me—it was a good one.

Glue in my hair, ending up in the hospital after getting my head slammed into the concrete, or having other students pull pranks and say I was the culprit in attempts to get me expelled—those were things that happened semi-regularly.

At parent-teacher conferences my social studies teacher didn't want to talk about my grades or my work. I was bright but distracted and didn't do a lot of my work. But she didn't see it as laziness like other teachers did; "Danny's chosen a hard life for himself," she said. She was concerned.

I didn't finish out my eighth grade year. I was just "passed" to avoid incidents. I was a liability to the school. And I didn't wear makeup or dress in girl's clothing. I didn't have long hair. I had a buzz cut and was forced to wear baggy Tommy Hilfiger because that made me manly or something.

In high school my parents didn't want me to be "out." They didn't want to deal with what had happened in middle school. And for the first semester I obeyed them until I couldn't anymore. Hiding is not a way to make things better.

"You can't advertise your life like that," my father told me. "You can't expect people not to react the way that they do. If you let it all out there, they're going to act out against you, so do yourself a favor and don't. Otherwise, you're asking for it."

I didn't listen. Hiding who you are is too much work and too much energy, and it seriously damages you. You question your self-worth, have zero self-esteem—it just leaves a mark on your soul. I didn't want that, but I didn't want to fear going to school or just survive each day either.

I guess I was asking for a lot.

Arik Hardin, Michigan

My parents realized I was gay when I was three years old. My peers in school figured it out in fifth grade. It took me quite a while longer. So when the laughing and name calling started, I was completely unprepared.

The first time I ever heard the word gay was during library in fifth grade. I was waiting in line to go back to class with two of my closest friends at the time, Claire and Katie. Everything was going as usual until Katie decided she should tell me the story of Sandy. Sandy was a boy (I'm unsure of Sandy's real gender identity, but when I was told the story, they referred to him as male, so I'll use the male pronouns) that was friends with Katie's older sister. According to her, Sandy was very girly, and he liked clothes and shoes and, most importantly, he owned a bright pink convertible with his name, "Sandy," written across the hood in cursive white letters. They told me that they were worried I was going to become like Sandy. That because I was friends with them, I would become gay (and, as was implied, I would then be a freak). They told me I had to stop talking to them and start finding friends that were boys. I didn't realize at the time why they were doing this, and so I assumed that I had done something wrong, or that they were just being mean to me. So I started to cry. That was the first time I cried about my sexuality (although certainly not the last).

Fifth grade continued, and slowly but surely the staring started. Then came the laughing and the muffled voices I would hear almost every day as I walked past in the hallway. Occasionally I could vaguely hear a few words as I walked by quickly. Usually they were "weird," "freak," and the occasional "gay" thrown in for flavor. This was a very difficult time for young Arik. Up until fifth grade, I had never really experienced any bullying of any kind. I was quiet, I kept to myself, and I was friends with almost everyone (and by everyone I mean all of the girls. Boys were weird to me then). I never had to deal with being called names, and it was a huge shock to the system.

Middle school brought an even bigger shock. There I was, a sixth grader, stuck in the middle of a building filled with multitudes of hormones and changing bodies. All of the anger, fear, and uncertainty that come with getting older was swirling all around us, and I happened to be a perfect target for my classmates to take out their frustrations. Not only was I very obviously gay, but I was also overweight and obsessed with my grades. In other words, I was the bullying trifecta; fat, gay, and nerdy.

There was no way I was going to make it through middle school unscathed out of my tiny town in Michigan.

The worst part about getting teased for being gay was that there was no real way for me to stop it. Being overweight wasn't so bad, because I could work out and eat healthier. Being nerdy was also fine with me, because I could stop raising my hand in class so often, and I could hide my grades from others so they wouldn't know how well I was doing. But I couldn't stop people thinking I was gay. I had (and still have) a very effeminate voice, and I've always been interested in more "girly" things (at the time I was into drawing cute monkeys and making friendship bracelets). That didn't stop me from trying, of course. Once I learned what it meant to be gay from friends (boys kissing boys? Eww), I did everything I could to try to change myself. I stopped talking about the things I liked. I hid my paper when I doodled in class, and I started to wear clothes I hated because I thought they would make me look more "normal" (I still shudder every time I see a T-shirt with a vaguely-clever yet cringe-worthy saying on it). These outward changes stuck with me until I graduated high school (and even a while after that).

Seventh grade was the worst year of my life. For some reason, the name-calling and laughter amped up almost immediately, and there was just about nothing I could do to stop it. There were also two very significant moments that happened to me during that year. The first happened when I was walking home from school one day. Two eighth grade boys who had often called me names in the past decided to follow me home on their bikes. I tried to ignore them, but they insisted on talking to me. They referred to me as "gay boy" (because they didn't know my real name, I assume), and they started to talk to me about sex. They asked me if I really was gay, and if I preferred to suck cock or eat pussy, among other questions. Eventually they realized I would never respond to them, so they gave up and rode away from me. I asked my mom to start picking me up after school that day. I never walked home again.

The second "moment" was really a collection of moments. I started band in sixth grade, but things really got interesting when I got into seventh grade. Our school was very small, and usually a lot of kids would drop out of band after their first year, so the seventh and eighth grade bands had to be combined. It was in this band that I met the biggest bully I would ever have, the eighth grader Christopher P. He decided that I was his biggest enemy the first day of class (partially because I was better than him at trombone, and partially because I was very obviously gay), and he decided then that it would be his personal mission to make every day of my life a living hell. He made fun of my voice, told me I was stupid, called me horrible names, and did everything he could to make sure that I both knew I was gay and that being gay was wrong. In fact, he once told me that I would never be able to get into college because I was gay and he had heard that they didn't allow gay people into colleges (I'm not sure why this hurt me as much as it did, but out of all of the horrible things he said to me over the course of the year, I have never been able to forget this one comment). Christopher bullied me so relentlessly that I quickly started hating band (a class that had been my favorite a year before), and I would go home crying nearly every day, thinking about the insult he had thought up to hurt me that particular day. He was the most directly and intensely hurtful person I had ever met, and every time I saw him in the hallway from then on, I recoiled from him, worried he would take up his old hobby of abusing me. (Many years later I learned that he himself was gay, and so I can only assume he was using me to deal with the frustration he had about his own sexuality. That doesn't make me feel much better about it, though.)

Thankfully, seventh grade was not only the worst year for my bullying, but in a way it was also the last. Early on in eighth grade I decided to listen to what my father often told me, and I stopped showing my classmates that their words hurt me. The clichéd phrase "The words can't hurt you if you don't let them" became my mantra. I stopped crying in class, I stopped replying to the names people would call me, and I stopped acknowledging the insults altogether. And slowly but surely the names stopped coming anywhere near as frequently, and I was able to go into high school with very few worries about bullying.

Of course, the name-calling kept happening, even until the last day of my senior year, and every single word felt like the prick of a very large needle in my chest, but I learned to deal with it internally. Plus, I met some phenomenal people online who let me be myself. They were the first people I opened up to, the first people I came out to, and the first people I could be comfortable with. Without them, I'm not sure how I would have ended up.

I'm not sure if my story can help anyone. I probably could have handled myself and my situation more pragmatically. I could have told my parents, I could have told a teacher. However, if you take anything from my story, I would like you to take these two things:

First, to kids: please do your best to find your tribe. Your tribe is the group of people who make you feel comfortable and safe, the people who love you and will support you no matter what. Not all kids get the chance to have parents that love them like I did, but everyone has the chance to make their own family. I found my tribe though the Internet, but you could find your tribe anywhere; in drama, on a sports team, in an after-school club, or anywhere else. As long as you know that there are people out there that will love and accept you for who you are, you'll be able to make it. Although if your parents are reading this book, then you've already won the gay lottery; you have parents that love you and are trying to be the best they can for you. Congratulations.

Second, to parents: please do anything and everything you can to normalize gay people (and, of course, people of all sexualities, gender identities, and romantic attractions). You don't have to say "If you're gay, that's okay" to your children (in fact, that might even be worse), but you should try to make sure they know that gay people are good, normal citizens worthy of respect. Take my parents, for example. They made the decision not only to not talk to me about my sexuality, but they also decided to act as if gay people didn't exist. They now tell me that they were worried they would influence me or somehow make it worse for me by telling me about other gay people. They were so committed to this idea that they didn't even tell me that my Uncle Jim was gay and in a committed relationship until I was sixteen years old. They missed out on a phenomenal and readily-available opportunity to validate my sexuality without even talking to me about my sexuality. Please don't miss that opportunity with your kid(s). (And please know that I don't have any ill feelings towards my parents for their decision. They made a choice while raising a gay kid and I know they love me very much. But you can do better. Please learn from their mistake.)

Resources

It Gets Better: Coming Out, Overcoming Bullying, and Creating a Life Worth Living by Dan Savage and Terry Miller

Odd Girl Out by Rachel Simmons

GLSEN www.glsen.org

It Gets Better www.itgetsbetter.org

Restorative Justice http://restorativejustice.org/

The ACLU LGBT Project https://www.aclu.org/issues/lgbt-rights

Trevor Project: Leading national organization focused on crisis and suicide prevention efforts for LGBTQ youth. They operate a 24-hour nationwide hotline to provide assistance.

http://cyberbullying.org/smart-social-networking Tips for students to be safe online.

http://www.athinline.org "MTV's A Thin Line campaign was developed to empower you to identify, respond to, and stop the spread of digital abuse in your life and amongst your peers. The campaign is built on the understanding that there's a "thin line" between what may begin as a harmless joke and something that could end up having a serious impact on you or someone else. We know no generation has ever had to deal with this, so we want to partner with you to help figure it out. On-air, online and on your cell, we hope to spark a conversation and deliver information that helps you draw your own digital line."

http://cyberbullying.org "This web site serves as a clearinghouse of information concerning the ways adolescents use and misuse technology. It is intended to be a resource for parents, educators, law enforcement officers, counselors, and others who work with youth. Here you will find facts, figures, and detailed stories from those who have been directly impacted by online aggression. In addition, the site includes numerous resources to help you prevent and respond to cyberbullying incidents."

http://www.wiredsafety.com "WiredSafety is the first online safety, education, and help group in the world. Originating in 1995 as a group of volunteers rating websites and helping victims of cyberharassment, it now provides one-to-one help, resources and extensive information, and education to cyberspace users of all ages on a myriad of Internet and interactive technology safety, privacy and security issues."

http://www.stopbullying.gov/index.html "StopBullying. gov provides information from various government agencies on what bullying is, what cyberbullying is, who is at risk, and how you can prevent and respond to bullying. StopBullying.gov coordinates closely with the Federal Partners in Bullying Prevention Steering Committee, an interagency effort led by the Department of

Education that works to coordinate policy, research, and communications on bullying topics. The Federal Partners include representatives from the U.S. Departments of Agriculture, Defense, Education, Health and Human Services, the Interior, and Justice, as well as the Federal Trade Commission and the White House Initiative on Asian Americans and Pacific Islanders."

Chapter 5

IT TAKES A QUEER VILLAGE—
BUILDING A SUPPORT SYSTEM

I have found that being a parent is one of the most difficult things I have ever done. And I have so many privileges and advantages! My husband and I had times in our 20s where we lived paycheck to paycheck, our two old cars were constantly breaking down, and I didn't have any health insurance, but since then we have been lucky financially. We've been able to afford tutors when our kids needed them, vacations, and to take the pets to the vet when they needed to go. We live in a safe neighborhood with good schools, we have good jobs, yet being a parent can *still* be so exhausting. Being a parent is also one of the most rewarding things I have ever done, but that doesn't mean that fatigue and the occasional frustrations are not real.

When I had Casandra, I got six weeks off from my job at 60 percent pay. Having a baby was considered "short-term disability." Casandra ended up in the hospital for nine days with jaundice and a broken collarbone. Because of that, breastfeeding was hard for both of us. I was so sleep-deprived; I cried all the time. Cried about how much I loved her, cried that I couldn't take her home, cried that I didn't know what I was doing. I felt isolated. I was the first in my group of friends to have a baby, and we didn't have any family in the same town. It was overwhelming.

I got my bearings and found a playgroup at my church, and things got so much better. I had a group of friends who were all going through the same stuff I was. Some were working part-time, some were working full-time, some were stay-at-home full-time moms. We all had kids about the same ages, and it was so nice to commiserate about potty training or to brag about a first soccer goal in Pee Wee soccer. That sense of comradery (my one friend calls it co-madre-y) saved my sanity and sense of self.

Even though my children are now young adults, some of my best friends are still other parents. You sit with these parents on the sidelines (or in my case, poolside). Your kids run in and out of each other's houses and into each other's cars. Your kids are around the same age, so together you worry about grades, boyfriends and girlfriends, teaching them to drive, and all the other milestones of parenting. These friendships can make the time-consuming, strange tasks of parenting (like making breakfast burritos for 25 hungry teenagers) more enjoyable.

It's no different when your child is LGBTQ. Suddenly you are in a world that maybe you didn't expect to be in, or the world you did expect is looking a lot different than you thought it would. It's a world where you could really use a listening ear and the occasional "I've been there/I'm there right now" hug. How do you find your people, both for yourself and your child?

Reaching Out

I don't know about you, but sometimes asking for help is hard for me. I think I should be able to do everything myself, and that if I just tried harder or organized my life a little better, I wouldn't need anyone else. This is a delusion I have to fight. My tendency, if left to my own devices, is to isolate myself. This is not good for me, and, I would argue, not good for anyone. Study after study has shown that those with close relationships, whether romantic or platonic, are healthier, happier, and have better survival rates for serious illnesses.[52] So both you and your LGBTQ child need to find some community (in addition to the community you already have).

First, you have to talk to your child after they have come out to you. Do they want to be out to anyone else? If you have a friend or family member who already has an LGBTQ child or is LGBTQ, mention that person to your child. "Is it okay if I tell Cousin Mary that you've come out to me? I think she might have some valuable insights for us." The very first thing I did after Casandra came out to me was to call my sister Tara. If you already have an LGBTQ family member, or a friend with an LGBTQ child, you have hit the jackpot.

If your child does not want to be out at school or to their school friends yet, *do not* tell other parents of children at their school, no matter how tempted you might be. Parents talk to their children, or their children might overhear or read something not intended for them, then their children repeat it to their peers, and all of the sudden, your child is out at school before they were prepared to be.

If you do not have any LGBTQ friends or family, the next thing to do is head online to pflag.org. You can type in your zip code and see what groups are available in your area. It will either link you to the web page of your area group or give an email contact for you to email about meetings and events. Depending on what area you're in, your PFLAG chapter could be very small and low-key, or very large and active. Get involved if you can! You will meet some great people and be helping to make your area more LGBTQ friendly. Parents with older kids can be a great resource for you, and you in turn can be a great resource for parents with younger kids when the time comes.

If your child is experiencing depression or having a hard time at school, you may want to seek out an LGBTQ-friendly therapist for them and/or your family. Sometimes children are reluctant to go to therapy because of the stigma still attached to it that going to therapy means something is "wrong" with them. If a child doesn't care for therapy or their therapist after several sessions, they may not get much out of the process. We cannot make our child talk or interact with someone; forcing them to go to therapy may be a waste of money. Try to talk to them about what their concerns are, or make a deal with them that they will make an honest effort for three months (or some other time period) and see if they feel better after that time. To get anything out of the process, they will need to feel safe and understood. Just as in every other profession (teachers, attorneys, mechanics, etc.), there are excellent therapists and there are not-so-good therapists. So if your child is complaining not about the actual therapy, but about the therapist, please listen to them and try another therapist. It may take a try or two to find a good fit. *Psychology Today's* website should have a listing of LGBTQ-friendly therapists, and there should be directories in your state as well—just google, or contact your local community mental health clinic.

Community

Are there out teachers at your child's school? These teachers can help you—not only can they be a listening ear, they may be good adults to ask about being the faculty advisor of a GSA if your school doesn't already have one, and they also can keep an eye on your child's friend-group and let you know if they hear about LGBTQ harassment at the school.

Does your child know of any other out children at school? While it might be a little awkward to email a parent you don't know and say, "So.... I hear your kid is LGBTQ...," the vast majority of the time, it will be worth this little bit of awkwardness. You may have a lot in common or you may have nothing in common, but either way you will (hopefully) have an ally at the school for LGBTQ concerns and issues.

If you child is okay with it, you both can talk to their counselor at school. The counselor may be aware of resources at the school and in the community that you and your child don't know about. The school counselor may also have information about LGBTQ-friendly high schools and colleges in your area.

If you live in or near a larger city, you are probably already aware of some of the amazing resources you have. Many people don't know that the United States is now home to over 200 LGBTQ centers in 48 of our 50 states. These centers (many of which are entirely volunteer staffed) offer help to over 43,500 people each week.[53] LGBTQ centers offer everything from social spaces to computer centers and crisis centers, and depending on the location, legal advice and mental and physical healthcare. LGBTQ Centers also help keep LGBTQ people and their families up-to-date on state and national initiatives that may affect them. Go to http://www.lgbtcenters.org/ and see what center may be in your area. They may have teen programs, free literature, and other programming as well. Plus you are bound to meet some really cool, loving, giving people.

Are you near a college or university? Chances are there is some sort of LGBTQ club, center, or organization there. While they may not have any programming for preteens or teens, they are usually happy to answer an email or set up a meeting to talk about resources in the area. (Buy them coffee if you can—they are usually broke undergraduate or graduate students.)

Again, depending on where you live, there might be a Pride celebration. Some activities might be a little much for a younger child, but a lot of times there are activities for teens around the time of Pride. Most Pride organizers remember very well what it was like to be an LGBTQ teenager. One year Casandra went to a teen White party in downtown Lansing. All of the kids wore white. There were snacks, soda, loud music, disco lights and dancing. Sweet drag queens drove golf carts, shuttling the kids back and forth downtown from the party location to the parking lot and to a parent pick-up and drop-off location. Casandra remembers one of the drag queens telling her and some other teens in the golf cart, "If anyone bullies you at school, you tell me, sugars, and *I will come f*ck them up.*" This loving acceptance, this atmosphere of normality and inclusiveness, is so important for your child. Yes, the LGBTQ community has problems (like all communities), but a community together can fix those problems. If there is no community to start with, we are all just trying to tackle our problems alone, which isn't very effective.

The Internet

The Internet is amazing—all this information at the literal touch of our fingertips. If you live in an area without a PFLAG chapter, or work at a job where you cannot make it to PFLAG meetings, the Internet can be a very important resource both for you and your child. Some of the students I have had in classes at Michigan State University have told me how important Internet communities have been to them in their coming out journey and for emotional support. (Be sure to go over Internet safety again with your teen. If they are a younger teen, you may want to give them a list of approved sites they may visit, and check their browser history or use parental controls to make sure they aren't straying off into more adult territory.)

Tumblr is a great resource, with many safe and approved organizations that have Tumblr pages: GLSEN, The Advocate, The Trevor Project, and many more. There are also "fan pages," so if your teen is into a certain show, movie, or book series, they may also meet people on those Tumblr sites. Many teens are more open about their sexual orientation and gender identity online, so they may find friends who like the same books and movies who are also LGBTQ. Many teens have made meaningful friendships with other LGBTQ teens through Tumblr pages.

Wattpad is a social site where LGBTQ people can connect through creative writing.[54] According to the *Daily Dot*, there are four to five million original stories tagged LGBT or LGBTQ on the site. This fulfills a need for LGBTQ people to read stories where they can see themselves in all their complexity, reflected back to them. So often in books and movies, it is still all about the main, straight character. These user-generated stories feature the wide variety of LGBTQ experiences that different people (well, I guess technically characters) have had.

The Trevor Project also maintains an online presence where LGBTQ people ages 13 to 24 can talk about anything they would like. If a teen isn't out at school, this can provide a great release valve to talk about harassment, bullying, fear, or even just not fitting into the "normal" high school experience.

Because Casandra has been pretty open about her sexual orientation, I have been able to help other people whose children just came out to them. I get questions from friends and friends of friends (as well as strangers from the Internet). "What does bisexual mean?" "My daughter told me she was gay, but she's only eleven. How does she know so young?" I try to give resources and websites and explain. I remember how concerned I felt when Casandra came out about what it meant to her life and to her future.

The LGBTQ community and their allies have made tremendous progress in the last years. I would like to say that that progress will continue to be a steady path forward, but like so many times in history, we make a giant stride forward (as with marriage equality) and then there is backlash (like the bathroom law in North Carolina, and "religious freedom" laws that would allow people not to issue marriage licenses if it was against their beliefs). You and your child need a community to help navigate a world that still isn't as safe for LGBTQ people as it should be, and to help make our world a better place for the next generation of LGBTQ children.

Do's and Don'ts

1) DO—reach out. I know it is tempting (especially if your child may not want to be out at school or with other family members yet) to just continue on with your day-to-day life. But fight against those instincts and begin making new friends and learning about new resources now.

2) DO—respect your child's wishes. If they only want you to know right now, don't tell other parents who have children at the school.

3) DO—use the resources that are available. They are there for a reason. You've now read the statistics about bullying, depression, mental health, and suicide in LGBTQ youth. These groups, websites, and Pride celebrations exist for a reason. Your love and acceptance of your child (while absolutely crucial) is not enough. It does take a village.

4) DON'T—be ashamed to ask for help or seek the guidance of an LGBTQ-friendly therapist (either for you, your child, or your family). Sometimes talking to an impartial third party can relieve stress and help you see things more clearly. This doesn't mean there is anything "wrong" with you, your child or your family. It just means you need some support.

5) DO—keep an eye on your younger teens and preteens Internet usage. There are various parental controls available on computers and through your Internet service provider and various apps to download. It is a good idea to

keep the computer in the dining room, family room, or similar common room in the younger years. Later in the high school years, this will be less crucial. They will be better able to navigate the Internet and make their own choices based on the values you've instilled in their younger years.

In Their Own Words

Kris Luce, Florida

In Tampa, the junction between I-275 and I-4 is notorious for turning into one giant parking lot. It doesn't matter if you're going from I-4 to 275, 275 to I-4, east or west, north or south, you're likely to be stuck for months if you hit that junction around rush hour. I am stuck here, waiting for traffic to clear seven exits before the junction. It is Thanksgiving Day.

I'm waiting to pick up my mom from the airport. It's the first time she has flown in nearly thirty years so I expect to hear about the flight: how takeoff and landing made her anxious, how she asked the flight attendant if the plane had been inspected, how during turbulence she grabbed the woman's arm next to her and screamed, "Just don't let me die! I haven't seen my kid since June!"

At the terminal I spot my mom standing under an American Airlines sign. She recognizes my car from the last time I visited Michigan; it's a "salsa" red Chevy Spark and hard to miss. I park and wait for her to walk to the car. She opens the door, "Hey," she pauses, "Where do I put my stuff?" She gestures to the back seat. I forgot that I brought my dogs along for the ride. They fell asleep in traffic and hadn't moved since.

"You can put them in the back with the dogs or you can hold them. They won't bother them."

Amelia, an over-social Doberman mix stands to greet the new person. Her tail wags against the window as she waits for a greeting. It never comes.

"So whose is the other dog?" She refers to Charlotte, a young white and tan Staffordshire Terrier mix.

"Mine. After Erika, my roommate, found that dog at the gas station Amelia made friends with him. When we rehomed him she was acting weird so when I took her to the vet they said to try getting her a friend." I threw my hands in the air, "I told the vet, 'I just rehomed a dog.'"

She laughs, "So now you have how many animals?"

"Too many." I list through our combined animals. Erika has two: a cat named Cissy and a rabbit named Dory. I have the bulk of our petting zoo: two cats, now two dogs, and a cage with seven rats. To top it off, our friend Sam's cat Berlioz is staying with us over his semester's break. We almost compete with my mom's ten cats and one dog.

"So does Erika," she pauses. I know what she is going to talk about. "Know? Is she okay with it?"

This is her way of asking if I am safe in my housing situation. On July 24, 2011, I came out to my mom as transgender. It wasn't a gorgeous moment, but it was the best I could have hoped for. I sent her a letter that I had written over the span of four or five days explaining that I wanted to transition from female to male, change my name, wear more masculine clothing, among other things. She was nervous to talk about it, but she did. Two days later she agreed to help me purchase clothing—something I had requested in the letter. I was eighteen, moving away to college, and didn't have a job.

Before I moved in with Erika I told her that I was trans and that if she wanted to learn more about the community that I would be happy to teach her and let her learn as we lived together.

"Yes, Erika knows. She's learning, but she's fine with it. I told her before I agreed to move in with her."

"What about her boyfriend? Does he care?" My mom adjusts herself in the seat. Her physical discomfort tells me she's not quite ready to have these kinds of conversations.

"Yes, Alex knows. He doesn't care."

I'm happy that conversations like these happen because I want her to know that I am safe and happy where I am. I try to surround myself with people who accept and love me and avoid those who don't. What's the point in being friends with people who can't be happy for me, my transition, and what I've worked so hard to achieve?

Every time I move in with a new person or a new person comes into my life my mom asks me the same things. Sometimes I can't help but laugh. Does she really think I would make friends with someone who hates me or my community? That would be like taking your dog to a groomer who is known to abuse animals. It just doesn't happen.

I think what is hardest for her to understand is that transgender people aren't that difficult to find and people who accept transgender people are even easier to find. Just like men like to hang out with other men and women with women, transgender people tend to flock together, and we enjoy flocking in public to challenge the fragile gender norms of society.

Even in school, with under 100 students in the entire English graduate department, more than 1,000 miles away from my Michigan home, I have met three other trans-identified people.

I want to tell my mom that there will always be a place for me. I want to tell her that I will always find a group of friends that accept me. I want to tell her that I will never stay friends with someone who puts me in danger or jokes about my identity as if it weren't legitimate. I want to tell her that she doesn't need to worry about me, but I know that she will anyway.

I return to her question, "They don't know much, but they're learning."

That's enough for her. On the highway we come to a complete stop behind hundreds of other cars.

"Is there an accident?"

"Nope. Just Tampa traffic."

Resources

www.pflag.org PFLAG's goals are "proud people, loving families, safe community, and a diverse and inclusive world."

Atticus Circle Dedicated to educating and mobilizing straight allies to advance equal rights for lesbian, gay, bisexual and transgender partners, parents, and their children.

ACLU's Get Busy/Get Equal Information and resources to improve the lives of LGBTQ people.

GLBTNearMe Find local social and support resources within the LGBTQ community.

GLBT National Help Center Provides free and confidential telephone and Internet counseling, information and local resources for LGBTQ callers.

https://www.wattpad.com/ Free stories to read. Upload your own.

Bisexual Resource Guide (4th Edition), Edited by Robyn Ochs, A guide providing information about bisexual organizations and events for social support, activism, and other general information about issues related to bisexuality.

Chapter 6

PARENTING YOUR NON-BINARY OR TRANSGENDER CHILD

Gender is ingrained in us, even before we are born. People excitedly ask expectant parents, "Do you know if you're having a boy or a girl?" Parents paint the walls of nurseries blue or pink, and buy frilly pink dresses for girls and blue masculine striped shirts for boys. Studies[55] have shown that people consistently treat boy babies and girl babies differently. Boy babies are held more and girl babies are talked to more. Boy babies get trucks and footballs. Girl babies get dolls and stuffed animals. Each and every day children (and adults) receive messages of what a man is supposed to do and be and what a woman is supposed to do and be. We watch commercials. We talk to other people. We participate in classrooms and meetings where women are interrupted and ignored, and men aren't allowed to express any emotion except for anger because crying and compassion are supposedly feminine. Gender is a fundamental underpinning of our society—and people get really upset and concerned when anyone questions why things are this way, and why things *have* to be this way.

Some people, who find the very discussion of questioning gender and gender stereotypes disturbing, talk about the way God intended things to be, or the way things are "naturally." As we talked about in Chapter 2, a lot of things have occurred "naturally" throughout the ages. And in addition to gender identity, about one in every 1,500 to 2,000 children at birth have "ambiguous" or "atypical" genitalia.[56] This, too, has happened throughout human history. These individuals are called intersex, and the response has been to surgically remake these children to adhere to one gender to make things "easier" for them in our culture. As science has evolved, we have realized that surgery is not necessarily always the best course of action. For example, in earlier times they would not realize that a boy's testicles had not descended, or that a baby who "looked" like a girl might have XY chromosomes. Now, being intersex and transgender are (sometimes) two independent constructs, but intersex people clearly illustrate that not every person is "naturally" born a man or a woman, as if genders were the North and South Poles. (A lot of people are born on the equator, too.) Like sexual orientation, gender too exists on a continuity scale or a spectrum.

Some parents are also concerned that if "everything is on the table" in terms of gender and sexual orientation, that the very fabric of our society will fall apart, all of our young people will start being super confused and trying everything, and all of a sudden every teenager will be a non-binary gender pansexual and the United States' streets will look like something out of Sodom and Gomorrah. Take a deep breath and think about this critically. For centuries we have had LGBTQ people in heterosexual marriages because they wanted to fit into our heteronormative society. And while I am sure they had good things in their lives too, they were probably pretty miserable. For centuries, we have had people who didn't feel comfortable with their gender either conform to their assigned gender (because they basically had no choice), or pass as their identity gender, and pray they didn't "get caught," because people have been literally raped and murdered for "tricking" people about their gender.

In no way is giving someone who is cisgender and/or heterosexual information about the gender spectrum going to "turn" them into a non-binary gender person. Take me. I met my sister's first girlfriend when I was 12. I have read consistently about homosexuality throughout my life, and I have so many LGBTQ friends and family I would be hard-pressed to sit down and name them all without the help of Facebook to remind me of who is straight and who isn't. And here I am at 48 years old, still cisgender and straight. What all of this reading and interaction has done is to help me to understand someone else's experience. That's it.

Might your child experiment? Might they dress as the opposite gender? Sure. And I promise you again that this type of thing has always taken place. But the difference is that for a trans child or teen, it isn't an experiment, they are trying to have their body conform to their interior experience. *You will be able to tell the difference by talking about their experiences with them. Trust your child.* No one sets out on this very tough road just to be different or for attention.

I am by no means an expert on gender identity. But I do know two things for sure. I know that no matter what your child is going through or what identity they are expressing, they need to know you love them and will support them, and that you will listen to them and, if need be, learn from them and grow in your own understanding of gender and our culture. The second thing I know for sure is as our culture evolves, so do our expectations and definitions of gender. Gender is not a fixed construct dependent on having a penis or a vulva; that is your biology, the makeup of your physical body. Gender is very much an *idea*. I believe if you can love your child and realize that to an almost impossible-to-believe extent we have been conditioned to believe that gender is fixed and polarized, you are going to do just fine parenting your transgender or non-binary child.

The statistics back me up on my knowledge of those two things. According to the 2012 Transpulse survey, 35 percent of trans teens who felt they had strongly supportive parents occasionally thought of suicide, but did not attempt suicide. Sixty percent of trans teens who felt their parents weren't supportive, or had parents who were strongly against their gender expression, contemplated suicide, but almost every single person in that 60 percent had attempted to take their own life. Teens who said they had supportive parents were *93 percent less likely overall to commit suicide.*[57]

Your love is a powerful antidote. Use it generously.

The World is Changing

If your teen has come to you and told you they might be trans or non-binary gender, they have probably done a lot of research themselves. They may have read articles online, talked to people they trusted, read books, or gathered information in other ways. Depending on your background and comfort zone, you may have some catching up to do. In a recent study, almost half of millennials surveyed believed gender was a spectrum, about half believed there were just two genders, and a small percentage said they didn't know.[58] If you posed that same question to middle-aged or senior people, you would get a very different response. So if you need to "catch up," you need to do so quickly, because your child wants to have conversations with you, and you need to know the language they are using to express themselves.

Your child was given what is called an "assumed" or "assigned" gender at birth. This gender assessment was made by looking at their sexual organs. Don't use the term "real" gender or "gender at birth" because a trans or non-binary gender person was also very likely born with their identity at that same time. To them, they have always been this gender, so to refer to their "original gender" or "real gender" marginalizes them further. This may seem like I'm being prissy about words, but language does matter and we want to use language that is respectful of our children and respectful of everyone's differences. I don't think this is being "politically correct," I think this is just trying to be a decent human being. Minority stress (which we cover in the next chapter) is a real thing. We can certainly do something as small as adjusting our language to make the lives of trans and non-binary gender children easier. Here are a few terms to get your started. (I highly recommend *The Transgender Teen: A Handbook for Parents and Professionals Supporting Transgender and Non-Binary Teens* by Stephanie Brill and Lisa Kenney for a more in-depth look at vocabulary as well as for more in-depth information about medical decisions that you and your teen might be facing.)

Cisgender—refers to those of us whose gender lines up with our assumed or assigned sex at birth.

Gender binary—boy/man vs. girl/female. Some people are firmly on one end or the other of this binary. But a lot of people fall in between those two poles.

Gender—the complex ways we interact with our body, and the way society interacts with us based on our body, how we present our gender to others, and our internal sense of self. Gender is changeable and mutable over time, and different culture to culture.

Non-binary gender—an umbrella term for people who are not exclusively boy/man or girl/female. This is not a perfect term, but helps in places like this book where it is simply impossible to capture every different person's experience on this deeply personal issue.

Transgender/trans/trans*—people who feel deep incongruity with their assumed or assigned sex, and feel aligned with perhaps the opposite end of the binary they've been placed on since birth. Being transgender does not imply sexual orientation. Trans people can be gay, straight, bisexual, etc. (The asterisk is used to indicate other people who are non-binary gender. Again, this is shorthand, generally used for books and articles where listing every potential identity would be impractical.)

The Science of Transgender

Even in the late 20th century, some doctors and therapists still believed that being transgender was the result of some childhood trauma or dysfunctional family dynamic. With further research and the increasing accuracy and new technology of brain scans, this old myth has been debunked.[59] Studies in 2013 and 2014 indicate that trans people have different brain structures than those who identify with their assigned birth gender. Scientists say these scans don't necessarily show a "male" brain or a "female" brain but a brain that is different than either one of those constructs. A trans brain.[60]

Another study done in Australia in 2008 also showed that the sex receptors in trans hormone genes were different than people who identified with their assigned birth gender. The preliminary findings from this study indicate that the sex hormones estrogen and testosterone act "differently" than with a different receptor. [61]

These studies are just the beginning of understanding the science and genetics of transgender. All of this to say once again that this is not something your child had a choice about.

Communication

This may sound like a cop-out, but it truly isn't. Everyone is different. You and your child are on a unique journey. Many transgender people never take hormones or have surgery. Many transgender people do take hormones. Some have surgery also. These are complex issues and deeply personal, and I am supportive of whatever a person needs to do to feel that they are in this world the way they are meant to be. The American Medical Association issued a statement in 2014 that a transgender person shouldn't have to have surgery to change their gender on their birth certificate.[62] I completely agree. Don't assume when your child says they are trans that there are costly medical procedures ahead. There might very well be, but just stay with your child in the right here and right now. They may like their body just fine. They may not even be able to sleep because they hate their body so much. Stay with them, wherever they are on their journey.

They are probably really scared, whether they will admit it or not. There will be many challenges ahead for both of you—potentially changing legal documents, acquiring letters needed for hormone therapy.[63] Try to take it one day at a time. Your child probably hasn't had time to fully consider gender and what it means in our world (heck, have any of us?), and it is okay if they are confused (or if you are confused) and if neither one of you have all the answers. Ask questions, do research together. Reach out for support. It is a journey and it will probably be a tough one, to be honest. But you will also be together as a team talking about this really meaningful thing, and that will make it so much easier for both of you.

Monitoring Your Child's Mental Health

Because of our current cultural values and stereotypes surrounding gender, your child is at a great risk for depression, isolation, loneliness, and suicidal ideation.

Professional counseling might be a good idea, but please make sure the therapist is an LGBTQ-affirming therapist. *The Transgender Teen: A Handbook for Parents and Professionals Supporting Transgender and Non-Binary Teens* has some great questions to ask a potential mental health provider. Depending on where you live, you may have to drive to find an LGBTQ-affirming therapist. Make the trip if you can possibly afford it. It is crucial. If a child ends up in a not-good therapy situation after already experiencing our society's rejection of non-binary gender people, it could be extremely damaging to them.

Do's and Don'ts

1) DO—notice how gender impacts us daily. Listen to the way that men and women talk. Notice how you feel when you see someone whose gender you can't immediately identify. Do you feel uncomfortable? Why do you suppose that is?

2) DO—express your love and support to your child frequently. Try to spend some extra time together.

3) DON'T—be too concerned if their notion of gender evolves as they get older and get more information. Remember, the identity they are experiencing is always real to them. Be supportive of it and suggest a LGBTQ-affirming mental health expert if they really are struggling. That person might be able to help guide them through their questioning.

4) DO—respect their pronouns and their new name if they choose one. Of course you may slip up occasionally—just correct yourself and move on. Be upfront with your child. "I've called you Erica for a long time, but I'll get used to calling you Eric. If I slip up, I'll either catch myself, or you let me know." Language is important and such an easy thing to change with a little patience and attention.

5) DON'T—force them to be "out" in the world if they are not ready to be. They are still trans even if they don't tell anyone.

In Their Own Words

Michael Whelan, Colorado

When your child wants to express who they are or their feelings, don't stop them. Don't warn them or discourage them. Don't even pause. Even if you want to stop them, warn them out of a place of love—because the world is a scary and sometimes hateful place and you reason you don't want it to be any harder for your child—that is still fear you're piling on them, instead of love and acceptance. The world has enough fear, which is so often tied to hate. Take your son to buy nail polish. Let your daughter take shop class and buzz her head. Let your children be happy. And when other people take out their fear or hate on your child, do not waver in your support. Comfort them and tell them that they are beautiful just the way they are. Then go get some more nail polish or talk shop with them. It seems small, but doing this will make the greatest difference in your child's self-esteem and self-worth. It's the greatest single thing I wish my parents had done. The thing I wish I could get across to every other parent out there.

Heidi Czerwiec, parent, North Dakota/Minnesota

My son Wyatt is lovely—liquid brown eyes with long lashes, and thick brown hair, which makes him stand out among all the towheaded toddlers in the Scandinavian Upper Midwest. He's always been an interesting mix—strong nurturing instincts combined with an intense desire to train to be a ninja. He enjoys dress-up, and is equally likely to want to wear a pirate vest and boots to preschool as he is his bright yellow bumblebee tutu skirt. It never bothered me what he chose to wear, though occasionally other kids and parents might comment on the tutu. (*Wyatt knows he's a boy, right?*) Fortunately, when I wasn't around, his amazing teachers had his back.

And yet I was surprised that it took me by surprise how upset Wyatt got at the dress-up clothes I bought him for his great-grandmother's funeral. Knowing we had that event, followed by my husband's law-school graduation and an aunt's wedding, I selected a set of khakis, white button-down shirt, and a sweet plaid vest. As soon as he saw the outfit laid out on his bed, he threw it to the floor and started sobbing. I pieced together that he had interpreted "dress-up clothes" to mean he would be wearing a dress. With only an hour before the funeral, I bargained with him: I apologized for the misunderstanding and offered to let him pick out a dress for graduation if he would wear this outfit now. He agreed.

As soon as we returned home, he demanded to know when we would go buy his dress. My husband was at first resistant—not opposed, but worried at how family and graduation attendees at his relatively conservative school would react. But he agreed that we needed to let Wyatt know that if this was important to him, it was important to us, that his comfort with his appearance took precedence over other people's, over ours. I took Wyatt shopping, and he chose a floral sundress with a tulle underskirt. In the dressing room, he preened and twirled; he smiled the whole way home. Once home, I called family who would be at the graduation to firm up details of their visit, and casually worked in that we were all excited, especially Wyatt, who bought a brand-new dress to celebrate.

And they were great. The day of graduation, they fussed appropriately over his outfit—which he paired with his Batman sandals and hoodie, then asked to wear some of my perfume and lipgloss—but didn't make too big a deal out of it. I was more wary of my husband's classmates, and we got some stares, but many of his friends complimented my son and snapped pictures.

The dress got hung up in his closet. That summer, he occasionally asked to wear it, and did, but because it was so delicate, I let him pick out a couple knit jersey sundresses for everyday play. He occasionally wore those. When it came time to cut his thick hair, he asked to grow it out, so we picked out some barrettes and headbands to keep it out of his face. Then, he asked to cut it short again.

I was confused—I thought Wyatt had been signaling that he was identifying as femme, and I tried to educate myself about what that meant and what to expect. But he wasn't consistently and persistently insisting on appearing feminine. He switched back and forth between shorts and sundresses, between Rescue Bots and beading bracelets. He is a child whose identity isn't defined by easy labeling.

Understand that my attempts at "easy labeling" didn't make it easy for me—I worried constantly about Wyatt and how the world would react to him, how he would react to their reactions. By trying to label his identity, though— potentially gay, trans, queer—I was trying to manage those reactions, lock them down by locking him down, so I knew how to parent him, how to protect him. The idea that he didn't fit any of those labels was at first terrifying.

How was I supposed to know how to parent Wyatt? Who is Wyatt?

Then I realized that I was the only one confused—Wyatt isn't confused. Wyatt is Wyatt. If he wants to wear a dress, he wears a dress. If he wants to be a ninja, he shows us his kicks and spins. Wyatt is not a gender. Wyatt is a spectrum. I don't know if this says more about his own emerging identity, or about a cultural shift in identity—that we're finally acknowledging that people can perform a range of self-expression. The old binaries, the old labels (male/female, gay/straight) are exploding in ways that, strangely, give me hope—not just for Wyatt, but for our future, and for the future of all our kids.

Resources

My Kid's First Dress (essay) by Yuvi Zalkow—a father, despite his initial misgivings, buys his four-year-old son a dress

How Rejecting Gender Made Me Healthier, Happier, Complete (essay) by D. Michael Whelan

A Guide to Hormone Therapy for Trans People

Middlesex (novel) by Jeffrey Eugenides

What Becomes You (memoir) by Aaron Raz Link and Hilda Raz

The Transgender Teen: A Handbook for Parents and Professionals Supporting Transgender and Non-Binary Teens by Stephanie Brill and Lisa Kenney

Chapter 7

BEING AN ADVOCATE

It seems like every time I open my web browser, I read another article about how this generation of parents sucks. We are helicopter parents,[64] raising a bunch of fragile narcissists. Supposedly this generation needs "safe spaces" and are "hurt by words" while previous generations were super tough and awesome. I have been skeptical of these articles from the beginning. The young adults I interact with every day—my kids, their friends, the students I teach—don't seem to fit this stereotype. Yes, Mom and Dad might be involved more financially in their children's lives than in previous generations, but our children are entering high school, college, and the workforce in one of the worst times in the United States' economic history. College is more expensive than it ever has been, and there has never been more pressure to be "advanced," do well in sports, take AP classes, and get good grades, because college acceptance is also more competitive than previously, as well. This generation has seen every major institution that previous generations believed in and trusted fall to scandal and corruption; the Catholic Church, Wall Street, our sports heroes, the political establishment. (I seriously cannot even keep up with all the scandals in Washington D.C.) It is hard to trust anyone or anything after seeing so much corruption at high levels. I don't believe for a second that our millennials have it easy. Some of them do, of course, but some kids in my generation had it pretty easy, too.

I think it is just human nature to talk trash about the upcoming generation. I am from Generation X, and I remember being called a slacker and being accused of living in my parents' basement when I was working two jobs, renting my own apartment (with roommates), and my parents didn't even own their own home (and the Michigan basement of that home was utterly terrifying. It could have been a set for a horror movie).

This attitude of dissing the upcoming generation has been going on for a while. Socrates said, "The children now love luxury. They have bad manners, contempt for authority; they show disrespect for elders and love chatter in place of exercise." I think our younger generation is just like previous generations, not better, not worse, just *different*.

I'm bringing up helicopter parenting for a couple of reasons. First, millennials face challenges we never had to face. Can you imagine trying to do your reading and homework for high school and college amidst social media and Netflix? My roommates and I wasted enough time in college playing the card game euchre, watching a black and white TV, and going to the snack shop in the basement of our college dorm to buy breadsticks. I can't imagine how much time we would have wasted with a world of entertaining content just a click or swipe away. This generation needs a lot of discipline to get even the most basic things done, and I admire their dedication. Second, I want to make it very clear that advocating for your LGBTQ child is not helicopter parenting. We hear these horror stories of parents calling professors and high school teachers to discuss their child's grades, and we don't want to be *that* parent. We don't want to do anything detrimental to raising a responsible adult.

Advocating means something different. When your child is a part of an institution—church, school, Boy Scouts, sports teams, 4-H, etc.—there is always a fundamental imbalance of power. Your child is a *child*, and your child has been indoctrinated from birth to respect authority and to do the best they can to please the adults around them. This is a good thing! Most adults in your child's life are just like you—they want to keep your child safe and help them grow and thrive, and they deserve respect when being spoken about and spoken to. But our LGBTQ children can run into trouble for several different reasons. The first is our heteronormative society. There is the assumption of straightness about everyone. Every day your child is steeped in heteronormative culture—99 percent of movies feature a mom and dad, not two moms or two dads. Everyone's gender identity is very clear. That is a man, that is a woman, and they act in man-like or woman-like ways. Same for popular songs, commercials, billboards, and a thousand other media messages. Novels are also guilty of this—yes, there is some great LGBTQ fiction, nonfiction, poetry, and films, but these are more difficult to find and they probably won't be at your child's library or suburban multiplex. Most of your child's friends are straight. And I don't think the high school prom has changed substantially in decades. The boy asks the girl. The boy dresses in a tux and the girl a pretty dress. Our entire American culture is telling your child they are abnormal and strange. (Things are getting better, but the assumption of straightness, traditional gender identity, and gender roles is still an underpinning of our daily lives.)

People within these institutions can have their own prejudices and biases as well. If your gay son likes to wear his hair long, knit, or bake cupcakes, or your lesbian daughter wears her hair cropped, likes to weld, and wants to go to the vocational tech center instead of traditional high school, those kids may encounter teachers and administrators who do not like them, their actions, or the way they are challenging cultural norms. And if this person is in a position of power over your child (the power to give grades, enroll them in classes, write letters of recommendation, or just make their daily life more or less pleasant), you may have some advocating to do.

The institutions themselves may be inherently biased as well. Take the Boy Scouts. Until 2013, you could not be a Boy Scout and be gay. Until 2015, you could not be gay and a Boy Scout leader. There are still institutions that are supposedly protecting "traditional values" by only letting straight or cisgender boys and girls participate. Here again, a parent would have some advocating to do.

There is also something called minority stress. This is stress from day in and day out interaction with a toxic culture as a member of a stigmatized minority group.

There are daily microaggressions (brief and commonplace verbal, behavioral, or environmental indignities, whether intentional or unintentional, that communicate hostile, derogatory, or negative slights and insults toward people of color and other marginalized peoples interpersonal conflicts, and discrimination).[65] So it's not just the one time someone calls your kid a faggot, or a classmate says something uncool is gay, it's the cumulative stress of these daily interactions.[66] Most people can ignore something that happens once in a while. But they can't ignore the daily harassment and disrespect even if it seems small. (If it happens regularly, trust me, it doesn't feel small.) Minority stress is another reason your child needs you as an advocate. They can't take on all of this on their own.

Advocating isn't necessarily solving the problem for your child. It's not doing their laundry or their homework. It's not saying they don't have to do any chores around the house, and it's not emailing their teacher to say they really deserved an A in pre-calc and not a B-. Advocating is correcting the imbalance of power that might occur in a situation where your child is at a disadvantage. Parents of special needs children spend huge chunks of their time advocating for their children—for IEPs, for accommodations, for opportunities for their children that the rest of us take for granted. Sometimes as parents of LGBTQ children we must do this, too.

To advocate, we must first gather information (and this includes asking questions—questions to our child, questions to the people involved, and questions to friends or family who may have encountered something similar while parenting). Then we need to learn the rules—

whatever the institution (schools, clubs, sports, etc.), there are always rules, handbooks, guidelines, and "proper channels." We have to find out what the processes are so we can navigate them and get to the person and/or people who can help us. We also need to plan—before meetings, what to say in an email, and how to present the information we've discovered, all these things. We need to keep written records of our conversations, emails, and meetings.

To be an advocate, we also have to listen. The person we are talking to might have a key piece of information, but if we are too angry or not listening, we won't be able to process what they are trying to tell us. Finally, we need to propose solutions. What is best for our child in whatever situation is occurring? What might be the outcomes? What might happen if we implement suggested solutions?[67]

Let's say your child has a teacher who is biased against LGBTQ people. We will call this teacher Mr. Jones. We don't know why Mr. Jones is a homophobe. Maybe he has experienced same-gender attraction himself. Maybe he was raised a strict, evangelical Christian. Maybe a gay person once stole his bicycle. We're not going to psychoanalyze Mr. Jones, we're just going to say he's kind of a dick. Your daughter Gina, who is a good student and has never gotten in any serious trouble at school, has Mr. Jones for health class (usually a requirement at every high school). Gina has a girlfriend, Sam. One day Sam walks with Gina to health class. They are holding hands, and Gina gives Sam a quick hug at the door as they separate to go to their different classes. Mr. Jones sees this, talks sternly to Gina about public displays of affection, and sends her to the principal. Gina has to go down to the office, where the principal warns her that with her next PDA she will be written up and it could lead to a three-day suspension. Gina comes home upset and tells you all about it.

Now, Gina has played volleyball forever. And you don't know how many times you have seen the volleyball girls hug after games, after a good block or spike, or in the hallways, goofing around with each other, sitting on each other's laps, taking photos for Instagram, etc. You've been to the school for conferences and other events and have seen heterosexual couples hold hands and hug in the hallways, and you really feel like Gina and Sam are being singled out because they are a same-gender couple and Mr. Jones doesn't like it.

You have several options at this point. You can ignore the whole thing and tell Gina she's on her own. You can tell Gina to be sure to not to touch Sam (or anyone else for that matter) at school. Or, you can advocate.

I would recommend you advocate. Your advocacy will depend on your school policies and rules, so be sure to get a copy of your school handbook. This is probably available on the school's website to download as a PDF. Check and see what the PDA policies are. Be sure to follow the procedures exactly. If the handbook says to contact the teacher directly, contact Mr. Jones and set up an appointment to talk to him. I would take Gina with you. You want to set this example for her. Like I talked about in the bullying chapter, take notes at this meeting. Express your concerns, in this case the unfairness of Gina and Sam being singled out for something that basically all the kids at the school do.

Unfortunately, things escalate after your meeting. Mr. Jones starts giving Gina bad grades, and sending her down to the office for other disciplinary concerns. This is the point in this stressful situation where you might start to lose sleep. Is it worth it to continue on with this? What's the point, you might think. The more you advocate, the worse things seem to be getting for Gina. Can she just suffer through the rest of the semester? You are so busy with work and your own father is sick and the cat needs to go to the vet. But this is also the point where you have to remind yourself that Gina is not the only gay student at that school, and that more LGBTQ students are going to have to deal with Mr. Jones, and even if you don't "win" this interaction, you will have left a paper trail for the next LGBTQ mom or dad who needs to take on Mr. Jones. It is also important to remember Gina, first and always. What messages are you sending her about what is acceptable behavior? What are you saying with your advocacy (or lack of it)? *She is worth it. You believe her. You will do your best to make sure that she is treated fairly.*

I hope while you are parenting your LGBTQ child that you don't run into a Gina-type situation, or an even worse scenario. If you do, use the resources in the previous chapters—your school and its district resources, any city ordinances, Lambda Legal, the ACLU, and anti-bullying legislation or policies. But also remember their greatest resource is you—an invested, caring, calm, but relentless parent, determined to seek a solution for their child.

Dos and Don'ts

1) DO—read the school handbook. Yes, I know it's boring. Read it anyway.

2) DO—keep your school allies close. Is there a teacher your child has had several times that they really like? Is there a teacher there you went to high school with, or a teacher who is there that was also there when you were in high school? Are you friends with one of those well-connected parents, you know the ones, president of the PTA and the coordinator of the teacher's lunch? Check in with these allies. Ask them what is happening and what the reputation is of the teacher or administrator your child might be having trouble with.

3) DON'T—waste your capital. Your child needs to be their own advocate where their grades are concerned (unless you feel they are being marked down because of being LGBTQ). Don't contact the administration over small stuff like a B- or a minor incident in the hallway. This way, when you bring something to the school's attention, they know you are not a helicopter parent who complains about every little thing.

4) DO—get involved at the school if you can. I know how busy work and other things can be. I know you might also be caring for an elderly parent on top of being a parent yourself and working. But if you can go to the occasional PTA meeting, or help when the school asks for volunteers, do it if you can. Not only will it give

you a better idea of the school environment, it will also make you a recognizable face, and this again will help you if a situation occurs where you need to advocate.

5) DON'T—give up. If it is a situation that is unacceptable, keep working your way up the hierarchy. This is especially true for a bully or a homophobic teacher or coach, who might go on making life miserable for other LGBTQ children long after your child has left the school. The stakes are too high to give up.

6) DO—follow the guidelines for complaints that are in the handbook and/or on the institution's website. It will make it too easy to dismiss your concerns if you are seen as not caring about the "proper channels."

7) DO—remember there is power in numbers. Has this happened to other students as well as your child? Reach out to other parents. See if they too will come forward and talk to the teacher/administrator/superintendent/board, etc.

In Their Own Words

Seth Fischer, California

The clearest image I have of my dad is from the day I told him I was bi.

The Alzheimer's hadn't yet hit him in any serious way, though if I had known to watch his behavior closely, I would've probably seen a few of the earliest signs. His bright orange hair was almost gone, and what was left was a mix of orange and white, toilet bowling around his head. He had newer frames on his glasses, the kind that blended in with his skin so you had to look twice from a distance to notice there was anything on his face.

He was the last parent I told. This wasn't because I was afraid of his reaction, necessarily. He always told me that he'd had a roommate in college who was gay; he'd said that it was horrible, all the oppression that man had to live through. I think I was scared to tell him because telling him would make coming out the most real. Of all my parents, he was always the most grownup of the grownups. This would cement it. There was no return to the closet after this.

I asked him to go for a walk with me. There's a park down the street from his suburban Boston home called Pequosette, but no one can pronounce it, so we called it PQ. I'd just started dating a guy I liked very much. I wanted to introduce my dad to him. But I had to come out first. His heart was bad. I didn't know what would happen if I just showed up with a guy and introduced him as my boyfriend. I wanted to do it gently. I was old to come out, twenty-five, and I had dated a long series of women, so I had a good feeling this would be a shock to him.

I was so nervous my hands were sweating, my back was sweating, my chest was sweating. It was a perfect sort of day, maybe in the low seventies. Perfect days don't come very often near Boston.

I said to him, "I need you to know that I'm bi."

For a second, he looked like I'd hit him. He took a deep breath, and nothing came out. We were in the middle of the park. There were kids playing on the swing set. The old video store still sat abandoned in the background.

"Okay," he finally said, and then he paused a moment before saying, "I don't understand why you have to tell people. Lots of men sleep with other men sometimes. It doesn't mean you have to tell people about it."

Some part of me knew this wasn't the right thing for him to say, but I needed to keep the moment normal.

"Well, it's important to me for several reasons," I continued, keeping my voice even, mimicking the intellectual, calm voice he favored, trying not to yell. I never have yelled at my dad as an adult, not since I was sixteen, and I wasn't about to start now. "I'm dating a guy I like, and I—"

But then, he kept going.

"I was ... assaulted ... by some older boys ... once when I was younger."

If your child ever comes out to you, please don't ever say that, even if it is true.

He was crying a little. There really wasn't much I could say. "I'm sorry," I think is what I managed.

Then he hugged me.

It wasn't fair, what he'd said, what he'd just done. It was maybe even cruel. Probably self-involved. Most definitely tragic. I was telling him something big about me, and it'd dredged out some horrible stuff about him that he couldn't keep down. But believe it or not, the hug made up for it. He held me tight, my head on his shoulder, with the kind of paternal affection I'd wished for when I was a teenager. For a second, I felt like a little boy again. For the first time since I'd come out to most people, I felt safe.

I could sit here and break down all the problems with what he said to me, how it is biphobic and homophobic all at the same time. How he had turned around and made it about him. How tragic it was that he had lived with this his whole life and it was this unresolved. How it reinforced my own fears, how it was exactly that kind of thinking that has kept the majority of bi people in the closet, how merging sexuality with sexual violence is something that homophobes and sexually repressed people have been doing for centuries. But I'm not going to go into that.

What I really want to say is that my dad was trying his best to connect to me, and I could see that. I was mad for a while, yes, but I could also see that the errors he made came from real concern and love and unresolved traumas from his past. He wanted to protect me from the bullies of the world. He wanted to connect with me. He wanted to understand me. He was in the early, early stages of a terrible disease. I wish he hadn't said what he said, but I forgave him because I recognized the love behind his kind of horrible reaction. Because I felt it in that hug. And if you show your kid love, they will see it, no matter how much you mess up.

Resources

This is a Book for Parents of Gay Kids: A Question and Answer Guide to Everyday Life by Dannielle Owens-Reid and Kristin Russo

Supportive Families, Healthy Children: Helping Families with Gay, Lesbian, Bisexual, and Transgender Children by Caitlin Ryan, PhD

Helping Families Support Their Lesbian, Gay, Bisexual, and Transgender (LGBT) Children (PDF) by Caitlin Ryan, PhD

Bi Any Other Name, Bisexual People Speak Out edited by Loraine Hutchins and Lani Kaahumanu.

Chapter 8

SIBLINGS AND OTHER FAMILY MEMBERS

You love and support your LGBTQ child (or you wouldn't be reading this book.) But one of the most painful things that can happen is when one of your parents, in-laws, or siblings do not support your child. In my family, three out of four of my and my husband's parents were dead before Casandra came out to us, and my mother (who was so cruel to my sister Tara when she came out) is now in a nursing home. But I did have a family member who told me it was "too bad" that Casandra had turned out gay. I think this family member had no idea how offensive they were being to me. I think that, in their own way, they were trying to be nice, to commiserate with me. I felt very angry, but I didn't feel able to talk about that anger to this person.

Which leads me to communication again. My dad could rarely express his emotions. I knew he loved me though he rarely, if ever, said those words. And I learned very early on that if I had a difference of opinion with my mother, she took it as a personal attack. If I wanted a relationship with her, I had to agree with her, or just not mention or talk about whatever it was. I also remember my mom getting angry, which was scary to me as a child. I remember one time, I don't even know how old I was, when my mom and dad were fighting, and my mother opened up the cupboard and started smashing all the plates in the cupboard on the ground, one at a time. I felt terrified at her loss of control, and I didn't know what she might do next.

My mother wasn't mentally stable, but I think the dynamic of "if you love me, you have to agree with me" can happen even in more functional relationships. A friend of mine's relationship with her parents decayed when they wouldn't respect her differing political beliefs. She would ask her parents, "I'm coming home for Thanksgiving. Can we please leave politics at the door?" And they would never do it. Her mother was always trying to persuade my friend that she was wrong. She took her daughter's rejection of her politics as a personal affront and lost her relationship with her daughter as a result of it.

It is hard to navigate conflicts in relationships under the best of circumstances. And I don't like confrontation. I'm a youngest child and I just want everyone to get along. I want everyone to like me. I want everyone to have a space to be heard. I want to respect everyone's opinions. The youngest child in me wants to build a consensus, a coalition. As I've gotten older, all those impulses are still there (please like me, please?), but I've also discovered that sometimes people's opinions are just wrong. And while we certainly can't stop someone from having a belief or an opinion, it is not okay for them to express a hurtful belief or opinion to your child. It is not okay to use harmful language around your LBGTQ child. No, your uncle may not tell your child, "All fags burn in hell." If that were to happen, you would need to confront that behavior.

We know this, right? We know it isn't good for your child to hear hurtful language or judgments about their eternal souls, but we also want to keep peace in the family. And there are no perfect families. Every family has strengths and weaknesses. I've had to work hard to be honest and open and express my emotions with the people I love, because that was not a strength of my family. I'm still not sure I'm great at this. We are also a divided country, and those divides (sometimes chasms) show up in our own families—some family members may be very religious, some might be atheists, and some may have different faiths or come from other countries. Some might be very educated, some may not be. Whatever your circumstances, you may have family members who may not be supportive of your LGBTQ child. What happens now?

Step One: Ask your child if they would like to be out to extended family. If the answer is no, you have nothing to worry about right now. Honor your child's wishes and stay quiet. Telling extended family, especially knowing that some family members may be hostile to your child's news, requires a lot of bravery and emotional and physical energy that your child may not want to expend right now.

If their answer is "yes, I would like to be out to my extended family," go to Step Two.

Step Two: Rally your allies. You know who in your family empathizes with LGBTQ people. Tell them first. You know your family, and you will know how best to tell them. Email might be best for some families, calling for others, or visits or texting, whatever you need to do to get the conversation started. Depending on your child's age and how close they are with some of these allies, you may want them to reach out as well. If you child is younger, you need to do this work yourself, but if they are a teen, you may want to involve them. You can talk to your child about this, too, whether or not to be involved with contacting empathetic family members. A sample script to an ally sister-in-law might sound something like this. "Hi Bianca. I was just calling with some news. Hannah came to us last week and told us that she is gay, and she's been dating a girl for about three months. She's told me it's okay to reach out to extended family, and I know how loving and supportive you've been of your nephew who is transgender. With Thanksgiving coming up..."

If you don't know how certain family members feel (it's unlikely, but it may have never come up), float a "weather balloon." Sometimes we make a mistake of stereotyping people based on external factors like their age or religion. People might surprise you. I know several women in their 70s and 80s who are all for marriage equality and are very happy that they've lived to see that Supreme Court decision.

So with these people, talk about something that is in the news pertaining to LGBTQ issues, or about an athlete or a celebrity who is LGBTQ. See what they say. Look for coded messages in their responses. "I don't mind what people do in their bedrooms, I just don't want to see it..." or, "We didn't used to have all these transgender people..." "You have to love the sinner but hate the sin..." These are all codes for someone who isn't where you need them to be right now. Sometimes people don't realize how homophobic they are. They really think they are good people who love everyone. And while they are certainly not evil, they are not in a place (as of this moment) where they are going to be truly accepting of your child.

Step Three: Identify the people in your family who are flat out homophobic assholes. I'm sorry to call them that, I really am. But we have to have real talk here. There are two kinds of homophobic assholes. The first kind will eventually grow used to your child and just not mention "the whole gay thing." They will not overtly say anything nasty, and your child's spouse or boyfriend/ girlfriend will be referred to as "their friend" until the day the homophobic asshole dies. These people are not fun, but you're probably not close to them anyway, and your child probably won't choose to be close to them, so this is someone you will have to tolerate at holidays and weddings.

The second kind of homophobic asshole is the worst. They will refuse to attend functions either if your child is there or if your child is there with their partner, or they will complain/gossip about your LGBTQ child (and probably you too) to other family members. They will make "jokes" about your child's queerness straight to their face and to other family members. If you ask them to not make "jokes" they will say they are "just kidding" or "can't you take a joke?" or "I see political correctness rules around here." They will quote biblical passages and say that it is their right to quote the word of God. I even know of an instance where a child's grandparent offered to pay for conversion therapy. I know of another instance where a mother told her father that her son was gay and the father never spoke to either one of them ever again. He *died* never talking to his grandson or his daughter again.

You probably already know who these people in your family are, but these are going to be the toughest situations. And it's going to really suck if you have a homophobic asshole in your family (maybe you won't?). It is going to be an even worse if one of the homophobic assholes is one of your child's grandparents.

Once in a while, the worst kind of homophobic asshole evolves into someone who can tolerate your LGBTQ child. But like Charlie Bondhus said in the first chapter's "In Their Own Words" writings, being tolerated isn't any fun. It is so much better to be accepted, affirmed, and celebrated. But if this is just a brother-in-law you see three times a year, it will work. Once in a great while (like seeing a unicorn), a homophobic asshole will evolve into a full-fledged ally who may never admit they were once wrong, but will fully celebrate and be proud of their LGBTQ relative. This is a big journey, too big for most people. And for the homophobic assholes who make it, well, they deserve an extra hug.

Step Four: You may have to go through unpleasant confrontations, which will have lingering effects on you and your family. This is up to you. We can pretend for a long time. Especially if you don't see your family a lot. But if you choose to pretend, or to not tell your family, it will have repercussions on you, on your child, and your relationships with your family members. It is less stressful and seriously better for your health to have satisfying relationships[68] and the definition of a satisfying relationship is usually an authentic one, a relationship that has as little hiding and/or omission as possible. I think it's a good call to be as truthful with your family as you can be about everything.

Let's say your mother is a homophobic asshole. And you know this. And your 15-year-old child has just told you that they are transgender. There is no way really to pretend about this one, because Michaela is now identifying and dressing as a girl and wearing make-up, and Thanksgiving is in two weeks and you all planned to get together.

Meet your mother face-to-face if you can. If not, if you can do a Google Hangout, Skype, or Facetime video conference, that would be the next best thing. The third choice is a phone call. I think it's important for your mother to hear your voice. Schedule a time to call/visit/ Skype when neither one of you is hurried or stressed. At the bare minimum, your mother must agree to not openly mock, shame, or even question Michaela. If she cannot agree to the minimum requirement, you probably shouldn't go to Thanksgiving. I know this is harsh. And some people might tell you, "Go and leave Michaela at home." What kind of message does that send to Michaela? That she is something to be left behind? Something to be ashamed of? That your relationship with your homophobic asshole mother is more important than she is?

I know there are things that may complicate these situations, and the decision about how best to proceed may be unclear. Perhaps your parents have given you financial help. Perhaps your parents are in bad health and you don't want to stress them out. Perhaps there have been family crises recently. But you have to find some space and navigate within it. You have to protect your kid from negativity like that—they are going to get enough of that in the adult world on their own. Maybe you don't go to Thanksgiving but try to go to Christmas or Hanukkah instead, to give her time to think about her relationship with you and with her granddaughter. Maybe you decide to go next Thanksgiving, when the newness of this has worn off and your child is a little older, with another year's experience in handling others' reactions to their queerness.

Regardless of what you choose, these will not be easy conversations and decisions. They will be hard, and they may have the result of fragmenting your family. I hope you never have to face this, but if you do please know that family is also made up of who we choose to have in our lives, people who have our backs, and the people who accept our children no matter their gender or sexual orientation.

Step Five: You can try to educate. The trouble with trying to educate people is that it gets exhausting, and you can't educate anyone who doesn't want to be educated. We all had our favorite subjects in school, right? Think about the difference between a boring class and one in which you were engaged. A lot of it had to do with the teacher, yes, but a lot of it also had to do with your interest in the subject. For me the humanities, biology, and the social sciences were fascinating. When I sat in trigonometry I could barely keep my eyes open. I'm not implying that learning about LGBTQ people is boring, what I'm saying is there are a lot of people in the world who don't want to learn, just like I didn't want to learn trig.

You can offer your knowledge and resources to your relatives. You can give them the movies, books, articles, or even some of the things I've listed in this book. But you can't make them read them, or watch the documentaries or YouTube videos. And sometimes when people read about homophobia, and they see some of their own behavior there, they get defensive. And sometimes when people get defensive, they lash out at the people who "made" them feel that way.

But there are also a lot of good people who maybe just haven't been exposed to a lot of differences. And with these people, education can make a huge difference. They may really want to read that book and watch that documentary, and that is wonderful. Just remember it can get exhausting explaining things, especially repetitively, year after year. It is important work, but take care of yourself, and don't let negative people take your joy and energy from your nuclear family.

Siblings

If your LGBTQ child has siblings, include them in some of these dialogues. They may have questions about what is going on with their sibling or with the family tensions. When at all possible, sit down together as a family and talk these things out as best you can. But it is also good to spend some time with your other child(ren) if your LGBTQ child has had a bad situation and needed a lot of your attention recently.

Don't forget that your straight child may be feeling some repercussions at school or in the family. They may be getting teased because their sibling is different, and that can be really hurtful. I do believe that things are getting better, but siblings still can be treated unfairly, can be asked if they are LGBTQ as well, and in general, can experience the same ignorance and/or bullying your LGBTQ child does. They can experience shame that their sibling is "different" but still love them. They may also feel guilty that they feel shame about someone they love. It can be hard. Be sure to talk to them about what's going on, and monitor their situation and circumstances at school as well. [69]

I have generally experienced and heard about situations where siblings are supportive of their LGBTQ brothers and sisters. Growing up with my sister Tara made me a very different person than I might have been otherwise, and I know I am a better mother to Casandra because of my relationship with my sister. It is difficult to grow up thinking that LGBTQ people are somehow "other" than you, when one of those "others" is your much-loved, idolized older sister. I generally find siblings of LGBTQ people to be an empathetic bunch, willing to learn, and with a unique way of looking at things.

The exceptions to that, however, are deeply painful experiences. If this is the case in your family, do think about trying family therapy to see if the situation can be healed. If your LGBTQ child does have a sibling who is not loving and supportive (especially if this is a half/step or older sibling not living in your home), you may have to take some of the steps mentioned above to make this a tolerable situation for your LGBTQ child.

Dos and Don'ts

1) DO—expect the best and prepare for the worst, especially if your child is the first out queer person in your family. Expect that everyone will be loving and accepting, but prepare yourself just in case they are not.

2) DO—give people space and time. Just as you may have needed some time to process when your child came out to you, so might your extended family. If they act poorly at first, or say something a little stupid, circle back around to them in a bit to see if they are in the same place. They may be sorry and not know what to do now that they've behaved badly.

3) DO—offer resources. I keep a couple of copies of several books I like to give to people who ask or to people who might need them. If you can afford to do this, I think it's great. It's a great way of offering a lot of information without a lot of pressure.

4) DON'T—let Uncle Ralph make homophobic jokes or engage in bullying behavior at family gatherings. Confront that behavior, even if the confrontation is awkward and painful. If Uncle Ralph continues his behavior, remove your child from that situation.

5) DON'T—forget to take care of yourself. I am the primary caretaker and "family maker" of my family. It can be exhausting and depleting on top of working and the everyday tasks of adulthood. If you throw in a homophobic family

and parenting stress, your BP can start to rise pretty quickly. Remember to breathe, exercise, and mind your nutrition. You need to be healthy and sane, and your child needs you to be healthy and sane.

In Their Own Words

Becky Woo Newcombe, sibling, Michigan

It was the early 90's. I was a high school sophomore, trying to figure out life as a teenager while my three older siblings were already out of the house. My sister Cynthia and my brother Lorenzo were living at Michigan State University, and my oldest brother, Harlem, was living in California at UCLA. It was early Christmas Eve and all my siblings were home for the holidays. It was an exciting time to have a break from being the only child at home, and I loved my time with them. I remember my brother Lorenzo being the only one up and saying, "Hey, I need to talk to you about something." The rest of the conversation stays in my head in bits and pieces all jumbled up together. What I heard was a lot to understand and digest as I lived my teenage, middle-class life in suburbia, and I honestly didn't see it coming.

I remember being asked if I knew what it meant to be gay. I remember him telling me that anyone can be gay and that I probably had friends that are gay but just don't know it. I remember him telling me that even guys on a football team could be gay. I remember my brother coming out to me for the first time. He just said, "I am gay."

At that time in 1992, as a high school sophomore, I had no tangible experience with what he was talking about. I felt so many emotions: confused, embarrassed, sad, happy, unsure, and scared. He told me how good it felt to come out, but why did it not feel as good to me? I did not quite understand. All I knew was he was different than I had expected, but I loved him.

In this conversation, I also didn't realize how hard it was to come out. I learned that an entire year before that that he had told my sister walking in the middle of Meijer while grocery shopping and that a year before that he had told my brother! My parents were the last to find out after my conversation. When retold, my dad's initial response was, "Oh, you'll change." Cold, uncaring, stiff Asian dad, sure that this was not going to affect him. It was a blow, it was a shocker and I don't think he really knew what to say. So dad went upstairs, and my brother and mom continued talking. And then it happened. This is a reminder of God's work in our lives. My dad came down the stairs sobbing and drenched with tears. He told my brother how much he loved him and that he will always be his son. He accepted it and was willing to learn. He opened his heart and let my brother in. It was not easy. Our Filipino/Chinese culture and our middle-upper class suburban life did not naturally open its hearts to the gay lifestyle in the 90's. All we really knew of was what was in the movies and news. Wild lifestyles and AIDS. It did not seem "normal." It's amazing how much we learned as the years went by.

So life continued. I slowly began to tell my friends about my gay brother. I remember a few jocks teasing me about it, whether it was to my face or behind my back. But I had other friends who were understanding. My family was still pretty private about it. But my brother would bring boyfriends home to visit and we would go out as a family with them, and every year, things seemed more and more normal. My brother was successful with good jobs and really didn't seem any different to me beyond the label. I know he had his struggles with living in

Michigan as a gay man, as a family though, it seemed like acceptance was coming together.

Fast forward about nine years from when my brother, Lorenzo, came out to me. I am now 24 years old, living in California with my first teaching job, a steady boyfriend, my own apartment and life is good! While my sister was raising a growing family and my brother and his partner had a nice house in Kalamazoo, my parents decided to come up to visit me out West. That weekend, my boyfriend asked my dad for his blessing and we got engaged the next day. To celebrate, we were off on a three to four day trip to Las Vegas with my parents and my older brother Harlem from LA, and then Jeremy and I would continue on to backpack alone in Utah for a few days. It was going to be a good weekend!

It was three and a half hours from where we lived in California to Las Vegas. The drive started in the mountains but then became mostly flat, dry desert the rest of the way. The midway stop was in Barstow where we usually got gas. Jeremy, my fiancée, and I were on cloud nine. My mind was on the ring on my finger and the man by my side. My parents and Harlem drove right alongside of us in a separate car since we were going to continue on camping. As we drove down the highway, we would pull up next to them and laugh and joke around, but they seemed wrapped up in conversation. When we got to a gas station in Barstow, it was really windy and my brother's car seemed out of sorts. My mom had either spilled something or lost her glasses, and my dad was running into the bathroom and newspapers were flying everywhere. I remember things feeling eerie, but couldn't pinpoint what was happening. Once we hit the glitz of Las

Vegas, I quickly forgot, and we had an amazing trip with dinners, shows, and shopping.

It wasn't until weeks later as my brother Harlem, Jeremy and I were driving the streets of Burbank on the way to a movie that my brother said, "I have to talk to you guys." And at that red light, my oldest brother came out that he was gay.

He had known forever. But then Lorenzo, only 10 months younger, had come out seven to 10 years before. My guess is, he felt trapped. How could he add to something so big? He and my brother were my father's only sons. What would become of our "Woo" name? He finally needed to tell them. And the best way he could think of was on a drive in the middle of the desert where there was nowhere to go. My parents found out Harlem was gay nine years after Lorenzo came out. They found out the day after I got engaged. They wanted to be happy for Jeremy and I but wanted to be there for their son. We never talked about it, but I am sure that was a difficult weekend for them. In the car, they made Harlem promise to give the weekend to Jeremy and I and to not make it about him. In retrospect, I can only imagine how awful that could have been. Harlem waited once again.

After growing up with two gay brothers, I see how it is just completely impossible to stereotype. My brothers live two completely different lives. Lorenzo and Joe have been married since 2008 and have a beautiful adopted daughter. They own a home, have successful jobs, and have really embraced family life. Harlem is single. He has never had a steady boyfriend that he has introduced to the family. He works a full-time job in hospital administration in LA and spends his spare time taking dance classes and singing around the city. As he approaches 50, I wonder if he sees a partnership in his future. He has always been independent.

Regardless of who they have become, one thing is for sure, my brothers are loved and supported. Through thick and thin, they are two amazing souls. I really think my parents, in the midst of all the dysfunction in their own marriage and lives, laid a strong foundation of faith, and that is what has brought us through the strange and uncertain times of living with two gay brothers/sons. Nobody ever gave up and nobody ever said you are alone. Nobody ever said get out or you are wrong. We forgave, we listened, we accepted, we learned, we continued and we always kept our eye on our faith.

Zahara, parent, Oregon

Ellis came out to us in a family text at a summer computer camp when she was fourteen:

"im tots hella gay," she texted.

"what?" her brother replied.

"im straight as a circle," she wrote.

"yay, Ellis!" her older brother texted back.

"Ellis, are you coming out as a lesbian?"
I asked.

"yes," she said.

"Okay," I replied. "I love you."

"Is this a joke?" my husband texted.

"No," she said.

Then why are you telling us in a text?

"my friends dared me"

"Okay. We all love you," I said. "Call me when you can."

Before this there had been no boy crushes, no pre-teen meetups or fledgling dates. Unlike other girls in her class, she liked hanging with her small group of girls. Her team earned the first place trophy in middle school flag football. She was the only girl on the team, but she was sad that the cheerleaders said the football players were hot, but not her. "I wish I were a dude," she said on the way home from school one day.

"Don't wish you are anyone but who you are," I offered. "You're fantastic. You are you." But I worried. She seemed depressed. There were no crying spells or acting out, but something was simmering. I took her to a psychiatrist, and he prescribed an anti-depressant. We didn't talk about the root of her depression. I assumed it was the pressured prep school she attended. All her shrink would say was, "Ellis is overwhelmed." She was only twelve. She had been attending rigorous prep schools since she was five. I thought she was overwhelmed with school and her environment, and maybe that was part of it.

We were living in a conservative upper middle class Los Angeles suburb, but within the year, my husband took a new job in a rural college town in Oregon. It was a good move for our family. We needed fresh air and a change of scene. Ellis was flourishing. She was becoming more herself. She became more willing to express herself and more open to her new world.

She called me soon after the text. "Mom," she said tensely. "I would have told you in person, but my friends dared me to."

"It's okay, it was funny. How are you? Are you okay?" I asked.

"I'm fine. Is Dad mad?"

"No, absolutely not. He was just surprised. He thought it was a joke."

"Okay," she said.

When she came home from camp she joined a local gay club called Out & About where she found like-minded high school friends. Unfortunately, some of her friends had been abused or neglected by family members, some were homeless, and many were very poor. Some had been subjected to conversion therapy. Some had tried to commit suicide.

Ellis became confused and angry, trying to work her way through her identity and the situation some kids faced. She started acting out. "Straight people are disgusting!" she said. "Straights always treat us like we are weird. They're weird!"

"Are Dad and I weird? Is anyone treating you differently?" I asked.

She always said no. But once we received a typed note in our mailbox from anonymous persons who said "they" were following Ellis's anonymous Tumblr. They warned us to be aware what she was saying. It was wrong. I checked out her page. There were rants about being a lesbian and how gross straight people were in colorful language. There was art, but there was nothing threatening, nothing ethically or morally wrong. It was just her observations, just her opinions. I dictated a note that she put on her page:

"To the Anonymous Person or Persons who left a note in my parents' mailbox,

> Please identify yourselves so that we can
> have a civil conversation about my personal,
> anonymous Tumblr. My parents wish you to
> know that they have read my Tumblr, and
> although they don't particularly agree with
> my language, they have no problem with my
> content. So who are you?"

We never heard from them again. Still, it left me feeling uncomfortable.

In the middle of Ellis's coming out year, she became very ill and was hospitalized with a life-threatening disease. She dropped all but two classes her first semester, but as she improved, she went to school more often. Even with her monthly infusions in the hospital, she still went to Out & About as often as she could, but her friends didn't visit her in the hospital or at home. At home, she was sick and isolated. She was struggling with the onset of a chronic lifelong disease, and it was hard. She still saw her psychiatrist, but I was worried about her.

One day, I received a call from her counselor. "Ellis says she is suicidal. Please come here immediately." I grabbed my car keys and left that minute.

I was led into the counselor's room. Ellis wouldn't look at me. She told me she wanted to live in a group home with other kids; she wanted a "break" from us.

"Ellis," I said, tears welling in my eyes. "I know you want a break from the doctors and hospitals and all of us hovering over you. You want a break from your disease, and I wish to God that I could make that happen. A group home is not for you. It's for kids who don't have a loving home or a compromised immune system. What you want is to have more friends visiting you. We need to talk about how we can make that happen."

"Ellis," said the counselor. "Look at your mother." I was full on crying. Tears were running down my face.

Ellis looked at me in all my fear and concern. "Okay, Mom. Let's talk." Things began to get better. Things always got better when we talked. But it takes a village. Her school, her psychiatrist, and her family pitched in. It wasn't easy, but knowing that we loved and respected her helped all of us through it. Ellis, though, did the heavy lifting. Because she willed things to be better and because she believed things would be, they were. We were just support.

Time passed. Ellis went back to school full-time, turned sixteen, got her driver's license, and took on honors and AP classes, and a part-time job working concessions for sports events. With her own money and a car she became more independent. She could drive to the movies, to friends' homes, to school. She experienced how we trusted her to make good decisions. She became the president of her high school's Gay Straight Alliance this fall. Her friends call her Queen Gay.

I'm proud of my daughter for being so brave and honest. I feel like I'm seeing her, the real her. I see her work, learn, and soldier on toward maturity through all the changes and difficulties life has handed her, and I am proud. She knows who she is and she's not afraid to live it. Bring it on.

What more can a mother ask?

Resources

Love, Ellen: A Mother/Daughter Journey by Betty Degeneres

I'm Their Mom by Denise Kestell

The History of Swimming by Kim Powers

Side by Side: On Having a Gay or Lesbian Sibling by Andrew R. Gottlieb

Chapter 9

ONLY PART OF WHO THEY ARE

Maybe you've always suspected your child was gay. Maybe you've just now gotten this book because they've come out to you unexpectedly. Whatever your circumstances, you know a lot of other things about your child besides their gender identification and their sexual orientation. My daughter, Casandra, likes to read and be outside. She likes walking, paddle boarding, swimming, and just in general being near water. She loves movies and board games and Pokémon (you are never too old for Pokémon). She likes being with her friends, writing, Tarot cards, listening to music, and she isn't very fond of math and hard-core science classes. Her sexual orientation is just one aspect of who she is. I don't spend time with my "gay daughter," I spend time with my daughter.

This is a really good time to focus on all aspects of your child. If your child has just come out, or is questioning their sexual orientation or their gender identity, it's a great time to encourage them to spend time with extracurricular activities, their friends, their family, and doing the things they love at home. In other words, keep them busy.

I know some people will say we are too busy. And I agree with those people 1,000 percent. We all need down time. And your young child shouldn't be overscheduled. Our rule for our kids was they could have activities two afternoons or nights before middle-school age. Casandra first chose swimming and gymnastics, and then switched to just swimming as she got taller and taller (she is now 6'1) and gymnastics became a less-than-ideal sport for her. Matthew chose swimming and fencing, and then fencing and Lego Club. When both kids hit middle school, the expectations of involvement for school sports increased, and Casandra ran cross country, swam, and participated in track in middle school. Matthew swam and played water polo, and played percussion in band and jazz band. I know extracurriculars are expensive and time-consuming. But as your child gets older, they have a lot of energy, and they need someplace to focus it. Studies have shown that the time of day when a student might make bad choices isn't necessarily at night (though weekends are an exception to this in the later teen years), it's after school, in those unsupervised hours after they leave the school and before parents get home. Smoking, drinking, drugs, and sex can be real issues in the hours between 3:00 p.m. and 6:00 p.m. if kids aren't supervised or don't have a structured activity to attend.[70]

Many studies have shown the benefits of extracurricular activities. Students who are involved in extracurriculars have better grades, are absent less, have higher self-esteem, are less likely to use alcohol and drugs, and statistically attain a higher level of education than kids who do not participate in extracurriculars.[71] GLSEN said in their research brief, "The Experience of LGBT Students in School Athletics," that LGBTQ students who played on school-based sports teams reported "better academic and mental health outcomes compared to LGBT students who did not participate in sports. Team leaders reported additional benefits (even higher GPAs and a sense of belonging at school), LGBT students on interscholastic or intramural sports teams reported higher GPAs than non-athletes." [72]

Clubs, sports, and music are also a great way to meet other students that your child may not regularly interact with. Depending on where you live, there are so many opportunities—sports, language clubs, GSA (!!!), debate, Boy and Girl Scouts, 4-H, SADD (Students Against Destructive Decisions), computer club, theater, dance, choir, and chess club, just to name a few. Extracurricular activities also look great on college resumes and let kids try out other areas of interest that might not be covered in a normal school day. The school curriculum is pretty locked down now, especially in the middle and high school years. There is little room for electives, especially if your child wants to take a language or band or choir or orchestra as some of the few electives allowed. Extracurriculars are a great way to explore interests and focus on something different, and in the case of sports, they also can help your child get some additional physical activity.

There are loads of hobbies and interests that your child might need a little encouragement to try. Don't put pressure on your child at this stage about "what career do you want when you graduate." But it is a great time to help them explore their interests. Casandra went through a knitting phase and one Christmas made hats for everyone in our family, as well as enough to drop off to our local cancer treatment center. Other kids might really like photography, or video-making and editing—all of which are fairly affordable to do now as technology and software become less expensive. Cooking, baking, volunteering at your church, synagogue, or mosque—all of these activities offer ways for your child to do something positive, stay connected to the wider world, and realize the contributions they can make to their family and community.

You don't want this to become a war or a control issue, but your average teen may balk at visiting a senior center once a week, joining a club at school, or going out for a sport, especially if they haven't done one before. (School sports like bowling, swimming, cross country, and track are really good for beginners. And our high school even has Intramural Quidditch and floor hockey teams.) You may hear the ultimate teen dismissals: "that's dumb;" "that's stupid;" "no one does that." I would be very flexible on what their choices are, but it is important that they *do* something. If they are in high school, you might ask that they choose two things, or one thing, depending on what financial commitment and transportation are needed for that activity. Do some scouting around before you eliminate an activity based on transportation needs. A lot of activities take place right after school, so you might be able to pick up your child after work. Some school districts also offer a late bus after practices and clubs. Sometimes your kid can catch a ride home with another parent, or another teen, if you are okay with that. Sometimes parents can set up a carpool so that each one only has an obligation once or twice a week to pick up or drop off. That goes for finances as well, don't eliminate activities until you see all the options. Many clubs offer scholarships. Many schools have athletic boosters for this exact reason. Sometimes you and your child can offer additional volunteer hours in exchange for a reduction in fees. I know it is hard to ask for help, but if your child is motivated and it might be an activity that is a good fit for them, do explore different options before saying, "No, we can't afford that."

Maybe they are spending too much time on their computer and on their phone, so you feel a sport or a physical activity is important to get them moving on a regular basis. And because you want them to give back to their community in some way, you think volunteering is important. Volunteering is great because more than likely they will be interacting with people of all different ages and backgrounds. Just as being with peers is crucial at this age, so is interacting with people of all ages and backgrounds. This helps them remember that school is kind of an artificial environment—that they will be interacting with really diverse people all the time after they graduate. You could have them volunteer at your place of worship, their local LGBTQ center, a senior center, a food bank, a local library, or a place that takes action about climate change. There are so many possibilities.

Have suggestions and a plan ready. If you get a lot of pushback, require them to try the activities for four weeks or six weeks (or whatever amount of time you feel is appropriate) and then tell them they can try something else. Try to be as flexible as you can, but hold firm. Parenting (as you know) is a lot of work. Sometimes it is too much effort to do a particular thing, or stay the course when you aren't getting much cooperation. But your child, while being an expert on themselves, doesn't know everything that is out there. This is no different than when they were five and threw a tantrum because they wanted more dessert or candy, and you told them no because you knew they'd either throw up or rot their teeth or both. You weren't doing that because you didn't love them or trust them, you did that because you knew, that in the end, it would be better for them. It is very important for your LGBTQ child to feel like a part of a team, a community, a club. It is fine to explain that to them, and walk through your thinking process. If they have good responses to your concerns, listen to them. But work hard to keep them connected to their school and larger community.

Friends

I remember Casandra's first playdate with a friend from the Catholic school. Casandra was in first grade and I had already seen some of the houses (mansions) her peers lived in, while we lived in a little house outside of town, with three small bedrooms and one bathroom. I felt insecure. Our living room carpet was stained from pets and kids. Our bathroom was so small two people literally could not be in there unless one person was standing in the bathtub/shower. I cleaned the whole day before the playdate, bought Casandra a new bedspread for her bed, and helped her pick up her room. When I called the other mother, I made sure to schedule the playdate during Matthew's nap time, and invited her to stay during the playdate because it was a bit of a drive to our house. Casandra wasn't nervous at all—she was excited to have her friend over. I was very nervous. The other mom was an extremely nice person, who didn't care at all that our house was one-third the size of hers. We had a great talk, found out we had mutual friends, and our girls had a nice time together. A successful and fun time, despite my worries and insecurities.

Fast forward fifteen years. We live in a bigger house in town now. As I'm writing, I'm looking at my china cabinet/buffet. It has a stack of important papers, two AP calculus books, a half-eaten bag of chips, a Halloween bowl no one has returned to the basement even though we are just days from Thanksgiving, last year's high school yearbook, an unhealthy Christmas cactus that needs to be repotted, and some random plastic silverware. In my "office," my workbag is on the floor, books are stacked everywhere and there is another pile of important papers on my desk. The living room is relatively clutter-free and recently vacuumed and dusted, but one of the dogs has pushed all the cushions off the couch again to make a nest. While we certainly aren't slobs or hoarders (we all work a little every day to keep complete house chaos at bay), we are not going to win any HGTV *Property Brothers'* award for keeping our house immaculate. Yesterday, my son had five friends over to play an RPG (role-playing game) called Sprawl. Outside of making sure there were snacks and wiping off the dining room table so their papers wouldn't get sticky, I didn't do much in terms of cleaning. I certainly didn't go buy a new bedspread.

Maybe you aren't concerned at all about people judging you. (If that's the case, share your secret with me, please?) But this is something I've had to work through. I worried at first that if my kids' friends were in and out of my house, they would judge us—our house would be too small, too messy, not decorated nicely enough, etc. The older I've gotten and the older my kids have gotten, the less I care. And the more I realize how important it is for your child's friends to be welcome in your home. I would rather have Casandra's friends here watching Netflix and eating popcorn than I would have them underage drinking at some party. I would rather have Matthew's friends here around my dining room table, rather than six of them wedged into a single car with a teen driver going God knows where. There may be that kid that reports back to their parents that my house is messy (I prefer "lived in"), that I'm slowly killing a Christmas cactus, and that our dogs track fallen leaves into our house that we ignore until they are at the point of crisis and have to be swept up. Yes, that might happen, but what of it? If a parent gets worked up because I have dishes in my sink, I'm not going to become BFFs with that person anyway, and neither will my kid.

It is especially important for an LGBTQ preteen and teen to have close friends. Peer pressure works both ways. We always hear about the negative peer pressure—drugs, alcohol, cutting class, etc., but we don't hear so much about the good peer pressure. If all of their peers are getting good grades and working toward their goals, chances are they will follow suit.[73] Because LGBTQ students are at such added risk of being bullied or seen as outsiders, it is especially crucial that they find their squad and have "normal," goofy-type fun with those peers. A few good friends (even two or three) who really get your child, and who your child can relax and have fun with, help make up for the times where they might feel different or excluded because of their queerness.

A note about "bad" friends: Your child may occasionally bring home a friend that you don't like. Here is another advantage to being willing to let your house be the hangout house. You can keep an eye on this kid—see how they talk to your child and yes, maybe eavesdrop on a conversation or two. There isn't much gained by telling your kid you don't like their friend. Sometimes they need to figure it out on their own. Obviously intervene if anything is destructive or dangerous in the relationship, but other than that let your child come to their own conclusions about their friend. They may see something in that friend that you don't, or alternately, they may have to learn that all friendships are not forever, and not all people can stay in your life always (something I myself have had to learn in my use of Facebook). These are important lessons to learn and process while they are under the safety of your roof, and these lessons will serve them when they are out on their own and making friends at their workplaces and in the rest of their adult lives.

Dos and Don'ts

1) DO—encourage your child to step outside of their comfort zone. Whether that's taking a painting class or joining the cross-country team, encourage them to spend these years trying new things and finding their passions. Never in their lives will they have more time and freedom to experience all the world has to offer.

2) DO—be firm. Even if your child is a homebody and seems perfectly content staying home with family, encourage them to find a couple of activities they enjoy.

3) DON'T—get into a power struggle. Talk about your reasoning and logic for wanting your child to be involved. Let them choose their activities (given your criteria of budget and time). They may choose something you think is weird (clogging and volunteering at the local arts and crafts festival). Do your best to support and affirm their choices.

4) DON'T—say I told you so. If clogging doesn't turn out to be something they want to continue with, let them try something else. Sometimes we have to quit things we don't like or that aren't a good fit for us, and those are important lessons as well.

5) DO—remember their queerness is an important part of who your child is, but it's just that, a part. They may be great at video games, love dogs, be an amazing badminton player, and love math. Never forget your child will be defined

in so many ways—and the number one way that you should define them and they should define themselves is as a unique, complicated individual.

6) DO—be kind to yourself and your child. Sometimes it really is all we can do to survive. In May 2009, both my sister and my brother-in-law died, and then in November 2009, my dear mother-in-law died of brain cancer. It was all I could do to keep groceries in the fridge, get the kids off to school, and do the bare minimum of what I needed to do for graduate school. Things like haircuts, dentist appointments, and extracurriculars just didn't happen with regularity. If you are having a year like my 2009, I'm so sorry. Just get through it and once you are back on your feet, think about bringing these activities back into your family's life.

In Their Own Words

Tara Morse, my sister, Colorado

The first time I laid eyes on a drag queen was at the Rubaiyat in Ann Arbor in 1981. They've improved their quality greatly over the years, trust me. There's a lot less visible hair and a lot less visible other stuff. Back then, it was more of a comedy/burlesque, very campy. (This was Bette Midler's Sophie Tucker period.) I even remember the drag queen's name, "Sofonda Peters." I ran into her in the bathroom. The bathrooms weren't labeled then, so peeing next to a trans person has never seemed weird to me. The bar then was a place to figure things out for myself and become more accepting of people. I was judgmental and weirded out at first when I saw two guys kiss. I just hadn't seen it before.

The bars were in a bad section of town, tucked away, unlit, and ID was optional. The locations made us vulnerable. Still today they aren't in the best part of town, so the "gay" has spread around them and renewed neighborhoods. This happened in San Diego. In some big towns, Houston for example, you can go to the gay store, etc., and never leave the gay part of town. How fun! My younger days were way before Google, so their location was passed by word of mouth, especially if you lived in a rural area like I did. LGBTQ people from rural areas went in groups and drove a long way and had that group sobriety test in the parking lot.

You could be yourself at the bar. About the only place you could be besides your house. You felt safe in the bar, around your kind, and occasionally you ran into someone you went to school with (or even your own cousin!) who even there, wouldn't acknowledge what you had in common.

Being from a rural area was especially difficult, and the groups were formed from someone knowing someone who had a "softball team." There were so few gay people that gay people sought each other out and included them. My group played softball and drank a lot of beer. We had sex with each other, it wasn't unusual to be sitting drinking next to your ex, who you broke up with two weeks ago, who was now with another member of the group. It may have seemed weird, but the rest of life was so hard.

Resources

The Secrets of Happy Families by Bruce Feiler

All Joy and No Fun: The Paradox of Modern Parenthood by Jennifer Senior

The Experiences of LGBT Students in School Athletics (GLSEN) PDF

Improving the Lives of LGBT Americans Starting with our Youth (article)

Chapter 10

OUT ON THEIR OWN (MOSTLY)

It seems impossible to imagine when we hold our child in our arms for the first time, that we will ever reach the point that they will be independent. They are so small and helpless and we spend so many hours taking care of them and keeping them safe. That independence comes in stages, of course. One day you put them on their blanket for tummy time, look away, and suddenly they are gone, rolling or crawling away, far from where you left them. Then walking and talking. Then reading. Having other relationships. Navigating learning and the social intricacies of school. They learn to help the family with chores, learn games, sports, or musical instruments, and learn to drive, and it seems impossible, but there you are with their 18th birthday in sight. What will happen? Where will they go? What will they do? How will they support themselves? Where will they go to college or for training for work? These very normal parenting questions all are even more urgent because a lot of times our queer children are going out into a hostile world, where queer people can still be fired from their jobs simply for being queer, and a dangerous world, where hate crimes are still altogether too common.

Finances

Hopefully, you've been giving your child an allowance, even if it's just a few dollars a week. I know there are mixed views on this, but I firmly believe that your child should be handling money as soon as they are capable of doing so. It seems like in the United States, we would rather talk about anything, even sex, rather than money. As a professor at a large university, some of the stories I hear about how ill-prepared students are to deal with their own finances are alarming. ("I still have checks in my check book. How can I be out of money?") Just as you've shown your child good personal hygiene and manners, they need to learn about budgeting, money, and the technology surrounding budgeting and money. You're probably saying to yourself, wait, isn't this a parenting-your-LGBTQ-child book? Well, money and how your child uses it are going to have a huge impact on your child's life. Good financial habits make our child happier, more secure, and allow them to have more options in life.[74] And since our children are already facing additional challenges in our heteronormative culture, we want to give them as many opportunities as possible to be happier and more secure.

Freshman year in high school is a good time to set your child up with a debit account. Hopefully, they already have a savings account, and you've taken them to your bank or credit union to make deposits and withdrawals. Other parents are sometimes shocked when I recommend this to them. Fourteen is too young, they say. What if they lose their debit card, they say. What if they overdraw their account, they say. I respond, "What if your teenager goes off to college or to their first job with no idea of how to use a debit card or handle money?" Just as driving a car, sports, and music require practice, so does becoming a financially-solvent adult. Wouldn't you rather your child make a mistake now with a debit card, when they are living with you at home and you can guide them, rather than spending all their freshman year book money on beer during Welcome Week and then being embarrassed to tell you because you've never talked about money with them? (This happens, people. This happens.)

I wish personal finances classes were required in high schools, but in most districts they are not. So our kids come out of high school knowing calculus, but not how interest, online statements, 401ks, the stock market, and mortgages work. Just as your child will need to know how to do their own laundry when they move out on their own, they will also need to be able to keep track of their balance and their expenditures, and to save money to reach their financial goals, whatever those may be.

In most families (maybe all but one-percenters?), money is a source of stress. Even if you have a good plan, a good budget, and good-paying jobs, an unexpected emergency (health problems, car repair, job loss, a move, even a vet bill) can throw even the most responsible family into financial crisis. Your child may not want to hear all the boring details of your financial story, but try to be as open as you can be about your plans for retirement, how you have been able to afford rent or a mortgage (and the pros and cons of both), and the expenses of running a household—utilities, repairs, taxes, insurance, cell phone bills, cable and/or Internet, groceries, etc. Talk to them about credit cards—the uses and the abuses. My husband and I are finally down to one credit card which we basically use for unexpected expenses, but this has been a hard thing for us. Again, when your child turns 18, they will be able to get a credit card in their own name (and these offers will be mailed to them, emailed to them, and handed out to them at community colleges and universities at the start of every fall semester). Many predatory companies cannot wait for inexperienced 18-year-olds to get buried under a 22 percent interest rate. I know saying "don't use credit cards" is sort of like saying "don't get sick" in today's society, but scare the living crap out of your kid about the danger of unsecured, high-interest debt so that when they do make the choice to use a credit card, it is for a true emergency.

Once your child hits high school, if at all possible, encourage them to get some work and/or volunteer experience. Babysitting is fine. Working in a fast-food restaurant is fine. If they are busy with extracurriculars during the school year, just working during the summers is fine. They need to start building references and a resume for future work, and again, get some experience with money. Casandra's first job was as a lifeguard, and I had completely forgotten how confusing the W-4/W-9 and direct deposit paperwork are when you're first hired at a job. Learn from me—before your child's first hire, print off a sample W-4/W-9 online and have your child fill it out while you are there to help.

Many banks and credit unions have online banking and smartphone apps. If your child has a smartphone, this will probably be the ideal way for them to monitor their expenditures, and at first, it is a good idea for you to monitor their balance and their expenditures as well. You may have to set up some rules about shopping online. You can buy almost anything on the Internet, both legally and illegally. Set the ground rules with the debit card. Are they allowed to have a PayPal or Google wallet account? Are they allowed to make Amazon, iTunes or Spotify or Playstation or Xbox purchases? Are they allowed to purchase but need to check with you first? I suggest giving them as much responsibility as you feel they are able to handle, and maybe a little bit more. If they have a clothes or school supply budget, I suggest you let them make these choices and purchases themselves.

Just as I've been encouraging communication about family relationships and expectations, I would also encourage communication about expectations for finances as your child gets older. Be honest. If they have to get a job for their high school spending money, clothes, and their cell phone bill, be clear about those expectations. If you can pay for their health insurance and cell phone while they are in college but nothing else, tell them that. If you have some money saved for their college, communicate how much that is, and what they may use it on. If they are going to continue to live at home after they graduate from high school, either to work or attend college, communicate what your expectations and their contributions should be. Have an open dialogue about this. Finances are much like the rest of growing up. Financial independence will probably come in stages and won't happen overnight between their 17th and 18th birthdays.

What's After High School?

College is more expensive than ever before, and many families simply cannot afford to help their child. So students are coming out of colleges and universities with a crippling level of debt, equal to a mortgage or sometimes even more. As parents, it is very easy to buy into the concept that if your child doesn't go to the "right" college, that they will not have the chance to be everything they can be. I'm probably prejudiced, as I did my undergraduate work at a big state school and I currently work at one, but I really believe that post-secondary education is a lesson in what you put into it, you will get out of it. There are opportunities at every major institution of learning. I've done a lot of things in my life, and I've sat at a lot of tables with people who went to Harvard, Yale, Columbia, and the like. Yes, they may be better connected than I am, but they aren't necessarily better educated. They may have had a few more opportunities because of the weight of the name of the college they attended, but a lot of state school students have had a different set of advantages. Like a fine education at one-third of the cost. I'm not putting down any college or university. If you can afford "the best" for your child's education, or they get a scholarship, go for it! But in my opinion, going $200,000 in debt just to receive a degree from a school with a "better" name or reputation than a state university or a community college just isn't worth it.

Community colleges are an amazing resource. There are many options where two years of study there might lead to an engaging and lucrative career. Not every person will want to pursue a four-year degree at a university. And many careers don't require it. There are successful mechanics, bookkeepers, cosmetologists, sales people, barbers, truck drivers, plumbers, electricians, construction workers, bakers, administrative assistants, certified nursing assistants, phlebotomists, retail managers, restaurant managers, and small business owners who do not have a four-year college degree, but who received some training and/or a degree at a community college. A community college is also an affordable way to start your four-year degree. In the Lansing area, many students do two years at Lansing Community College, do all of their prerequisites there, and then transfer to Michigan State University or another state university where they complete their studies in the major they desire.

Regardless of what career path your young adult thinks they might be interested in, if they plan on pursuing a degree or further training after high school, it is imperative that you both do some research on the institution they will be attending to make sure it is LGBTQ-friendly. A great place to start on this is the Campus Pride Index, which rates college campuses on LGBTQ concerns.

If your child does plan to pursue post-secondary education, look for LGBTQ scholarship funds. Many colleges and universities, recognizing the unique challenges of LGBTQ students, offer them some form of funding. Search the <u>Human Rights Campaign's LGBTQ</u> <u>Student Scholarship Database</u> and <u>FinAid: The Smart</u> <u>Student's Guide to Financial Aid.</u>

It is time-consuming to apply for scholarships, and you may need to do a little nagging to get your young adult motivated to do this work. Help them come up with a plan to tackle this big task. Make sure they have their high school resume (listing all their activities, awards, clubs, employment, etc.) up-to-date. Have them approach the teachers and/or coaches they think will write letters of recommendation. Figure out the transcript procedure at your high school—sometimes they send transcripts electronically by email or through a service on the Internet, other times the school will make paper copies and mail them to the requestor, so you will have to provide postage and an envelope. Sometimes you have to fill out a form each time you send out a transcript to a college or scholarship. Every high school has some sort of procedure. Look at the various deadlines and help your young adult come up with a goal, like applying for two scholarships a week, or whatever you think is feasible given scheduling, financial need, and other considerations. Many of these scholarships may be for small amounts—$100, $250 and $500. But if your student can string together a few of these, it will make a nice dent in a book bill or tuition.

Relationships

We've talked a little bit about the importance of peers and friendships, but it will also be quite normal if during the young adult years your child starts to date for the first time and has their first serious romantic relationship. (It is also quite normal if they are not ready for this yet and aren't dating.) Any romance at any age, straight or queer, can be fraught with drama, joy, and/or heartbreak, and it can be really tough to watch your young adult navigate their first relationship(s). Unfortunately, we can't protect our children from heartbreak, messy break-ups, or a less than ideal first relationship, and we can't make their romantic decisions for them, but we can and should set some ground rules.

1) *Are "sleepovers," platonic or otherwise, allowed?* This is a good time to go over the safe sex talk again. Yes, it is embarrassing. Yes, they will probably roll their eyes at you, but this is crucial information, and they will need this information as they make choices within their relationship.

2) *Are they allowed to use Tinder or other online dating apps?* Once your child hits 18, you can still offer them guidance and advice, but you really have no more power to set rules for them (unless they are still living with you, of course.) This can be a tricky decision. It is difficult for LGBTQ teens to date traditionally. Your teen might get up all their courage and ask their crush out for coffee. Well, their crush might be straight and just think two friends are going out for coffee. Dating apps reduce these misunderstandings, and your child can also find people with their same interests, so you don't end up with an introvert who loves to read with an extrovert who likes to party all the time. But there are a lot of lying,

creepy people online and in these dating apps. Safety is also an important thing to discuss if they are going to use these apps to meet people in real life.

3) *What is an appropriate age difference? And why do you feel that way?* I know many happy long-term couples who are a decade or more apart in age. I think I've come to the conclusion that age doesn't matter as much as what stage in your life you are in at present. If a 40 year old starts dating a 30 year old, I don't think too many people would consider it inappropriate and creepy. But if a 26 year old asks your 16 year old out on Tinder, that would be cause for alarm.

4) *How much time is your child's significant other allowed to be over at your house, or vice versa?* Yes, I know I said it is important to open your home to your children's friends. But there is a difference between opening your home and your child's significant other de facto living with you. Now, you might be totally fine if they are there all the time. This is especially true if you like them. But first relationships can come in all shapes and sizes, and you may want to draw some boundaries about how and when their significant other can visit. Or maybe your child has disappeared seemingly permanently over to their significant other's house. Like you make dinner and no one shows up. Don't seethe. Talk about a schedule and the expectations of that schedule.

Most Important

Remind your young adult that everyone's path isn't always clear. If they have a dream, they should pursue it. If they want to dance or sing or write or act or paint or design clothes, those are all just as important as scientific research or becoming a doctor or an attorney. But their path might look a little different than the alleged "ideal" of four years of school followed by a good-paying job with health insurance. They may go to college, take an unpaid internship, or work a day job while they pursue their dream. They may need a graduate degree. They may need to move to a bigger city, or conversely, move to a place where rent is more affordable, and yes, they may need to work at Starbucks for a while. I've worked many different jobs, and I went to graduate school later in life. I don't regret it. My path has definitely not been straightforward, but I wouldn't change all my experiences for anything in the world.

Try to have faith in the process of your child finding who they are and what they want to do. Some people have a dream and a calling from a young age, but some do not. There are many ways to be a successful person. Believe that your child will find their way.

Dos and Don'ts

1) DO—be honest about finances and what will be expected of them in the high school and college years. No one likes surprises, and your child may have to adjust where they want to go to school based on financial aid, scholarships, and what you can and cannot contribute.

2) DO—realize that our society has significantly changed and our young adults may need our help (our health insurance and maybe their bedroom) for longer than some previous generations. This does not make them worthless or lazy. It's just different.

3) DON'T—think that now that your child has graduated from high school that they won't need you. Current research show that the young adult's brain doesn't fully mature until they are 25 years old.[75] This is really good to remember if your child has gotten into a car accident or overdrawn their debit account. They are still learning.

4) DO—get to know your child's significant other if possible. Invite them over for dinner. If your family plans on going to a movie, invite them too. If you are visiting your child at college, see if their significant other wants to come for lunch, too. Whether this will be the person they settle down with for the rest of their life or someone they only date four months, you will be glad to be a part of your child's expanding life and relationships.

In Their Own Words

Nancy Conyers, Sweden

When my now spouse/then partner Libby and I made a commitment to each other in 1988, there were no protections for gay people either individually or as a couple. We weren't able to legally marry, so we moved in together and privately vowed to be there for each other for better or for worse. While we were happy, we also felt a bit diminished. Sitting on the floor eating pizza, clinking our slices together and saying, "We did it," wasn't the wedding or reception either of us had imagined for ourselves.

ACT UP had been formed the year before as a response to Ronald Reagan's complete and utter mishandling of the AIDS crisis. It felt as if, to most of the straight world, to be gay meant you had AIDS. The "gay ghetto" offered protection from that misconception and scorn in big cities like New York, San Francisco, Los Angeles— and in Jamaica Plain—the gay ghetto of Boston where we lived for the first three years of our relationship. A rundown, originally blue-collar Irish neighborhood that had seamlessly absorbed gays and lesbians, Chinese, and African-Americans, JP was a rare pocket of Boston. There, we felt safe, able to be open about who you were and who you were with. Once you left that series of safe streets, however, you had to watch how you behaved, and decide who you could trust. This felt like work, and it was often exhausting.

When you come out as a gay person, you don't just do it once. You do it over and over and over again. It's tiring and annoying. Why do we have to announce we're gay, as if it were an apology or a proclamation? Straight people don't have to say who they are, they can just *be*. Why did it have to be such an issue for us?

Libby and I lived on Woodlawn Street in JP, a diverse yet cohesive dead end street that backed onto Forest Hills Cemetery, where E. E. Cummings, Eugene O'Neill and Anne Sexton are buried. There were Irish families, Cantonese families, African-American families, leftover hippies from the 60's and gay and lesbian singles in addition to Libby and me. We had a great neighborhood association that met regularly and had fun social events that turned street clean ups, Halloween, and all the summer holidays into daylong block parties. The neighbors called me "the mayor of Woodlawn Street" and the neighborhood kids loved to hang out on our porch and play with our golden retriever, Beau. Libby was working for Frito-Lay, and when the kids saw her Astro van coming up the hill they'd run out of their houses and wait for her to park, hoping to snag some of her free samples.

Libby was promoted in 1993 and we moved to Ann Arbor, a gay friendly town in Michigan, where we already had friends that were a part of a like-minded, gay-friendly community. We were beginning to feel like we could be comfortable anywhere in the wider world—two cities and two positive experiences. But right after we moved, Bill Clinton instituted the "Don't Ask, Don't Tell" policy, making it legal for people to be dismissed from the military if they said they were gay. It was ok to be gay. You just couldn't say you were gay. So much for being comfortable. Gay Americans had helped elect Bill Clinton. He had huge support from the wealthy gay community in

Hollywood, and for the first time gay people around the country openly rallied around a presidential candidate and were instrumental in putting him in office. After "Don't Ask, Don't Tell" it felt as if first he had come for the military, then he would come for us.

In 1994, Libby received another promotion—this time into a real management position—and we were off to Princeton, NJ. I was so proud of her, but I was also mad at Pepsi, Frito-Lay's parent company. There were no domestic partner benefits. I had to buy my own health insurance instead of being covered under the Pepsi group plan. Nobody at the company knew I existed except the other gay people Libby had sussed out by using her "gaydar" to come out to them and form a group they called The Gays at Frito-Lay. In addition to the issue with health insurance, I wasn't eligible for the standard spousal relocation benefits—two look/see trips for housing, airfare to the new location—and Libby was only eligible for housing benefits based on one person. We were a two-person family, even if nobody recognized this fact.

We wondered if our suburban townhouse development in Princeton would be a safe place for us, so we decided to just introduce ourselves as 'we' to everyone we met, not to officially come out but to say things like, "We moved here from Ann Arbor," or "Before Ann Arbor we lived in Boston," and let people make their own determinations. Everyone accepted us right away, but it was a little strange to not have said anything declaratory about being gay or have anyone ask us anything about our relationship. It still felt a bit like living a secret, living out "don't ask, don't tell" in our real lives. That changed in 1996, two years after we moved to Princeton, when Bill Clinton signed DOMA, the Defense of Marriage Act into law. One day I went outside to get into my car, when my next-door neighbor approached me and said, "I don't care who marries who. All I care about is if they are good people. I don't agree with that law. It's ridiculous." That family became dear friends of ours.

In 2000, after many promotions in Princeton, Libby was promoted yet again and we moved to Dallas, Texas. We were scared about Dallas. Besides big hair, conspicuous consumption, and the Lone Star state flag, when you think of Texas you think of white, evangelical born-again Christians. I didn't want to go, but agreed after we consulted a locational astrologer who told us we should go, but not for too long. "Dallas will be good for you two, will give you a sense of home and rootedness and be great for both of your careers, but don't stay more than three years. It's Dallas, after all." We ended up moving into an unbelievably diverse neighborhood and loving Dallas for the three years we lived there. Our time in Texas—not exactly known for progressive thinking when it comes to gay rights or anything else—was bookended by two monumental shifts in gay rights. Shortly after our move to Dallas, Vermont became the first state to legally recognize civil unions, but stopped short of recognizing marriage. Right after we left Texas, the Supreme Court, in *Lawrence v. Texas*, ruled that sodomy laws were unconstitutional.

In 2003 Libby again was promoted at exactly the three-year mark the astrologer had mentioned. When it was time for us to move to Connecticut, she'd had enough of me being ignored. She went to see the head of human resources and told him she had a domestic partner who had been with her since the beginning of her career at

Frito-Lay and Pepsi, who'd made every move and received no spousal benefits. He immediately said, "Libby, I'm sorry, I had no idea," and sat down and wrote a letter giving me all the benefits accorded to the other spouses, with the exception of health insurance. Then he asked Libby what would cause her to leave Pepsi and she said, "If another company with domestic partner benefits recruited me, I'd leave in a minute." He told Libby that the company was exploring such benefits and asked if he could tell the CEO, who valued Libby's work, what she said. I like to think that Libby played a big part of Pepsi offering domestic partner benefits in 2004 right after Massachusetts became the first state to legalize same sex marriage.

2005 was a watershed year for us because we moved to Shanghai, China, our first international assignment. We were now officially called expatriates. This was the first move we'd made for Pepsi where I was also officially a spouse, allowed on the company health insurance plan, and fully included in all the move preparations. Everyone in human resources and upper management at Pepsi knew about me, which was a wonderful feeling, but the irony was that we were explicitly told not to say anything to anyone about our relationship. China had no laws against gay people, but there were no laws protecting us either. Since the company was jiggering around with my visas because we couldn't move on a family visa like the other expats, they felt it was important to keep quiet. Looking back on that now, it seems crazy that we agreed to those conditions, but at the time we just wanted to move to Shanghai so badly. Libby is half Chinese and had always wanted to explore the Chinese side of herself. We also wanted to see if we could find out what happened to her Chinese grandfather during the Cultural Revolution and find the grave of my missionary ancestor who was buried near Ningbo, a town outside of Shanghai. The astrologer who had given us the green light for Dallas also said, "I don't know what it is with you two and Shanghai. That is the best place in the world for you to live, starting in 2005."

Even though China was the most fascinating place we've ever lived and Shanghai is the most incredible city in the world where my heart will continue to live for the rest of my life, the stress of having to be closeted took its toll. We, of course, didn't keep completely quiet and made decisions about who to tell and who not to tell, but now that we're not there anymore I realize the day-to-day anxiety I lived with. Every time there was an unexpected knock at the door, I jumped. After living there for four years, I was hauled in to the immigration police and questioned two times, purposely separated from the human resources director of Pepsi who accompanied me. I was kicked out of the country (kindly asked to leave) and even though I eventually got back into China, it was never the same. I was living on borrowed time.

While we were living semi-closeted in Shanghai tremendous strides in gay rights were made in the U.S. In those five years, civil unions became legal in Connecticut and New Jersey; the House of Representatives approved a bill ensuring equal rights in the workplace for gay men, lesbians and bisexuals; Oregon allowed same-sex couples to register as domestic partners allowing the same spousal rights as married couples; the California Supreme Court ruled that same-sex couples had a constitutional right

to marry, then California voters approved Prop 8, a ban
on same-sex marriage; the Connecticut Supreme Court
ruled that same-sex couples had the right to marry; the
Iowa Supreme Court overturned the law banning same-
sex marriage; Vermont legalized same-sex marriage as
did Maine and New Hampshire and Washington DC; and
President Obama signed a referendum allowing same-sex
partners of federal employees to receive benefits with the
exception of health insurance. Libby and I cheered all this
on from afar, mindful that while there was still a long way
to go, things in our home country were finally progressing.

When another company recruited Libby away from
Pepsi in 2009, we were ready to leave Shanghai and move
to Hong Kong where the job was based. Hong Kong,
while not nearly as fascinating as Shanghai, was much
less stressful for us, and my visa situation was much
easier to navigate. We were, for the first time in five
years, comfortable and able to speak openly about our
relationship. In 2011, during our last year in Hong Kong,
New York passed a law allowing same-sex marriage. This
was a big deal to us as we had met in New York, and it was
a big deal to the national gay rights movement as well.
Momentum was rising.

In 2012, we moved to Italy. We were feeling free,
the first time in seven years we weren't living in
pollution, and I was easily able to obtain a ten-year
Italian retirement visa, which gave us incredible peace
of mind. Days after we unpacked our lamps and books
for the umpteenth time, President Obama came out and
endorsed same-sex marriage days after VP Joe Biden
and Arne Duncan, the Secretary of Education, announced
their support. We were thrilled. Even though we had no

idea when the U.S. would make same-sex marriage legal everywhere, we decided that soon we would wed in New York. We'd always wanted to marry and have a beautiful wedding, but we didn't want to do it until we could do it legally and on par with straight couples.

In August of 2013, for our 25th anniversary, Libby and I had the wedding of our dreams. I'd been planning this wedding the whole time we'd been together, down to every last detail, but what I hadn't planned on, what we hadn't known, was the surge of feelings and emotions and love that would envelop us as we began walking down the aisle together. It made up for having to wait 25 years for this moment. The night was truly magical where we felt like we were floating inside the dream we had long ago conceded would never, ever happen. Yet, there we were, declaring our love for each other openly, legally, clinking champagne glasses in front of the people we loved most in the world instead of slices of pizza by ourselves.

We left New York right after our wedding, and traveled to our house in Santa Fe only to realize our marriage wasn't legal in New Mexico. It was a sobering reminder.

It still gives me goose bumps to think about June 26, 2015, the day the U.S. Supreme Court ruling was handed down in *Obergefell v. Hodges* granting same-sex couples the fundamental, constitutional right to marry. We were in our house in Santa Fe, watching all the coverage on TV, grateful to be in the U.S., grateful to be American.

In August of 2015, Libby and I moved to Sweden, where same-sex marriage had been legalized since 2009. Since the early 1990's, discrimination against gays has been virtually nonexistent in this country. We were still riding high on the Supreme Court decision, and the move to Sweden was the first time in almost 11 years of living abroad that we moved to a country officially as a couple—and a legally married one at that. On the resident visa application form where it asked, "What are the circumstances of your move to Sweden?" I don't have words to describe the joy and thrill I felt writing, "I am a trailing spouse." When the case-worker read our applications, she asked to see our marriage license, made a copy of it and said, "Welcome to Sweden." Simple as that.

We'd come full circle, but it had taken 27 years. We were finally able to just *be*, something straight couples take for granted. Libby was 27 and I was 36 when we made our commitment to each other, and we'd spent our adult lives trying to get to this point. Welcome to Sweden indeed.

Resources

Campus Pride Index—research the most LGBTQ friendly colleges in the United States

The Princeton Review's Guide to College for LGBTQ Students

The Advocate College Guide for LGBT College Students by Shane L. Windmeyer

The Gay and Lesbian Guide to College Life by The Princeton Review

The Opposite of Spoiled: Raising Kids Who are Grounded, Generous, and Smart About Money by Ron Lieber

Human Rights Campaign's LGBTQ Student Scholarship Database.

FinAid: The Smart Student's Guide to Financial Aid

Queer: The Ultimate LGBT Guide for Teens by Kathy Belge

The Interrogation by Nancy L. Conyers

The Bisexual's Guide to the Universe, by Nicole Kristal, Mickey Skee, & Mike Szymanski

Acknowledgments

This book has been a team effort in every sense. I couldn't have possibly completed this book without my "In Their Own Words" contributors. I have only my one experience of raising a gay daughter, and the "In Their Own Words" contributors made sure that this book reflects the diversity and richness of the queer community. Their contributions show the challenges and joys of LGBTQ life in this country, for this they have my tremendous gratitude.

This book also could not have been written without my editor, Marva Hinton. Marva is an intelligent and thoughtful editor. She always believed in me and in this book. I so appreciate her comments and support. I would also like to thank Mango Publishing and all of Mango's design, marketing, and editing staff. You have all been a pleasure to work with.

I would not have had the time or focus to write this book without the support of my family. I would like to thank my husband, Andrew, who has been my partner, my love, and my friend for over a quarter of a century now; my daughter, Casandra, who has been brave and fierce to let her mother write about her, and my son, Matthew, for providing much needed comic relief, as well as for taking my work hours in stride amidst his busy life. I don't know where I would be in my life in general without my sister Terese, my sister Tara, my sister Tina, my niece Hannah, my niece Jessica, my brother-in-law Neil (the best water polo uncle ever), and lifelong friends Carol, Dave, Amy, Bill, Beth, and Steve. I love you all. And for Tonya and Lorin, who are gone from our world, I am a better person because of you both.

I would also like to thank my supportive colleagues at Michigan State University—Robin Silbergleid, Janine Certo, Marcia Aldrich, and Glenn Stutzky.

Thank you to Nancy Schertzing for being my good friend these many years, and for sitting down and talking to me about restorative justice.

Thank you to the carpool crew—Jenny & Bill and Coni & Will. I will miss the group texts when Matthew graduates! I also heard a rumor that Will is happy to drive to the Lake Orion water polo away-game again next year. Thank you to Coach Ron Marsh for including and encouraging LGBTQ student-athletes of all skill levels, and for providing them with leadership opportunities.

I have been blessed with amazing writer/editor friends. I would like to thank Stephanie Glazier, Yuvi Zalkow, LeVan Hawkins, Seth Fischer, Kara Waite, Charlie Bondhus, Meredith Landry, Alice Dreger, Kate Maruyama, Alan Stewart Carl, Imani Williams, Kristin Lieberman, Michael Whelan, Marianne Peel, Chelsea Cristene Bock, Heather Mingus, and LaToya Jordan, who are pretty much the reason for everything. Ever.

I would like to thank the One Book/One Community Program at Michigan State University/East Lansing and Professor Anita Skeen.

Thank you, Antioch University Los Angeles and my dedicated mentors there—Richard Garcia, Sharman Apt Russell, and Emily Rapp Black. (Also, Sages!)

Finally, for the LGBTQ civil rights activists, the words "thank you" are inadequate for how hard you have fought for the rights that my daughter now enjoys. I know you've paid for this activism with the loss of relationships, the loss of jobs, and sometimes even your lives. No words can compensate for the debt we all owe you for your courage and tenacity.

Author Bio

Telaina Morse Eriksen was born in rural Michigan, the youngest of seven children in a working-class family. She received a B.A. in journalism with concentrations in history, English, and political science from Michigan State University in 1990. She worked for many years in the educational software industry writing technical manuals and doing marketing and public relations. She returned to school at age 39 to study for her MFA in creative writing, concentrating in both creative nonfiction and poetry. She graduated from Antioch University Los Angeles in December 2009. She has taught creative writing for the Department of English at Michigan State University since 2011. Her work has appeared (or is forthcoming) in *By One's Own Hand: Writing About Suicide Loss* (an anthology) *Mother is a Verb* (poetry anthology), *Under the Sun, The Fem, The Good Men Project, Role Reboot, The Manifest-Station, ARS Medica, Hospital Drive, Marco Polo Quarterly, The Truth About the Fact, poemmemoirstory* and in many other online and print publications. Her essays have been nominated for the Pushcart Prize in 2010, 2011, and 2016. She lives in East Lansing, Michigan with her husband of 24 years, her 16-year-old son, and her two dogs, Sprite and Clement. (Her 20-year-old daughter drops in from college for free Wi-Fi and laundry once or twice a month as well.)

Endnotes

1   "Surviving A Broken Neck And Cancer, Jillion Potter Becomes An Olympian And Part Of History—The Denver Post". 2017. *Denverpost. Com.* http://www.denverpost.com/2016/08/07/jillion-potter-us-womens-rugby-olympics-cancer-broken-neck/.

2   "Growing Up LGBT In America: View Statistics". 2017. *Human Rights Campaign.* http://www.hrc.org/youth/view-statistics/#.V4zGPzW18yc.

3   "Our Work | True Colors Fund". 2017. *True Colors Fund.* https://truecolorsfund.org/our-work/.

4   Mustanski, B.S., Clifford, A., Bigelow, L., Andrews, K., Birke, M.A., Ashbeck, A., & Fisher, K. (2012) *A Healthy Chicago for LGBT Youth: An IMPACT Program White Paper on Health Dispari es in Chicago's LGBT Youth.* Chicago, IL: The IMPACT Program at Northwestern University. Retrieved

from http://www.impactprogram.org/youth/
whitepaper.

5   Koebler, Jason. 2012. "Scientists May Have
     Finally Unlocked Puzzle Of Why People Are Gay".
     www.usnews.com. http://www.usnews.com/
     news/articles/2012/12/11/scientists-may-have-
     finally-unlocked-puzzle-of-why-people-are-
     gay.

6   "Prevalance Of Homosexuality Study".
     Kinseyinstitute.Org. Accessed January 5, 2017.
     https://www.kinseyinstitute.org/research/
     publications/kinsey-scale.php.

7   Fink, Richard. 2016. "Kinsey's Scale Is So 1948".
     The Huffington Post. http://www.huffingtonpost.
     com/patrick-richardsfink/kinseys-scale-is-so-
     1948_b_2362996.html.

8   "Box Turtle Bulletin » Today In History: APA
     Removes Homosexuality From List Of Mental
     Disorders". 2008. *Boxturtlebulletin.Com*. http://
     www.boxturtlebulletin.com/2008/12/15/7128.

9   "WGBH American Experience. Stonewall
     Uprising | PBS". *American Experience*. Accessed
     January 5, 2017. http://www.pbs.org/wgbh/
     americanexperience/features/introduction/
     stonewall-intro/.

10 "Stonewall Riots: The Beginning Of The LGBT Movement". 2009. *The Leadership Conference On Civil And Human Rights*. http://www.civilrights. org/archives/2009/06/449-stonewall.html.

11 "President Obama Designates Stonewall National Monument". 2016. *Whitehouse.Gov*. https://www.whitehouse.gov/blog/2016/06/24/ president-obama-designates-stonewall-national-monument.

12 Campaign, Human Rights. "The Lies And Dangers Of "Conversion Therapy" | Human Rights Campaign". *Human Rights Campaign*. Accessed January 5, 2017. http://www.hrc.org/ resources/the-lies-and-dangers-of-reparative-therapy.

13 McCoy, John. 1998. "Evidence Of Gay Relationships Exists As Early As 2400 B.C.". *Egyptology.Com (Citing The Dallas Morning News)*. Accessed on January 5, 2017. http://www. egyptology.com/niankhkhnum_khnumhotep/ dallas.html.

14 Crompton, Louis. 2003. *Homosexuality & Civilization*. 1st ed. Cambridge, Mass.: Belknap Press of Harvard University Press.

15 Wilhelm, Amara. "GALVA-108: Gay & Lesbian Vaishnava Association". Accessed January

6, 2017. *GALVA-108: Gay & Lesbian Vaishnava Association.* http://www.galva108.org/single-post/2014/05/08/A-Timeline-of-Gay-World-History.

16 Munn, Bonnie. "Dancing To Eagle Spirit Society - TWO SPIRITED PEOPLE". *Dancingtoeaglespiritsociety.Org.* Accessed January 5. http://www.dancingtoeaglespiritsociety.org/twospirit.php.

17 "Gay Popes: Sixtus IV (R. 1471-1484)". 2011. *Queerhistory.Blogspot.Com.* http://queerhistory.blogspot.com/2011/07/gay-popes-sixtus-iv-r-1471-1484.html.

18 "Thomasine/Thomas... Clothes Make The (Wo)Man". 2000. *Mohicanpress.Com.* http://www.mohicanpress.com/wwwboard/messages8/17269.html.

19 Jason, Koebler. 2012. "Scientists May Have Finally Unlocked Puzzle Of Why People Are Gay". *Www.Usnews.Com.* http://www.usnews.com/news/articles/2012/12/11/scientists-may-have-finally-unlocked-puzzle-of-why-people-are-gay.

20 "Congenital Adrenal Hyperplasia (CAH): Your child: University Of Michigan Health System". *Med.Umich.Edu.* Accessed January 5, 2017.

http://www.med.umich.edu/yourchild/topics/caheffects.htm.

21 Colapinto, John. 2000. *As Nature Made Him*. 1st ed. New York: HarperCollins Publishers.

22 Rahman, Qazi. 2015. "'Gay Genes': Science Is On The Right Track, We're Born This Way. Let's Deal With It.". *The Guardian*. https://www.theguardian.com/science/blog/2015/jul/24/gay-genes-science-is-on-the-right-track-were-born-this-way-lets-deal-with-it.

23 Parens, Erik. 2006. *Surgically Shaping Children*. 1st ed. Baltimore, Md.: Johns Hopkins University Press.

24 McBride, Hugh. "What Is A 'Locus Of Control' And How Does It Affect My Teen's Behavior?". *Aspen Education Group*. Accessed January 5, 2017. http://aspeneducation.crchealth.com/article-locus-of-control/.

25 Dreger, Alice. 2014. "What's Wrong With Trying To Engineer Your Child's Sexual Orientation?". *Pacific Standard*. https://psmag.com/what-s-wrong-with-trying-to-engineer-your-child-s-sexual-orientation-688e1036381a#.2p59u2gdo.

26 Parens, Erik. 2006. *Surgically Shaping Children*. 1st ed. Baltimore, Md.: Johns Hopkins University Press.

27 Duggan, Maeve, Amanda Lenhart, Cliff Lampe, and Nicole Ellison. 2015. "Parents and Social Media". *Pew Research Center: Internet, Science & Tech.* http://www.pewinternet.org/2015/07/16/parents-and-social-media/.

28 Hamblin, James. 2015. "The Key To Healthy Facebook Use: Don't Compare Yourself To Others". *The Atlantic.* http://www.theatlantic.com/health/archive/2015/04/ways-to-use-facebook-without-feeling-depressed/389916/.

29 Dentith, Jessica. 2015. "Highlight Reels Vs. Reality". *Thought Catalog.* http://thoughtcatalog.com/jessica-dentith/2015/02/highlight-reels-vs-reality/.

30 "Equal Access To Public Restrooms". *Lambda Legal.* Accessed January 5, 2017. http://www.lambdalegal.org/publications/trt_equal-access-to-public-restrooms.

31 "How The Law Protects LGBTQ Youth". *Lambda Legal.* Accessed January 5, 2017. http://www.lambdalegal.org/know-your-rights/how-the-law-protects-lgbtq-youth-0.

32 "Same-Sex Dates And School Dances". *Lambda Legal.* Accessed January 5, 2017. http://www.lambdalegal.org/know-your-rights/youth/same-sex-dates-and-school-dances.

33   "Your Speech Rights At School". *Lambda Legal.* Accessed January 5, 2017. http://www. lambdalegal.org/youth/student-speech-and-expression

34   Marshal, Michael P., Mark S. Friedman, Ron Stall, Kevin M. King, Jonathan Miles, Melanie A. Gold, Oscar G. Bukstein, and Jennifer Q. Morse. "Sexual Orientation And Adolescent Substance Use: A Meta-Analysis And Methodological Review". Accessed on January 17, 2017, *Https:// Www.Ncbi.Nlm.Nih.Gov/.* https://www.ncbi.nlm. nih.gov/pmc/articles/PMC2680081/.

35   "Preventing Substance Abuse Among LGBTQ Teens". *Human Rights Campaign And The Partnership For Drug-Free Kids.* Accessed January 17, 2017. http://www.drugfree.org/wp-content/ uploads/2015/10/HRC-Youth-Substance-Abuse-issue-brief-rev4.pdf.

36   Preventing Substance Abuse Among LGBTQ Teens". *Human Rights Campaign And The Partnership For Drug-Free Kids.* Accessed January 17, 2017 http://www.drugfree.org/wp-content/ uploads/2015/10/HRC-Youth-Substance-Abuse-issue-brief-rev4.pdf.

37   Grimm, Joe and MSU School of Journalism. 2012. *The New Bullying-How Social Media, Social Exclusion, Laws And Suicide Have Changed Our*

Definition Of Bullying, And What To Do About It. 1st
ed. Front Edge Publishing.

38 "Risk Factors | Stopbullying.Gov". *Stopbullying.
Gov.* Accessed January 5, 2017. http://www.
stopbullying.gov/at-risk/factors/index.html.

39 Walsh-Sarnecki, Peggy and Teresa Mask. 2005.
"Power And Control Drive School Bullies (The
Detroit Free Press)". *Bridges4kids.Org.* http://
www.bridges4kids.org/articles/2005/5-05/
Freep5-23-05.html.

40 Gordon, Sherry. 2016. "10 Reasons Kids Get
Bullied". *Verywell.* https://www.verywell.com/
reasons-why-kids-are-bullied-460777.

41 "GLSEN Shares Latest Findings On LGBTQ
Students' Experiences In Schools". 2013. *GLSEN.*
http://www.glsen.org/article/2013-national-
school-climate-survey.

42 "The GLSEN 2015 National School Climate
Survey: The Experiences Of Lesbian, Gay,
Bisexual, Transgender, And Queer Youth In Our
Nation'S Schools". 2015. *Glsen.Org.* https://www.
glsen.org/sites/default/files/GLSEN%202015%20
National%20School%20Climate%20Survey%20
%28NSCS%29%20-%20Full%20Report.pdf.
(p. xvii)

43 "Vice President Joe Biden: Transgender
Discrimination 'Civil Rights Issue Of

Our Time' | Transgender Law Center". 2012. *Transgenderlawcenter.Org*. http://transgenderlawcenter.org/archives/2312.

44 Wakefield, Mary. 2014. "Bullying Prevention In 2014: HRSA'S Perspective". *Stopbullying.Gov*. https://www.stopbullying.gov/blog/2014/10/22/bullying-prevention-2014-hrsas-perspective.

45 Walsh-Sarnecki, Peggy and Teresa Mask. 2005. "Power And Control Drive School Bullies (The Detroit Free Press)". *Bridges4kids.Org*. http://www.bridges4kids.org/articles/2005/5-05/Freep5-23-05.html.

46 Walsh-Sarnecki, Peggy and Teresa Mask. 2005. "Power And Control Drive School Bullies (The Detroit Free Press)". *Bridges4kids.Org*. http://www.bridges4kids.org/articles/2005/5-05/Freep5-23-05.html.

47 Lenhart, Amanda. 2007. "Cyberbullying". *Pew Research Center: Internet, Science & Tech*. http://www.pewinternet.org/2007/06/27/cyberbullying/.

48 De Lench, Brooke. "10 Tips For Teens To Prevent Cyberbullying | Momsteam". *Momsteam.Com*. http://www.momsteam.com/health-safety/10-tips-teens-prevent-cyberbullying.

49   "What To Do If Your Child Is Being Bullied And Resources". *Stompoutbullying.Org.* Accessed January 5, 2017. http://www.stompoutbullying. org/index.php/information-and-resources/ parents-page/what-do-if-your-child-being- bullied-and-resources/.

50   "The GLSEN 2015 National School Climate Survey: The Experiences Of Lesbian, Gay, Bisexual, Transgender, And Queer Youth In Our Nation'S Schools". 2015. *Glsen.Org.* https://www. glsen.org/sites/default/files/GLSEN%202015%20 National%20School%20Climate%20Survey%20 %28NSCS%29%20-%20Full%20Report.pdf. (p. xix)

51   Holing, Wes. "Local Schools Give New Look To Resolving Conflicts". *Lansingcitypulse. Com.* Accessed January 6, 2017. http:// lansingcitypulse.com/print-article-1230- permanent.html.

52   McHenry, Erin. 2015. "How Relationships Affect Health And Wellbeing—Health Talk". *Health Talk.* http://www.healthtalk.umn. edu/2015/02/13/relationships-affect-wellbeing/.

53   CenterLink and MAP Project. 2016. "2016 LGBT COMMUNITY CENTER SURVEY REPORT: Assessing The Capacity And Programs Of Lesbian, Gay, Bisexual, And Transgender Community Centers". *Lgbtcenters.Org.* http://

www.lgbtcenters.org/Data/Sites/1/SharedFiles/
documents/news/2016-lgbt-community-
center-survey-report.pdf.

54 Fabian, Renee. 2016. "6 Of The Safest Spaces
For LGBT Youth To Hang Online". *The Daily Dot.*
http://www.dailydot.com/irl/lgbt-youth-safe-
spaces/.

55 "Baby Boy? Baby Girl? Baby X! | Neurotic
Physiology". 2011. *Scicurious.Scientopia.Org.*
http://scicurious.scientopia.org/2011/03/09/
baby-boy-baby-girl-baby-x/.

56 "MYTH #10: Intersex Is Extremely Rare |
Intersex Society Of North America". *Isna.Org.*
Accessed on January 5, 2017. http://www.isna.
org/faq/ten_myths/rare.

57 Bauer, Greta and Ayden Scheim. 2015. "Project
Report - Trans Pulse". *Trans PULSE.* http://
transpulseproject.ca/research-type/project-
report/.

58 "Explore Topics". 2017. *Gender Spectrum.* https://
www.genderspectrum.org/explore-topics/.

59 Boston University Medical Center. "Transgender:
Evidence on the biological nature of
gender identity." ScienceDaily. Accessed
January 6, 2017. www.sciencedaily.com/
releases/2015/02/150213112317.htm

60   Russo, Francine. 2016. "Is There Something
     Unique About The Transgender Brain?".
     Scientificamerican.Com. https://www.
     scientificamerican.com/article/is-there-
     something-unique-about-the-transgender-
     brain/.

61   Erdely, Sabrina. 2014. "Understanding The
     Science Of Transgender". *Rolling Stone.* http://
     www.rollingstone.com/culture/news/the-
     science-of-transgender-20140730.

62   Human Rights Campaign. 2014. "American
     Medical Association Adopts Two Important Pro-
     LGBT Resolutions | Human Rights Campaign".
     Human Rights Campaign. http://www.hrc.org/
     blog/american-medical-association-adopts-
     two-important-pro-lgbt-resolutions.

63   "A Guide To Hormone Therapy For Trans
     People". *www.teni.ie.* Accessed January 5, 2017.
     http://www.teni.ie/attachments/9ea50d6e-
     1148-4c26-be0d-9def980047db.PDF.

64   Joyce, Amy. 2014. "How Helicopter Parents
     Are Ruining College Students". *Washington
     Post.* https://www.washingtonpost.com/news/
     parenting/wp/2014/09/02/how-helicopter-
     parents-are-ruining-college-students/.

65   Sue, Derald. 2010. "Racial Microaggressions
     In Everyday Life". *Psychology Today.*

https://www.psychologytoday.com/blog/
microaggressions-in-everyday-life/201010/
racial-microaggressions-in-everyday-life.

66   Sue, Derald. 2010. "Microaggressions: More
     Than Just Race". *Psychology Today*. https://www.
     psychologytoday.com/blog/microaggressions-
     in-everyday-life/201011/microaggressions-
     more-just-race.

67   Wright, Pamela. 2016. "Advocating For Your
     Child: Getting Started". *Wrightslaw.Com*. http://
     www.wrightslaw.com/advoc/articles/advocacy.
     intro.htm.

68   Harvard Publications. 2010. "The Health Benefits
     Of Strong Relationships - Harvard Health".
     Harvard Health. http://www.health.harvard.edu/
     newsletter_article/the-health-benefits-of-
     strong-relationships.

69   LaSala, Michael. 2011. "Brothers And Sisters Of
     Gays And Lesbians". *Psychology Today*. https://
     www.psychologytoday.com/blog/gay-and-
     lesbian-well-being/201110/brothers-and-
     sisters-gays-and-lesbians.

70   Dean, Terry. 2001. "Teens Alone After School
     Ripe For Trouble, Survey Finds". *Tribunedigital-
     Chicagotribune*. http://articles.chicagotribune.
     com/2001-03-07/news/0103070230_1_ymca-

programs-unsupervised-teens-after-school-
activities.

71   "Extracurricular Activities". *Kidshealth.Org.*
Accessed January 5, 2017. http://kidshealth.org/
en/teens/involved-school.html.

72   GLSEN. 2013. "The Experiences of LGBT
Students in School Athletics (Research Brief)".
New York: GLSEN https://www.glsen.org/sites/
default/files/The%20Experiences%20of%20
LGBT%20Students%20in%20Athletics.pdf.

73   "How Positive Peer Pressure Works". 2013.
Secureteen.Com. http://www.secureteen.com/
peer-pressure/how-positive-peer-pressure-
works/.

74   Palmer, Kimberly. 2014. "10 Money Tips For
Teens". *Money.Usnews.Com.* http://money.
usnews.com/money/personal-finance/
articles/2014/11/05/10-money-tips-for-teens.

75   "At What Age Is The Brain Fully Developed?".
Mental Health Daily. Accessed on January 5, 2017.
http://mentalhealthdaily.com/2015/02/18/at-
what-age-is-the-brain-fully-developed/.

D0188420

THE

100

BEST

*R*OMANCE

NOVELS

THE
100
BEST
ROMANCE
NOVELS

From Pride and Prejudice
to Twilight, *books to*
fall in love—and lust—with

JENNIFER LAWLER and the Editors of Crimson Romance

Avon, Massachusetts

Published by
Adams Media, a division of F+W Media, Inc.
57 Littlefield Street, Avon, MA 02322. U.S.A.
www.adamsmedia.com

ISBN 10: 1-4405-6098-6
ISBN 13: 978-1-4405-6098-9
eISBN 10: 1-4405-6099-4
eISBN 13: 978-1-4405-6099-6

Printed in the United States of America.

10 9 8 7 6 5 4 3 2 1

*This book is available at quantity discounts for bulk purchases.
For information, please call 1-800-289-0963.*

Contributors

Jennifer Lawler has her dream job: As the acquisitions editor for Crimson Romance, she gets to read romances and look at pictures of male cover models all day. A former college English teacher (but don't hold that against her), she turned to writing and editing as an alternative to grading papers and realized too late that she'd guaranteed herself homework for life. She is the author or coauthor of more than thirty books.

A fan of romance since she was in her teens, she has a particular soft spot for wisecracking heroines. She writes romances herself under several pen names.

Julie Sturgeon has been a journalist for more than twenty-five years, covering everything from business analysis to college basketball. As an avid romance reader for even longer, she was the romance columnist at *Pages* magazine. Today, she is a development editor for Crimson Romance and owner of Indianapolis on the Cheap.

Jessica Verdi used to dream about getting paid to read about true love and super-sexy heroes all day . . . and now, as Crimson Romance's assistant editor, she actually gets to do it! Jessica is the author of the young adult contemporary novel *My Life After Now* and received her MFA in creative writing from The New School. She is also one of the founders of TeenWritersBloc.com, a popular blog dedicated to the world of children's and YA literature.

Jessica watches the Keira Knightley version of *Pride and Prejudice* more often than is probably healthy and remains firm on her stance that vampires beat out cowboys and rugged police detectives as romance's sexiest heroes any day of the week.

Contents

Introduction: The List—and How We Came Up with It ♥ 13

The Top 100 Romance Novels ♥ 17

For all of the Crimson Romance readers and writers, without whom there'd be no Crimson Romance editors.

Acknowledgments

We'd like to thank all of the staff at F+W Media, for all of their unflagging support and confidence in Crimson Romance, and in this book. All books start with an idea, and every author needs someone who believes in that idea.

Special thanks to Halli Melnitsky for her patience and ability to deal with 500 "Oh, wait, I have an idea!" e-mails on any given day. And a shout-out to Meredith O'Hayre, managing editor extraordinaire, without whom we would all be drinking a lot more tequila than we should, and probably during the Friday morning edit meeting.

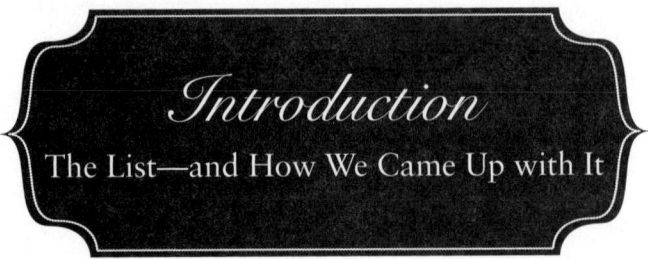

Introduction
The List—and How We Came Up with It

IN BETWEEN LOOKING AT PICTURES OF SHIRTLESS MEN (purely for book cover research—this is work related) (we swear), we at Crimson Romance also spend a lot of time talking about our favorite romances and why we love them.

"Mary Stewart really knew how to set a scene," we'll say, or "You can always count on Jennifer Crusie to make you smile," or "Did you read the new Eloisa James?"

We also spend a lot of time talking about the kinds of romances we're looking for at Crimson—romances that our readers will love. "Does it have enough heart?" we ask. "Does it give enough emotional satisfaction at the end? Does it have that spark?" We know what we like, and you should hear us when we find a manuscript with that passion and that payoff. We're happy not just because we love good romances, we're happy because we know that's exactly what readers like you are looking for.

Even though we eat, drink, and breathe romance all day long, we can't get enough of it. So after a long day of reading and editing romance, we go home and read some more. Junkies are like that.

The Idea

One day not too long ago, one of us (~~it was Julie's fault~~) (~~actually, it may have been Jess~~) (~~or possibly~~ Jennifer did it) said, "We should make a list of the top 100 books in romance. The books that we would publish here at Crimson, if they hadn't already been published."

"Great idea!" we said and went back to editing.

Then someone else said, "Not just a list, a book! You should write a book. You could name each romance and tell what it's about and include cool facts and the reason why Crimson would publish it!" The person who said that was our publisher, Karen, and suddenly there was a deadline and writing assignments and an editor editing the editors (hi, Halli!). Karen *gets things done*. It was a bit like boot camp and we enjoyed every minute of it. Really.

The Criteria

We knew from the start that certain criteria had to be met for a book to be included in our list of the top 100 romances. Any book we considered had to be a romance—a romance as we publish them here at Crimson. That is:

1. Whatever else happens, the novel must focus on the development of the love relationship between the main characters in the book. If the main point of the book is the heroine completing her personal journey, we love that, but it's not romance. If she completes her personal journey in the context of a romantic relationship, then that's romance.
2. There must be an emotional payoff for the reader—in the form of a satisfying happily ever after.
3. It must be full length—a novel, not a short story, play, blog post, or tweet.
4. Something about the book must make it important enough that we would publish it at Crimson. For example, perhaps it pushed the boundaries of the genre or was a pioneer in some way. Or maybe it simply has emotional staying power.

So you won't see *Romeo and Juliet* on this list. Even though it is a beautiful love story, it is not a novel. And we don't think we'll be spoiling the ending if we say it also doesn't end happily ever after.

Beyond that set of basic criteria, we wanted to choose from a variety of subgenres (romantic suspense, paranormal, contemporary, historical, and more) and publishing eras (nineteenth century, the 1980s, just this year).

We have presented the titles in alphabetical order rather than trying to rank them. You should see the vicious arguments that break out when you try to tell Jess that Jane Austen can't have all of the top slots. In order to keep the peace at Crimson, we felt that it made sense to leave the ranking up to you, Dear Reader. Make your argument for who deserves the top spot, and why, and we'll listen!

You may find your favorite authors and titles on this list—or you may not! If not, send us your pick and your argument as to why it should be in our Top 100, and we'll talk about it on the Crimson Romance blog (*www.crimsonromance.com*) and possibly include it in a future volume.

The Top 100
Romance Novels

16 Lighthouse Road

DEBBIE MACOMBER

CONTEMPORARY / 2001

> *"Cecilia Randall had heard of people who, if granted one wish, would choose to live their lives over again. Not her. She'd be perfectly content to blot just one twelve-month period from her twenty-two years."*

Macomber portrays realistic, truthful events in a heartwarming, uplifting way. She doesn't shy away from dealing with heart-wrenching circumstances—in this book, a couple loses a newborn child—but she always finds a way to show how grace, hope, and love can ultimately triumph.

* This is the first book in Macomber's celebrated Cedar Cove series. Others include *311 Pelican Court* (2003), *8 Sandpiper Way* (2008), and *1225 Christmas Tree Lane* (2011).
* Macomber's hometown created a five-day Cedar Cove Days festival in 2009 to celebrate the success of these novels.

In *16 Lighthouse Road*, connected stories trace the trajectory of various characters' love relationships. Cedar Cove family court judge Olivia Lockhart hears—and ultimately denies—the divorce petition of a young couple, Cecilia and Ian Randall—a couple seeking a divorce despite having signed a prenuptial agreement promising to love each other forever. Olivia sees hope and promise for them when they cannot see it for themselves.

Olivia's court decision leads to some challenges in her own romantic life, for the newspaper coverage of the case brings newspaper editor Jack Griffin into her orbit. Long divorced, Olivia finds Jack appealing.

Olivia's daughter must also grapple with a decision about marriage, Olivia's good friend must deal with her husband's disappearance, and Olivia's mother befriends a disabled man with a secret.

Throughout the novel, Macomber uses her warm and sympathetic style to explore issues of trust and to reject the idea that relationships—and love—can be thrown away.

All Through the Night

CONNIE BROCKWAY

HISTORICAL / 1997

> "The landlady shuffled into the long narrow room ahead of Colonel Henry 'Jack' Seward and headed right for the curtained window overlooking the square."

Brockway's warm and intelligent style shines in all of her stories—but we find this one particularly riveting.

*+. Meticulous research makes Brockway's historical romances richly textured and finely drawn.
*+. Brockway is an eight-time finalist for Romance Writers of America's RITA Award. And don't worry, this isn't a case of "always the bridesmaid" syndrome—Brockway has won the award twice (so far)!

Set in Regency England, this tale follows the exploits of the widow Anne Wilder, a thief who targets the richest members of society. Unfortunately—or perhaps fortunately—Colonel Jack Seward sets a trap to catch the thief. Anne seduces him and escapes his snare, but the colonel isn't one to give up: He chases her all over England, never realizing that the criminal he pursues (and desires) is the same person as the widow he is growing to love.

While Anne does have a noble reason for her thievery (think Robin Hood), she is also motivated by the daring and risk involved. The colonel, a ruthless agent, adds a dark intensity to the story. The characters are troubled, with pasts that must be confronted, who make decisions that aren't always defensible, but they aren't the stereotypical troubled characters of romance—they're complex, sensual, tender, and likeable.

Top Five Romantic Movie Proposals

1. *Pride and Prejudice*—Elizabeth Bennet (Jennifer Ehle) and Mr. Darcy (Colin Firth). The second proposal. Sigh.

2. *Walk the Line*—June Carter (Reese Witherspoon) and Johnny Cash (Joaquin Phoenix).

3. *Love, Actually*—Jamie (Colin Firth) and Aurelia (Lúcia Moniz).

4. *Jerry Maguire*—Jerry Maguire (Tom Cruise) and Dorothy (Renée Zellweger).

5. *Pride and Prejudice*—Elizabeth Bennet (Keira Knightley) and Mr. Darcy (Matthew Macfadyen). I know, we cheated. No, we didn't.

Almost Eden

DOROTHY GARLOCK
HISTORICAL / 1995

> *"Jason Picket was mesmerized. His mind scarcely registered what he was seeing, but he was alert enough to grasp the possibilities this chance encounter could mean to his miserable life."*

The romance trope of the half-breed rejected by society is given a fresh take in this adventure story.

- ✳. Garlock doesn't gloss over historical truths—her historical romances capture the true flavor of the Old West.
- ✳. Characters in *Almost Eden* also appear in Garlock's *Wild Sweet Wilderness* and *Annie Lash*.
- ✳. Garlock was one of the launch authors for Bantam's Loveswept line.

The two main characters—Baptiste Lightbody (Light) and Maggie—are both outcasts in their respective societies. He's called a half-breed; she's called a witch (mostly because she's beautiful and adept with animals). They meet when Light rescues Maggie from a rapist; Light immediately senses they are two parts of the same spirit.

Though connected by this spiritual bond as well as by a common desire to find a home, they must confront a number of challenges—not least of which is a band of pirates—as they undertake a journey to reach their "almost Eden."

Along Came a Duke

ELIZABETH BOYLE
HISTORICAL / 2012

"The day dawned like it always did in May in the village of Kempton, with a bright sprinkle of sunshine, a hint of dew on the grass and the birds singing happy choruses in the garden. There was no indication whatsoever that on this day, Miss Tabitha Timmons would not only find herself betrothed, but fall madly and deeply in love. And not necessarily with the same man."

Boyle has written any number of wonderful historical romances, but this brand-new title is a delightful rags-to-riches Cinderella story.

- ✴ This is the first in Boyle's Rhymes with Love series—and we're eagerly anticipating #2!
- ✴ Expect tongue-in-cheek wit from Boyle rather than a perfectly realistic portrait of Regency England.
- ✴ We give Boyle the award for most intriguing book titles—come on, who wouldn't want to pick up a book called *Confessions of a Little Black Gown* or *Memoirs of a Scandalous Red Dress*?

Impoverished Tabitha Timmons is the perfect Cinderella—hardworking, smart, with an independent streak and troublesome relatives. And she has the chance to inherit a vast fortune if she weds the right man. Tabitha knows what the sensible thing is—marriage to the proper Mr. Barkworth.

But the Duke of Preston has other plans for Tabitha, which she would be more willing to participate in if he weren't such a scoundrel. He's arrogant (as a duke should be!) but ultimately softhearted and worthy of Tabitha's love. Despite their differences, they make a believable and genuine match.

Boyle writes with a Jane Austen touch—witty, intelligent, and arch.

Top Five
Romantic Dinners

Don't forget the candlelight!

1. Chilled shrimp and champagne.
   Substitute oysters for the aphrodisiac
   quality.

2. Steak and lobster.

3. Asparagus risotto for the vegetarian.

4. For women, anything on a picnic!

5. For men, anything on the grill!

Bait

KAREN ROBARDS
ROMANTIC SUSPENSE / 2004

"It was a professional job, Sam McCabe saw at a glance. The bare minimum of muss and fuss. A couple sprawled on the floor of their cathedral-ceilinged great room, hands bound behind their backs, blood from the bullet wounds in their heads soaking into the already deep red of their Oriental carpet."

Robards balances page-turning suspense with an emotionally moving romance, and adds in just the right touch of humor, a juggling act few can accomplish as well as she.

- ✦ Robards was in law school before she sold her first romance (at age twenty-four).
- ✦ Robards started her first romance novel as a class assignment for the University of Kentucky. Go Wildcats!

A case of mistaken identity starts *Bait* off with a bang. There are two Maddie Fitzgeralds staying at a hotel in New Orleans. One is an advertising executive on a business trip. The other is an FBI informant. The FBI informant is killed, but the advertising executive barely escapes with her life.

FBI agent Sam McCabe swoops in to question Maddie. McCabe believes the attacker is a serial killer he's been chasing—and who has been taunting him with his failure to stop the murders. But the murderer has been successful in killing the informant, so Maddie should be safe . . . right?

When Maddie is attacked again, McCabe knows the only way to trap the killer is to use her as bait—but first he'll have to convince her to play along. And she doesn't want to have anything to do with the FBI, because Maddie's got a secret.

Like all of Robards's novels, this one is character driven and engaging.

Bet Me

JENNIFER CRUSIE
CONTEMPORARY / 2004

> "Once upon a time, *Minerva Dobbs thought as she stood in the middle of a loud yuppie bar,* the world was full of good men. *She looked into the handsome face of the man she'd planned on taking to her sister's wedding and thought,* Those days are gone."

This is Crusie at her wry best—an appealing opposites-attract novel with memorable characters, a heartfelt and humorous look at how two different people can find their common ground.

- ✴. To research her PhD dissertation on the different ways men and women tell stories, Crusie set a goal to read 100 romance novels. She was immediately hooked and started writing romances herself—much to our delight!
- ✴. Crusie keeps a witty, insightful, and very current blog on her official website, where she writes about all sorts of stuff, from things she finds funny to her favorite TV shows to what's going on in her life at the moment. Don't you just love when authors give you a sneak peek into their personalities like that?

When Minerva Dobbs (an actuary of average looks but quick wit) is dumped by her boyfriend just before her sister's wedding, she's more concerned that her overbearing mother will be annoyed that she's dateless than emotionally wounded by the end of her relationship. So when gorgeous Calvin Morrisey picks her up at a bar, she goes right along with him. She thinks he's trying to win a bet by dating her, and she's immune to his charm. Sort of.

Min's not Calvin's usual type—she's overweight, attractive but not beautiful, and not nearly as adoring as he's accustomed to. They have nothing in common, so there's no reason they should pursue a relationship. They both agree about that.

Fate, and their friends, have a different idea. Through a variety of comic but believable incidents, Min and Calvin find themselves forced together—and battle their growing attraction (unsuccessfully, of course!). They learn to see the truth about one another, and to admire what they see.

Bet Me is an affirming, never-a-dull-moment story with a fun subplot about a beautiful psychologist who thinks of falling in love as an intellectual and biological exercise, only to learn the heart has a mind of its own.

Top Five Romantic Chores

Yes, housework can be sexy!

1. **Gardening**—working together to make those flowers bloom can be a great way to spend time together.

2. **Cooking**—you chop while he sautés, or vice versa.

3. **Walk the dog**—and catch up with each other on how the day has gone.

4. **Grocery shopping**—and pick out some fun, sexy food for play!

5. **Do something your sweetie hates as a gesture of love**—or offer a bedroom game in exchange for his doing a chore you hate!

Blue Heaven, Black Night

SHANNON DRAKE

HISTORICAL / 1986

"Fulk the Black, Count of Anjou, was descended from Rollo, the great Viking who laid claim to Normandy."

A terrific example of the tempestuous romance many of us grew up loving—the strong-willed heroine battles the somewhat (okay, more than somewhat) obsessed hero until she can finally admit her love for him. How enjoyable when they finally come together as true lovers!

Shannon Drake also writes romantic suspense under the name Heather Graham. (Not to be confused with the actress Heather Graham who is best known for playing a porn star in *Boogie Nights* and a stripper in *The Hangover*—hey, maybe *she* should write a romance novel!)

A complex backstory gives texture and depth to this medieval romance (it's of the "sweeping" variety—"a sweeping romance"); the author works hard to ensure her characters act in an historically accurate way without sacrificing the compelling storyline.

Elise is the bastard daughter of Henry II, the king of England; Sir Bryan Stede is known as the Black Knight. Much to Elise's chagrin, Bryan engages in a bit of bride stealing, as medieval warriors were wont to do. (You know you already want to read it.)

Elise, of course, being stolen, can't admit that she grows to care about Bryan or we would have no book, but when he goes off to the Crusades, Elise recognizes her love for him and sets off to join him. This being the Middle Ages, travel is not quite as easy as boarding a plane, and she is abducted (a very favorite staple of 1980s romance), with drama and conflict galore. It's a roller-coaster ride, so hang on tight till you get to that oh-so-satisfying conclusion.

Breaking the Rules

Suzanne Brockmann
Romantic suspense / 2011

"It happened so fast."

This is the culmination of Brockmann's fabulous Troubleshooters series, and it's everything a romantic suspense should be—fast paced, engaging, heart wrenching, heartwarming, and when you finally put the book down, you want to grab her by the throat and ask her why she ended the series. All this "new direction artistically" is just not a good enough excuse, Suze.

- ✶ If you thought military suspense was the province of Tom Clancy, you've never read Suzanne Brockmann.
- ✶ Brockmann's Tall, Dark and Dangerous series of books featuring Navy SEALs sparked a huge trend in romance. And we're grateful for it.
- ✶ Brockmann's husband Ed Gaffney is also an author. The couple, along with their son Jason, cowrote the feature film *The Perfect Wedding*.

Izzy Zanella, Eden Gillman, and Danny Gillman have a long, long history. Izzy and Danny are SEAL teammates who've never gotten along. Their dislike for one another is complicated by Danny's sister, Eden, a troubled young woman whom Izzy marries when another man abandons her after getting her pregnant. When Eden has a miscarriage, the relationship between Izzy and Eden ends.

Oh, but this is romance, so it doesn't end *forever*. It just takes a breather in order to make things way, way more complicated than they otherwise would be.

Eden resurfaces in Izzy's life when she tries to get custody of her younger brother Ben. Her abusive stepfather has destroyed her life; she

won't let him destroy Ben's. Danny agrees to help, but what would help most is if Eden could prove that she and Izzy have a solid marriage.

Yep, a marriage-of-convenience storyline that is nothing like any other marriage-of-convenience story you've ever read. Throw in a child prostitution ring, an abduction, and a handful of determined Navy SEALs, and you've got a sizzling page-turner.

Ultimately, this is a story about family, trust, and the kind of happily ever after that comes after the infatuation wears off.

Top Five Real-Life Romances

Happily ever after happens in the real world, too!

1. Spencer Tracy and Katharine Hepburn

2. Nicole Kidman and Keith Urban

3. Will Smith and Jada Pinkett Smith

4. Paul Newman and Joanne Woodward

5. Kirsten Dunst and Jake Gyllenhaal

Bride of Pendorric

Victoria Holt
Romantic suspense / 1963

"I often marveled after I went to Pendorric that one's existence could change so swiftly, so devastatingly."

Who doesn't love a retelling of *Rebecca*? Holt is a suspenseful, romantic writer, sadly neglected these days. We'd publish her in a New York minute.

- ✦ Victoria Holt is the pen name of Eleanor Hibbert, who also wrote under the names Jean Plaidy and Philippa Carr.
- ✦ Pick this modern-day Gothic romance if you're interested in getting started reading Holt.
- ✦ By the time she died in 1993, Holt had sold over 100 million books. And that was in the pre-social media/Internet hype/über-marketing era!

Young orphan marries a man she hardly knows. What could possibly go wrong?

Favel Farrington has lived on an Italian island (Capri) with her father all of her life—until Roc Pendorric sweeps her off her feet. He seems to adore her, and it looks like they are destined for a happily ever after.

When Favel's father dies, Roc brings her to his estate on a cliff in Cornwall. (These mysterious estates are always on a cliff in Cornwall, have you ever noticed that? Apparently it's a slightly crowded cliff in Cornwall.)

There, Favel learns all about the brides of Pendorric, who have an alarming tendency to die young and oh-so-tragically. A series of events (of the unfortunate kind) make Favel wonder if she'll escape the curse of the Pendorrics—and whether she's really in danger or just a victim of her own overactive imagination.

There's a wonderful Mrs. Danvers character that you'll want to smack, a ghost (maybe), a sister and her family who *seem* welcoming, and a sense of foreboding that will keep you up for approximately three nights after you finish the book.

This is one of Holt's most suspenseful novels, and even though you think you know whodunnit, you don't.

Captive Bride

JOHANNA LINDSEY
HISTORICAL / 1977

> *"The weather was pleasantly warm on this early spring day in the year 1883. The slightest of breezes played daintily with the great oak trees that lined the long driveway leading to Wakefield Manor."*

The language isn't as flowery as Woodiwiss's and the plotline isn't as involved as a Rogers tome, which makes it just right for many casual readers who enjoy a classic tale of a spirited Western gal redefining the rules on how to be a sex slave. It's not politically correct, but desert romances rarely are.

- ✦ *Captive Bride* was the first of fifty-two bestsellers for Johanna Lindsey. She is one of the few pioneers still actively publishing today.
- ✦ Rather than sticking to one subgenre, Lindsey's books run the gamut. Sci-fi, the Old West, the Vikings . . . nothing is off-limits to Lindsey's fantastic imagination. And as long as she keeps writing those dreamy heroes and steamy love scenes, we'll follow her anywhere.

Beautiful Christina Wakefield gives in to the lure of the Arabian desert and impulsively follows her brother to Cairo, but her plans for adventure get a new definition when she bumps into someone she knows.

Sheik Abu is known as Philip Caxton back in the London ballrooms, where Christina didn't deem him worthy of her hand in marriage. He has remained a bachelor because he's looking for a wife with intelligence rather than merely a flair for fashion. He jumps at

this opportunity to show her a new side to him by kidnapping her and holding her prisoner as his slave.

The danger, however, stems from a rival tribe that succeeds in capturing Christina and dragging her away from the relative safety of Philip's tent. She becomes the lure to bring him to their camp, where they plan to take revenge on their rival for a past slight. As Abu, her lover rescues Christina and escapes a slow death—then lies about his feelings to convince her to return to England and safety before he eventually joins her for their happily ever after.

The tale begins with total male dominance, the usual flavor of the times, and evolves to an emotional dance where Christina and Philip lean toward each other only to pull back when the L-word starts to hover on the edge of their physical relationship.

Carolina Moon

NORA ROBERTS
ROMANTIC SUSPENSE / 2000

> *"She woke in the body of a dead friend. She was eight, tall for her age, fragile of bone, delicate of feature. Her hair was the color of corn silk, and slid prettily down her narrow back. Her mother loved to brush it every night, one hundred strokes with the soft-bristled, silver-backed brush that sat on the graceful cherry-wood vanity."*

As if we need a reason to pick a Nora Roberts title. Bah. [*We really need to give a reason.*—The Editor.] [*All right, all right.*—The Authors.] We picked this title, written well into Roberts's career, because it showcases her ability to engage her readers with a heartfelt, gripping story.

* *The New Yorker* calls Roberts "America's favorite novelist" and she's one of ours, too!
* The prolific Nora Roberts also writes under the pen name J. D. Robb.
* Roberts met her husband when she hired him to build bookshelves for her. A gorgeous handyman comes over to the single writer's house and she finds herself attracted to more than just his skills with a hammer? Jeez, if that doesn't sound like the plot of a romance novel, we don't know what does!

Tory Bodeen, a child with a psychic gift, grows up in an abusive home. Her gift is neither respected nor appreciated by her unredeemable, soul-crushing parents, causing her to develop understandably ambivalent feelings about it. Despite her horrific home life, she is able to seek refuge with her friend Hope Lavelle—until the day Hope is murdered. Hope's life isn't the only one that's destroyed with this brutal act: Tory's life comes undone as well.

Years pass and as a grownup, Tory returns to her home of Progress, South Carolina, trying to make peace with the past. She has friendships she wishes to renew and a point she wishes to prove—but moving home is going to be harder on her than she ever imagined.

Hope's family blames Tory for her role in Hope's death, although Cade Lavelle, Hope's older brother, steps in to shield Tory from his family's dislike—and if you can't guess what happens between them, you are not a romance reader, my friend.

Reclaiming her past and rebuilding her life isn't complicated just by the mixed emotions she and those around her feel—the murderer is still on the loose, and Tory is next on his list.

Here Roberts shows off the reason why she's the queen of southern Gothic.

Chance McCall

SHARON SALA
CONTEMPORARY / 1993

"A strange anxiety seized him. It was time! Suddenly he couldn't get away fast enough. He grabbed the can he'd brought from the station and began walking through the house, methodically pouring a thin, steady stream of gasoline on and over everything."

This early Sharon Sala novel makes a common fiction trope—the hero who loses his memory—something special and heartwarming.

- ✶ Sala is the author of more than eighty novels, including those written under the name Dinah McCall. In fact, on the cover of many of her books, her name is actually written as "Sharon Sala, also known as Dinah McCall." Add that lengthy moniker to a book named after a character with the same surname as the author (i.e., McCall), and things are bound to get confusing— surely only a writer as good as Sala/McCall would be able to get away with it!
- ✶ Sala began writing in 1980 but it wasn't until after the deaths of her father and sister several years later that she decided to seriously pursue her dreams of being a published author.
- ✶ Sharon Sala has won both the National Reader's Choice Award and the Colorado Romance Writers Award of Excellence five times each!

For years, Jennifer Ann Tyler has had a thing for Chance McCall, who came to her father's ranch looking for work when he was just

a teenager. Though Chance becomes like family, he hasn't dared to pursue a romantic relationship with her because of his past.

This stalemate is upset when Chance loses his memory—knowing only that he cares for Jennifer but not remembering anything beyond that. He sets out to learn who he is—and Jennifer finds the courage to go with him, not caring what she may risk to do so. Together they must face the secrets of Chance's past that have kept them apart for so long.

In this novel, Sala explores the theme of "love never dies" but ultimately the story is one of love renewed, love restored.

Chasing Perfect

SUSAN MALLERY
CONTEMPORARY / 2010

"Charity Jones loved a good disaster movie as much as the next person—she would simply prefer the disaster in question not be about her life."

Fool's Gold is the town you wished you lived in. Mallery has a deft touch with creating a vivid sense of community in this novel.

- ✦ This is the first book in Mallery's popular Fool's Gold series, already up to nine titles at the time we wrote this.
- ✦ *Booklist* has said of Mallery's writing, "Novels don't get much better than Mallery's expert blend of emotional nuance, humor, and superb storytelling." And we agree!

Settle in for a round of excellent storytelling with Mallery's characteristic humor and emotion. City planner Charity Jones comes to Fool's Gold, Nevada, to help create jobs so that the men of the town don't have to leave to find work. The itinerant Charity sees Fool's Gold as a chance to put down some roots. She is absolutely not interested in dating, no siree, no how. She's been stung too many times.

Enter Josh Golden, whom the town has taken to their collective heart. A former professional cyclist, his womanizing reputation precedes him and Charity wants no part of him. None at all. *Really.* The other women in town have no problem with his past, and of course he could pick one of them, but he doesn't. He wants Charity.

Despite her reluctance to get involved again, Charity doesn't stand a chance, especially when the townspeople start playing matchmaker. Everyone knows they're meant for each other, and eventually Charity figures it out, too!

The Convenient Marriage

GEORGETTE HEYER
HISTORICAL / 1934

> *"Lady Winwood being denied, the morning caller inquired with some anxiety for Miss Winwood, or, in fact, any of the younger ladies. In face of the rumour which had come to her ears it would be too provoking if all the Winwood ladies were to withhold themselves. But the porter held the door fully open and said that Miss Winwood was at home."*

Heyer's meticulous research—and her captivating style—make this a must-read for any fan of historical romance.

- ✦ She's been called a modern-day Jane Austen—and we agree! (That is, of course, if you consider the 1930s "modern-day.")
- ✦ Heyer wrote her first novel, *The Black Moth*, when she was seventeen. Since 1921, it has never been out of print.

Not surprisingly, given the title, this is a story about a marriage of convenience—which eventually turns into a true love relationship. Although Heyer is probably best known for her Regencies, this novel is set in the Georgian era.

When the Earl of Rule proposes marriage to Elizabeth Winwood, a marriage that would help her entire impoverished family, her younger sister Horatia steps in. Elizabeth is in love with someone else, and if Horatia were to marry Rule then Elizabeth would be free to follow her heart.

But don't worry! Horatia's noble sacrifice shall be rewarded eventually. After his marriage to Horatia, Rule continues his relationship with his mistress, Lady Caroline Massey (tsk tsk). Horatia doesn't particularly mind at first—she knew exactly what she was getting into. But as she finds herself drawn more and more to Rule, the knowledge that he is intimate with another woman becomes a source of pain to her.

Horatia begins a friendship with Lord Lethbridge, who has an ulterior motive for cultivating their relationship: He wants revenge on Rule and hurting Horatia is an excellent way to get it. Rule begins to fall in love with his wife, but she keeps her distance, believing he is still attached to his mistress. A series of calamities set in motion by Lethbridge could drive Rule and Horatia apart—but they finally learn to tell each other their true feelings, robbing Lethbridge of his revenge and living (you saw this coming, didn't you?) happily ever after.

15

The Cove

CATHERINE COULTER
ROMANTIC SUSPENSE / 1996

> *"Someone was watching her. She tugged on the black wig, flattening it against her ears, and quickly put on another coat of deep-red lipstick, holding up the mirror so she could see behind her."*

Fast-paced suspense and a compelling romance jump-start the first book in Coulter's popular series of FBI suspense thrillers. We love page-turners, even when they're a little . . . preposterous.

✴ Coulter has had sixty *New York Times* bestsellers!
✴ Coulter says she writes every morning from 7:30 to 11 A.M.

To escape her past (and her arms-dealing father's murderers) Sally Brainerd moves to a small town that appears to be picture perfect—and ideal spot for her to hide. But the townspeople have a secret. . . .

FBI agent James Quinlan has no intention of letting Sally hide. To him, she's a witness (possibly a hostile one, and potentially a murderer). He goes undercover to find a way to bring her into custody.

Loads of twists and turns keep you turning the pages, and, okay, the plot is not the most realistic you've ever read. You'll love it or you'll hate it: We love it!

Dark Lover

J. R. WARD
PARANORMAL / 2005

> *"Darius looked around the club, taking in the teeming, half-naked bodies on the dance floor. Screamer's was packed tonight, full of women wearing leather and men who looked like they had advanced degrees in violent crime. Darius and his companion fit right in. Except they actually were killers."*

Erotic vampires. Yum.

- ✦ This is the first book in Ward's The Black Dagger Brotherhood series.
- ✦ Sherrilyn Kenyon fans will love Ward's books.
- ✦ The book opens with a superhandy glossary of terms that you'll need to know as you embark on your journey through the pages, such as, "Needing period (n): Female vampire's time of fertility, generally lasting for two days and accompanied by intense sexual cravings."

Vampires. Vampire slayers. Vampire warriors. Oh, my, our hearts are racing! This is not just another vampire story, but a vampire story with a twist! (Which we are not going to reveal; you're going to have to find out for yourself.)

Wrath, the leader of The Black Dagger Brotherhood (a.k.a., band of vampire warriors), is consumed by the desire to revenge himself on the vampire slayers who murdered his family. That any number of centuries have passed doesn't deter him from his vendetta.

Beth Randall is the orphan of one of Wrath's warriors—and she doesn't have any idea what her father was or why she's having such weird changes happening to her body. It's up to Wrath to help her understand what she's getting into—and to protect her from their enemies. Despite Beth's uncertainty about the world Wrath lives in— and that she is now part of—she also craves his touch.

Sexy, sexy, and did we say sexy? We wouldn't mind a little nibble from Wrath ourselves. . . .

Dark Possession

CHRISTINE FEEHAN
PARANORMAL / 2007

> *"Manolito De La Cruz woke beneath the dark earth with his heart pounding, bloodred tears streaking his face and grief overwhelming him. A woman's despairing cry echoed in his soul, tearing at him, reprimanding him, drawing him back from the edge of a great precipice. And he was starving."*

Feehan reaches her peak with this sexy, captivating novel. We reached our peak, too.

* Feehan is also the author of the manga comic *Dark Hunger*.
* At last count, Feehan's Dark series included twenty-three titles.
* On her official website, Feehan says, "Once I create my characters, I try very hard to have them react to situations as they really would. Sometimes I have preconceived ideas of what I would like them to do, but they don't mind me, because it would be out of character for them. They take on a life of their own." That might sound crazy to some of you, but we at Crimson know that wayward voices in your head is the mark of a great writer!

We know, we know. It's not the first book in the Dark series. It's not the last book in the Dark series. It's the eighteenth book in the series! Why'd we pick the eighteenth? 'Cause we liked it the best! C'mon, it's got a guy whose afraid he's about to become a vampire, it's got jaguar-men, it's got a werewolf, it's got any number of evil persons who must be outwitted.

Manolito De La Cruz, one of the Carpathians*, knows that his life mate is MaryAnn Delaney, who really has no intention of getting embroiled with a Carpathian man. They're aggressive, territorial, possessive. A relationship with a Carpathian would sort of be like a rabbit becoming a lover to a wolf. Possibly interesting, definitely way, way too risky.

Okay, wipe that visual from your mind. Sorry.

So, standoff: He wants her, she doesn't want him. If you were an alpha male (e.g., Carpathian man), what would you do?

Exactly.

*_You_ know, the Carpathian Carpathians. People who are not what they seem.

The Devil in the Junior League

LINDA FRANCIS LEE
CONTEMPORARY / 2006

> *"The Junior League of Willow Creek, Texas, is* très *exclusive, one of the oldest and most elite women's societies in the country. And we work hard to keep it that way. Outsiders need not apply."*

This story pokes fun at every rich society gal stereotype and leaves you clutching your sides.

- ✦ Linda Lee herself is a member of the Junior League.
- ✦ Linda Lee says she got the idea to write a story about "the secret handshakes of life we learn to prove we fit in" when she realized that, as a transplanted Texan living the cosmopolitan New York City life, she didn't fully "belong" anywhere.
- ✦ Lee is a social media queen! She's constantly updating her blog, her Twitter feed, her Facebook page, and her YouTube "Linda Francis Lee in NYC" webisodes.

Fredericka Mercedes Hildebrand Ware—a.k.a. Frede—knows the rules of Willow Creek, Texas's high society life inside out: Never dominate a conversation, don't look at yourself in a mirror in public, do not give your children a middle name like Sue or Jo, and always wear make-up, even to the gym. Oh, and it simply won't do to show up for meetings and charity work without a Luis Vuitton messenger bag.

But how do you uphold your genteel lifestyle when your husband runs off with his girlfriend and all the money, leaving you high, dry, and embarrassed? You let the tackiest guy in the neighborhood blackmail

you into getting his gaudy wife, Niki Grout, into the Junior League in exchange for legal action against your thieving, cheating husband.

Sawyer Jackson is the dashing but reclusive artist Frede turns to when she needs to make her hobby art gallery pull its weight as a true profit-churning business. She instantly labels him "A Shame"—her category for men who possess a sheer waste of good looks because they have no money or status—and assumes he's gay. It's the perfect introduction for two lovers with very little in common, but everything in the world to teach each other.

The laughs never stop as this unlikely group bonds to track down her ex-husband and make him pay, all while learning what really holds a society together.

19

Devil May Cry

SHERRILYN KENYON
PARANORMAL / 2007

> *"Vengeance. Some say it's a poison that infiltrates the soul and strips it bare. That its path only destroys the one who treads it. But to others, it's mother's milk. It nourishes and thrives—gives them a reason to survive when they have nothing more to hold them to this world. This is the story of one such creature."*

The hero is a Vegas-casino-owning god. Yes, a literal god. Well, a former literal god. What's not to love?

.✦. This is one of the many books in Kenyon's Dark-Hunter series. Classical mythology has never been this much fun before.

.✦. Kenyon calls being a #1 *New York Times* bestselling author "the most miraculous and surreal thing imaginable to me." And she's been in that coveted spot no fewer than sixteen times!

This madcap adventure is worth your time. Sin is—or, rather, *was*—a powerful Sumerian god until that nasty goddess Artemis overthrew him and stole his godhead. Sin's been waiting a long, long (long!) time to get his revenge.

But that's not Sin's only problem. There are also those pesky gallu, demon-like creatures that are trying to escape to devour all humanity.

Artemis, sensing that Sin is going to make her regret her past, sends an acolyte (Katra, called Kat) to kill him, but Kat recognizes the danger the gallu present and joins forces with Sin instead of killing him. High jinks and hot sex ensue. Also, love.

Actually, we feel kinda bad getting you started on Kenyon's Dark-Hunter series. Your "to read" pile just got way bigger.

Devil's Bride

Stephanie Laurens
Historical / 1998

> "'The duchess is so very . . . very . . . well, really, most charming. So . . .' With very an angelic smile, Mr. Postlethwaite, the vicar of Somersham, gestured airily. 'Continental, *if you take my meaning.*'"

Not your ordinary historical—and not your ordinary historical heroine!

* This is the first book in Laurens's popular Cynster series.
* Laurens was born in Ceylon (now Sri Lanka), which is also the birthplace of Rosemary Rogers, author of *Sweet Savage Love* (#82 on our list). There must be something extra-romancey in the water over there!

This is a rollicking good time. If you like your romances brimful of sex and adventure, Laurens knows how to deliver the goods!

Governess Honoria Wetherby tries to help an injured man (Tolly Cynster) and ends up turning her life upside down. As a result of going to Tolly's aid, Honoria ends up in a compromising position with Tolly's cousin Devil (an unrepentant scoundrel who lives up to his nickname). Devil surprises everyone (society, his family) by offering to marry her.

If this were an ordinary historical romance, they would get married and then discover they truly love each other. But it's not. . . .

Honoria doesn't see why she should marry Devil just because they were caught unchaperoned. She longs for a life of adventure, not marriage, and Devil is determined to show her that life with him is just the adventure she's looking for.

Dreaming of You

LISA KLEYPAS
HISTORICAL / 1994

> *"The lone figure of a woman stood in the shadows. She leaned against the wall of a crumbling lodging house, her shoulders hunched as if she were ill. Derek Craven's hard green eyes flickered over her as he came from the back-alley gaming hell."*

An historical with a hero who isn't an earl. Or a duke. Cockney street rat Derek Craven is unforgettable.

- ✴ Lisa Kleypas is a former Miss Massachusetts and competed in the Miss America pageant. She says that because "Massachusetts" is such a long word and she's only 5'2", she had to tuck the end of her banner into her swimsuit, thereby inspiring her nickname "Miss Massachu." We think a story that quirky and endearing is begging to be put in one of Kleypas's romance novels!
- ✴ Derek Craven, the hero of *Dreaming of You*, was a minor character in Lisa Kleypas's previous book, *Then Came You*. She just couldn't get him out of her head, and knew he needed a book of his own. We couldn't agree more! Now, she writes on her website, the only problem is that he overpowers whatever story he appears in. That's okay by us!
- ✴ Kleypas published her first novel when she was only twenty-one years old!

Derek Craven came from nothing but has managed to make himself the wealthy owner of a famous London gambling house. He has all the scars to prove it. Gently bred Sara Fielding, a popular novelist, is going to be no match for him . . . is she?

Sara enters Derek's world merely for the sake of research—she wants her latest novel to be realistic and she's taking notes. She ends up saving Derek from a group of thugs and he grudgingly allows her to conduct her research in his realm.

Derek, the orphaned child of a prostitute, doesn't allow anyone to get close to him, but he is enchanted by the innocent Sara, whose practical exterior covers up a deep desire for love and adventure.

We love the nuanced characterization and a fast-paced plot—don't be surprised if you reread this one again and again!

A Duke of Her Own

ELOISA JAMES
HISTORICAL / 2009

> "'The duke must be here somewhere,' said Mrs. Bouchon, née Lady Anne Lindel, tugging her older sister along like a child with a wheeled toy. 'And therefore we have to act like hunting dogs?' Lady Eleanor replied through clenched teeth."

As the reigning queen of historical romance, James is welcome at Crimson anytime!

* This is the sixth, best, and last book in James's Desperate Duchesses series.
* Each of the previous Desperate Duchess books closed with a party; the next book in the series opened with that same party.
* James is a well-known Shakespearean scholar and professor of English literature; her novels have a delightful literary feel.

Don't read this one until you've read all the others, because that will make the Duke of Villiers's finally meeting his match oh-so-satisfying.

Once the epitome of the bored, irresponsible aristocrat, Leopold Dautry (the aforementioned duke) has grown into a mature man. He has decided to raise his (illegitimate) children in his own home. For that purpose, he needs a wife.

Which is how he finds himself betrothed to Eleanor, the Duke of Montague's daughter and really the only proper match for him. Eleanor is chaste and respectable. Or is she?

Lisette, the daughter of a different duke, is completely unlike any other woman in the society where Leopold spends his days. He thinks she's nutty. He thinks she's many things. He can't, in fact, *stop* thinking about her . . . even though she is also betrothed to someone else.

Which woman will capture Leopold's heart?

Emma

JANE AUSTEN

CONTEMPORARY AT THE TIME BUT HISTORICAL TO US! / 1815

> *"Emma Woodhouse, handsome, clever, and rich, with a comfortable home and happy disposition, seemed to unite some of the best blessings of existence; and had lived nearly twenty-one years in the world with very little to distress or vex her."*

With *Emma*, Jane Austen proved the power of love stories—a good romance can even make the most unlikable of characters become likable!

* Before writing *Emma*, Jane Austen said she was going to write a heroine "whom no one but myself will much like." And she stuck to her word—Emma Woodhouse is spoiled, self-aggrandizing, oftentimes rude, and ignorant of how damaging her penchant for interfering with other people's lives can be. But even so, by the end of the book, thanks to Austen's brilliant writing, readers can't help but fall in love with her.
* The 1995 film *Clueless*, starring Alicia Silverstone, is a modern-day adaptation of *Emma*, set in Beverly Hills.
* Emma Woodhouse has been portrayed on film by Gwyneth Paltrow and Kate Beckinsale. Don't even get us started on the "who played the role better" argument—we might be here a while.

Emma Woodhouse is a beautiful, smart, and privileged young woman who lives with her hypochondriac father. Her only friend is the handsome George Knightley—who also happens to be the only person

who seems to think her newfound interest in matchmaking couples is a bad idea.

Emma gets it into her head that her new friend Harriet Smith is meant to be with Mr. Elton, the town vicar. When Harriet is presented with an offer of marriage by Mr. Martin, a farmer, Emma convinces her to refuse him, stating that he's not good enough for her. Emma tells Harriet to direct her sights toward Mr. Elton instead, and Harriet complies. But when Mr. Elton proposes to Emma instead of Harriet, Emma's plan falls apart. Harriet is heartbroken, and, after being refused by Emma, Mr. Elton runs off and marries someone else.

Over time, Harriet falls for a new man—and Emma is astonished when she learns who it is: Mr. Knightley! She instantly objects to the match, and comes to realize that it's because she's jealous. She'd been spending so much time meddling into other people's love lives that she never took the time to tend to her own. And now it may be too late—if Mr. Knightley returns Harriet's affections, Emma may never get a happily ever after of her own.

Faking It

JENNIFER CRUSIE
CONTEMPORARY / 2003

> *"Matilda Goodnight stepped back from her latest mural and realized that of all the crimes she'd committed in her thirty-four years, painting the floor-to-ceiling reproduction of van Gogh's sunflowers on Clarissa Donnelly's dining room wall was the one that was going to send her to hell."*

No one does romantic comedy quite like Crusie!

* *Faking It* is connected to (and comes after) Crusie's delightful *Welcome to Temptation*.
* Crusie is a former art teacher—a background she puts to good use in this novel.

Matilda Goodnight has a secret. In fact, she has a lot of secrets. Davy Dempsey does, too. In fact, practically the entire cast of characters is hiding something with the possible exception of the dog.

Matilda comes from a long line of art forgers, but she is determined to make sure the reputation of her family's art gallery remains squeaky clean. No one has ever connected the Goodnights with their forgeries, and their forgeries hang in some hallowed halls.

To protect that reputation, Matilda has to steal back a painting from the conniving Clea Lewis (who may or may not have killed all of her previous husbands). But Matilda's a better forger than she is a thief and in her attempt to get the painting, she falls in with Davy, a reformed (sort of) con man who is himself trying to steal something—

the fortune that was embezzled from him by Clea's lover, who is (or make that *was*) Davy's financial advisor. Davy and Clea also have a past: He stole the money from her in the first place.

Whee! And that's just for starters. The plot snowballs from there, but Crusie runs the show with her usual skill, blending in subplots and backstories, crazy relatives, FBI agents, and hit men, not to mention muffins, doughnuts, piña coladas, paper umbrellas, and Double Crostics. Her larger-than-life characters (like Michael, Davy's impossible, unrepentant thief of a father) will charm you even as they pick your pocket. You'll be cheering when Davy finally figures out the truth, frees Matilda from her self-imposed goodness, and—with the good-natured aplomb of all Crusie's heroes—shows her how to solve all of her problems.

Fat Tuesday

Sandra Brown
ROMANTIC SUSPENSE / 1998

> "'He'll walk.' Burke Basile extended the fingers of his right hand, then formed a tight fist. This flexing motion had recently become an involuntary habit. 'There's not a chance in hell they'll convict.'"

Emotionally charged, this page-turner hauntingly evokes all the tangled complexities of life in the Big Easy.

- ✦ Brown has written sixty *New York Times* bestsellers.
- ✦ She is also a recipient of the Romance Writers of America's Lifetime Achievement Award.
- ✦ She's also written under three pen names: Laura Jordan, Rachel Ryan, and Erin St. Claire.

New Orleans detective Burke Basile is a pretty good cop until the day he mistakenly kills his own partner during a raid. When the man ultimately responsible for the death is acquitted and Basile comes home to find his wife cheating on him, Basile can't take anymore and sets in motion a series of events that will change his life—and the lives of many others.

Frustrated with a criminal justice system that doesn't seem to work and angered by the corruption he sees all around him, Basile resigns from the police force and seeks his own kind of justice.

Pinkie Duvall, one of the creepiest villains ever written, is the man Basile blames for his partner's death. Basile will do just about anything to see his nemesis suffer—including kidnapping Duvall's beautiful

wife, Remy. What Basile doesn't realize is that Remy is suffering, too: Her husband is abusive and domineering; she is only with him because he holds her sister's life in his hands; and she doesn't believe she can trust anyone.

As they come to know each other, these two broken souls find hope for the future and determine to bring Duvall down together.

The Flame and the Flower

KATHLEEN E. WOODIWISS
HISTORICAL / 1972

> *"Somewhere in the world, time no doubt whistled by on taut and widespread wings, but here in the English countryside it plodded slowly, painfully, as if it trod the rutted road that stretched across the moors on blistered feet."*

The Flame and the Flower launched the modern romance, as women delighted in both a rollicking tale and satisfying sex—a refreshing change from the kiss-and-a-smoldering-stare approach of older romances.

- The book was the first single-title romance novel to be published as an original paperback.
- Woodiwiss settled for 4 percent of the royalties after an Avon editor pulled it out of the slush pile.
- Raised by her mother and many sisters, Woodiwiss attributes her own plucky and determined heroines to the strong females surrounding her as a child.
- As one of the first steamy romance writers, Kathleen E. Woodiwiss changed the romance genre forever. We have her to thank for many of the spicy books on this list!

Heather Simmons is on the run for killing a man who tried to rape her, and ends up on the London docks, where she's captured by men who think they're providing a prostitute for the captain of the *Fleetwood*. Heather goes aboard the ship on the misunderstanding that she's been arrested for murder, and Captain Brandon Birmingham ends up bedding her as the hooker he thought was on offering.

When she ends up pregnant, the magistrate forces them to marry, and two unhappy strangers set sail for his home in America. Brandon's former fiancée and a pack of mean girls who had an eye on the handsome captain are also unhappy at the news when they land.

Heather withstands cutting jealousy from Charlestonian belles, and then blackmail when someone from her past threatens to spill her murderous secret. Brandon himself ends up accused of murdering his ex-betrothed. Through these trials, she finds her self-confidence, and he allows love to soften his rougher always-in-control edges.

The couple discovers love in the transformation, and the reader immerses herself in the rich details of two worlds—the well-ordered England of 1799 and the brawling newness of America.

Flowers from the Storm

LAURA KINSALE
HISTORICAL / 1992

> "He liked radical politics and had a fondness for chocolate."

It's rare to mix religious devotion and sex, but Kinsale found a way to respect both, converting readers who considered romances a guilty pleasure.

✴ Kinsale spent six years as a geologist before writing her first romance novel, putting her at the forefront of a wave of professional women who weren't afraid to say they loved this genre.

Christian Langland, Duke of Jerveaux, is a combination of a genius mathematician and a complete rake whose initials (D of J) are found often in the London newspaper gossip columns. Then a stroke seizes him just before he engages in a duel, which leaves him permanently unable to speak. His embarrassed family declares him insane and ships him off to a sanitarium, giving out the story the duke was killed on the field of honor. Meanwhile, he is trapped in a hell of understanding his circumstances but is unable to communicate his plight.

Along comes Maddy, a righteous Quaker and do-gooder, who is well aware of Christian's profligate past, as he once tried to flirt with her while working on an academic paper with her father. But when the two recognize each other during one of her charity rounds, she adheres to her Christian duty to care for the sick and becomes his caretaker and often protector from the guards.

Through her gentle patience and understanding, she is able to live with Christian's intense anger and frustration, and eventually ferrets

out what others overlooked: This man is sane, and merely mute. She becomes his champion and coach to help him improve to the point where he can pass a competency hearing and prevent greedy relatives from stripping his title and worldly possessions.

Maddy's struggle to reconcile her love for this man and her faith is genuine, and the author is careful not to ridicule or pooh-pooh the young Quaker's devotion. Meanwhile, Christian's experience is a classic tale of a proud man being stripped of everything to learn his lesson, but his refusal to quit fighting and despair at the roadblocks will soften the strongest cynic's heart.

Forever and a Day

JILL SHALVIS
CONTEMPORARY / 2012

> *"Tired, edgy, and scared that she was never going to get her life on the happy track, Grace Brooks dropped into the back booth of the diner and sagged against the red vinyl seat. 'I could really use a drink.'"*

In this sweet and sexy romance, Shalvis combines a delightful contemporary sensibility with an old-fashioned, heartfelt embrace of community and family.

✶ This is the sixth (and most recent) book in Shalvis's Lucky Harbor series.
✶ Shalvis has written more than fifty romances.

Like a lot of romance heroines, Grace Brooks has lost everything and is starting over again. Which is how she ends up in the small town of Lucky Harbor, working as a dog walker for Josh Scott, the ER doctor. Before she knows it, she's helping to take care of Josh's son, too. The dog, the son, and the doctor all capture Grace's heart, but she's not ready for a commitment and Josh hasn't got the time for love.

As their relationship grows, Grace rebuilds her life and discovers what she was meant to do. And Josh learns that sharing the burden means . . . more time for love!

Lighthearted and humorous, this is the epitome of the summer beach read.

Forsaking All Others

LaVYRLE SPENCER
CONTEMPORARY / 1982

"'North Star Agency,' answered the voice on the phone."

Spencer's romances focus on the family as much as on the couple in the relationship, making her novels the precursors of today's women's fiction.

- ✦ Spencer has won five RITA awards from the Romance Writers of America.
- ✦ Kathleen E. Woodiwiss was instrumental in getting Spencer's first novel published—she sent it to her editor at Avon.
- ✦ Much to the regret of romance readers—and the writers she inspired—Spencer retired from writing in 1997.

In this novel, one of Spencer's earliest, Allison Scott is a photographer who is deeply wounded when her model-turned-lover abandons her. She finds herself heading down the same road with Rick Lang, her new model who, in addition to being gorgeous, is also kind. But can she trust her heart with him?

Though an early 1980s book, don't mistake this for the typical bodice-ripper of the time. Spencer's characters feel like real people in your neighborhood, coping with the same problems everyone else has, yet always able to find hope and love.

The Grand Sophy

GEORGETTE HEYER
HISTORICAL / 1950

> *"The butler, recognizing her ladyship's only surviving brother at a glance, as he afterward informed his less percipient subordinates, favored Sir Horace with a low bow, and took it upon himself to say that my lady, although not at home to less nearly connected persons, would be happy to see him."*

One of Heyer's best Regencies, with a playful sense of humor and a meticulously rendered historical setting.

✴ Heyer is considered the mother of historical romance.

Sophia Stanton-Lacy has traveled around the world with her father, a diplomat, for many years, but when he receives a posting to South America, he sends Sophy to live with his sister—it being time for Sophy to find a husband and settle down in England.

Sophy's cousin, Charles Rivenhall, who is responsible for the household, does not view Sophy's arrival with favor. Sophy, tall, confident, and brash, is not one who is easily overlooked. Charles's fiancée, Eugenia, does not care for Sophy's presence in the household, either, and does her best to make Sophy miserable.

But Sophy is not so easily subdued, and thus the dueling of wits begins. Sophy takes the household in hand, dispatching one problem after the other, and ultimately Charles realizes that she is, indeed, the one for him.

Guilty

KAREN ROBARDS
ROMANTIC SUSPENSE / 2008

"Where the sweet hell do you think you're going?"

No one does "past-coming-back-to-haunt-you" as well as Robards.

✴ "I read, I write, I chauffeur children. That's my life," Robards says on her website, describing her daily life. Most of us can probably relate!

Prosecutor Kate White, the single mother of an eight-year-old son whom she adores, has a secret: When she was a teenager, she and a group of friends robbed a store—and one of them killed an off-duty police officer.

Now, years later, she's in a courtroom when chaos erupts and someone starts shooting. Kate is grabbed as a hostage—and then to her surprise, one of her friends from that night, who is in a jail holding cell, kills her captor—and expects Kate to protect him. If she doesn't? Well, no one has ever been convicted of killing that cop, and maybe it was Kate who did it. . . .

The case is being investigated by Tom Braga, a homicide detective she's had plenty of run-ins with before as prosecutor, and he thinks she's got a secret she isn't telling—which she does.

The stakes are upped when Kate and her son are threatened. Someone is trying to kill them. She's going to have to trust someone with the truth about her past—but how can she do that without destroying the life she has built?

The fast-paced suspense does not overshadow the emotionally satisfying relationship that develops between the two as they learn to love each other.

32

High Country Bride

LINDA LAEL MILLER
HISTORICAL / 2002

> *"Angus McKettrick hated every thorn and cactus, every sprig of sagebrush, every juniper tree and jackrabbit and hunk of red rock for fifty miles in all directions, and if he could have scorched the land bare as a pig's hide at rendering time, he'd have done it, yes, sir."*

Miller's Western-flavored romances have enormous appeal to romance readers—and this is one of her best.

- ✳ Miller is the daughter of a town marshal.
- ✳ Miller has written more than 100 novels.
- ✳ *High Country Bride* is the first book in the McKettrick Cowboys trilogy; there are also any number of related McKettrick novels.

Angus McKettrick has one ranch and three sons. He'll give the ranch to whichever son marries and produces an heir first. Thus, the McKettrick Cowboys core trilogy is set up.

The oldest son, Rafe McKettrick, looks around their little town and decides a mail-order bride is just the ticket. Emmeline, who comes West for her own reasons, agrees to his proposal. It is basically a business decision for both of them.

But it doesn't stay business forever! Though Rafe can be a bit thick-headed, he's sincere, and he and Emmeline grow closer through some tender moments. Their love is threatened when Emmeline's past shows up at the door and a most surprising secret is revealed!

Ice Storm

ANNE STUART
ROMANTIC SUSPENSE / 2007

> "*Mary Isobel Curwen had never shot a man before. She stood there, numb, unmoving. She'd never fired a gun before, and the feel of it in her grasp was disturbing.*"

The heroine heads up a covert mercenary organization! She kills people without remorse! We love us some kick-ass heroines!

⚬ Anne Stuart has written contemporaries, romantic suspense, historicals, paranormals—and more! But we think she may have invented the genre of black ops romance.

Isobel Curwen is the head of The Committee, a covert mercenary organization. Dealing with some of the most dangerous people in the world doesn't shake her. But confronting her past does.

Serafin, an assassin, seeks help from her organization—help only she can give. But it turns out that Serafin is a man she thought she killed a long time ago. What does he really seek? Is he looking for revenge? And what are they supposed to do about the attraction that has flared up between them now, just as it did then?

Serafin is a bad boy extraordinaire, and Isobel just might be the only one who can tame him.

In Too Deep

JAYNE ANN KRENTZ
PARANORMAL / 2010

> *"Paranormal fire burned in the darkness. Auroras of psi splashed across the ether. The night sky of San Francisco was ablaze with light from across the spectrum. Fallon Jones gripped the condo balcony railing with both hands, fighting to anchor himself to reality."*

This is a wonderful example of a paranormal that anyone can enjoy— even readers who aren't fans of the genre. No blood-sucking vampires, no werewolves, just a lot of conflict and suspense.

* Krentz also writes under the names Amanda Quick and Jayne Castle. She has also published as Amanda Glass, Jayne Taylor, Jayne Bentley, and Stephanie James. We're exhausted just reading that list.
* *In Too Deep* is the tenth novel in the Arcane Society series. We love this one because Fallon Jones finally gets what's coming to him. Krentz juggles the mystery/detective story, the paranormal suspense, and the romantic relationship with consummate skill, all the while exercising her trademark wit.
* Thirty-two of Jayne Ann Krentz's 122 romance novels have made the *New York Times* bestseller list. We like those odds!

In a slightly futuristic world, Fallon Jones lives in Scargill Cove, a place where otherworldly phenomena thrive. And Fallon is a paranormal investigator, so he's in his element. He runs Jones & Jones, which might best be described as a detective agency for things that regular

law enforcement can't handle. Things like . . . dark energy and people who can bend the will of other people.

Fallon's also a recluse, dour, cynical, and the last person you'd ever expect to see starring in his own book. He's sort of an accidental romance hero, which makes him extra-delightful.

Isabella Valdez, a talented intuitive, arrives in Scargill Cove and takes over Fallon's office—and his life. But she's on the run from danger, and it's not just the physical kind. An encounter with an object of dark energy puts them both in danger and they must unravel its secrets before it destroys them. Krentz creates two unforgettable characters here.

It Had to Be You

Susan Elizabeth Phillips
Contemporary / 1994

> *"Phoebe Somerville outraged everyone by bringing a French poodle and a Hungarian lover to her father's funeral."*

Sassy, sexy, heartwarming, and oh-so-emotionally satisfying. SEP, we adore you.

✦ *It Had to Be You* is the first in Phillips's enormously successful Chicago Stars series.

We dare you to read that first line and not be hooked.

Phoebe Somerville, a blonde bombshell, inherits the Chicago Stars football team from her despicable father. She doesn't know the first thing about football, and she can't imagine anything she cares about less. She knows her father's will is his final slap in the face: If she doesn't lead the team to the playoffs, she'll lose the inheritance and it'll go to her creepy cousin Reed. And if there's one thing Phoebe is least likely to do, it's succeed at running a football team.

Dan Calebow is the stubborn, sexist coach of the team, the type of man she heartily dislikes. The feeling is mutual: The last thing Dan needs is a boss like Phoebe. What he wants is a new owner, so he has no intention of helping her figure out what to do.

But they can't help their attraction. And they come to realize that they are both more complex than they seem to be at first glance. Their attraction grows, and so does their ability to work together as a team. In the end, Dan has a chance to ride to Phoebe's rescue, and they both get to enjoy the fruits of their success.

Jade Island

ELIZABETH LOWELL
ROMANTIC SUSPENSE / 1998

"The man was frightened."

Romance, adventure, and treasure hunting! No one does it quite like Lowell.

✦ This is the second book in the Donovan family saga—the others are *Amber Beach* and *Pearl Cove*.

Kyle Donovan, of the Donovan gem empire, prefers the allure of hunting for treasure to sitting in an office negotiating deals. When Lianne Blakely, a jade expert and the illegitimate daughter of the powerful Johnny Tang (a jade collector), is accused of stealing a precious cultural artifact from China, Kyle has to figure out what happened or Lianne and his family will be in jeopardy.

In one fun twist, Tang asks Lianne to seduce Kyle for the good of their family, and Kyle is asked to seduce Lianne for the good of *his* family, and neither knows what the other is up to.

The two must work together to find the true thief, and you know what that means! Love amidst the jewels.

Sensual and fast paced, this is the best book of the Donovan trilogy. The characters are nuanced and complex, their motivations compelling and sympathetic—even when they're at odds with each other.

Jane Eyre

CHARLOTTE BRONTË

CONTEMPORARY AT THE TIME BUT NOW HISTORICAL / 1847

> *"There was no possibility of taking a walk that day. We had been wandering, indeed, in the leafless shrubbery an hour in the morning; but since dinner (Mrs. Reed, when there was no company, dined early) the cold winter wind had brought with it clouds so sombre, and a rain so penetrating, that further out-door exercise was now out of the question."*

Though *Jane Eyre* is considered a classic love story today, when it was first published it was truly ahead of its time, as it features a strong-willed, individualistic female main character and explores the issues of sexuality, religion, and feminism, paving the way for contemporary romance novels.

✦ *Jane Eyre* was originally published in three volumes, which was a common publishing practice in the nineteenth century. Volume One consisted of chapters 1 to 15, Volume Two—chapters 16 to 26, and Volume Three—chapters 27 to 38.

The novel begins with ten-year-old Jane Eyre living with her deceased uncle's wife and children in a home where she is routinely emotionally and physically abused. When she is given the opportunity to leave the family and attend school at the Lowood School for Girls, Jane finally stands up to her aunt and tells her what she really thinks of her. But her school life doesn't turn out to be much better, as the headmaster is

a cruel man who subjects his students to cold rooms, thin clothing, and insubstantial meals.

After six years as a student and two as a teacher, Jane leaves Lowood and takes a job as a governess, where she meets the handsome Mr. Rochester. The two quickly fall in love and are preparing to get married when Jane learns that Mr. Rochester is actually already married—to Bertha, the mentally ill woman living locked up in the house.

Ashamed and brokenhearted, Jane flees from Mr. Rochester's home. She soon meets St. John, a clergyman who asks to marry her and take her away to India. Now Jane must make a decision—live a life of duty with St. John or go back to the man who lied to her and shamed her.

Kiss Me If You Can

CARLY PHILLIPS
CONTEMPORARY / 2010

> *"News flash!* The Daily Post *is happy to announce a partnership with the Bachelor Blogs, bringing you news of New York's hottest men, both online and in print!"*

Feel-good, fun romance with a contemporary voice.

✦ Phillips was an attorney before trying her hand at writing romance.
✦ This is the first book in Phillips's Bachelor Blog series.

Reporter Sam Cooper (Coop) is not a man who likes change. But things are about to get turned upside down in his world when he stops a robbery at a jewelry store and is rewarded with an antique ring—and shows up in the city's Bachelor Blog.

Free spirit Lexie Davis is interested in the ring, which was stolen a long time ago and which she thinks belongs to her family. Events get complicated when someone tries to steal the ring from Coop.

As they try to figure out why the ring matters, Lexie and Coop are drawn to each other, but will Coop find a way to change, and can Lexie be content settling down?

A Knight in Shining Armor

JUDE DEVERAUX
PARANORMAL (TIME TRAVEL) / 1990

> *"Nicholas was trying to concentrate on the letter to his mother, a letter that was probably the most important document he would ever write. Everything depended upon this letter: his honour, his estates, his family's future—and his life."*

Deveraux does an excellent job putting both Douglass and Nicholas in fish-out-of-water scenarios and showing the reader just how difficult yet funny a culture swap can be.

✱ The original release, which was the author's hardcover debut, didn't give romance readers the expected happily ever after—the hero dies alone in his time and the heroine ends up in the twenty-first century with his reincarnation. But despite some readers' restlessness, Deveraux left this plot twist in place with her 2002 rerelease.

American schoolteacher Douglass Montgomery finally stands up to the boyfriend who is constantly taking advantage of her and pays a high price in the short run: She finds herself abandoned in a churchyard in England sans money, passport, or a plan. Who wouldn't shed a few tears of panic? But Douglass's tears conjure up Sir Nicholas Stafford, a womanizing, roguish Earl of Thornwyck who died in 1564, in the flesh before her—and not exactly happy to find himself whisked into the wrong century.

Once Nicholas manages to convince Douglass that his story is real, they build their romantic relationship on a friends-in-need basis

rather than a friends-with-benefits arrangement as they team up to find the passage to this time travel portal. When they find it and he leaves her behind, she realizes her emotions are love and she must follow him. The kink in this plan? She lands in 1560—several years before Nicholas's time-travel jaunt.

Naturally, he has no recollection of his lady love, so Douglass must set out to nurture their bond all over again despite the fact that ancient Nicholas's personality is nothing like the man he became in 1988. The tender ending leaves even casual readers with tears as these two begin a third time to regenerate their connection—a solid definition of true love.

Lessons in French

LAURA KINSALE
HISTORICAL / 2010

"Lady Callista Taillefaire was a gifted wallflower. By the age of seven and twenty, she had perfected the art of blending into the wallpaper and woodwork so well that she never had to dance and only her most intimate friends greeted her."

A sexy, humorous romp that also delivers a poignant love story.

✦ Known more for her darker stories, this novel is a delightful departure for Kinsale.

Shy, plain Lady Callista Taillefaire has resigned herself to spinsterhood. She has been dumped (there's no way to put it politely) three times, even though she comes equipped with a fortune. So she has turned her attention to other matters. Like raising her bull, Hubert.

Hot bad boy Trevelyan d'Augustin is a scoundrel from Callista's past—the man who gave her lessons in French. And also *French*. Oh-la-la! Though he's the worst possible choice for Callista, when he returns home, the sparks fly—and so do the adventures! And yes, Hubert is involved in them.

These are deeply believable characters drawn with a touch of whimsy.

Lion's Bride

IRIS JOHANSEN
HISTORICAL / 1995

> *"'I have it!' Thea whirled to see Selene running through the city gates toward her. The child's red hair had come loose from her braid and was flowing wildly down her back, and her narrow chest was lifting and falling as she tried to catch her breath."*

This medieval romance keeps you biting your nails as you try to figure out how Thea and Ware will ever be able to outwit the Knights Templar.

- Best known for her Eve Duncan forensic thrillers, Johansen got her early start writing category romance.
- Although she's switched from romance to suspense, she writes on her website that she still tries to put a love story in each of her books.

Set during the Crusades, this is a story of romance, adventure, and intrigue. Johansen evokes the reality of the time with all of its many abuses of humans—everything from child labor to slavery. But she doesn't forget that she's writing a romance; where there's romance, there's hope.

Thea of Dimas is an indentured servant, working for a silk merchant. She steals some silk worms, intending to set up her own silk shop, and travels to Damascus, hoping to free her sister Selene. But her caravan is set upon, everyone is killed but her, and Lord Ware rescues her and carries her off to his castle.

Ware, who is in danger from the Knights Templar, knows that just

being near him puts anyone in jeopardy and he doesn't intend to get close to Thea. Thea likewise has her own plans, and Ware isn't going to thwart them. In fact, she intends to have him help her.

At first, they battle each other, and then they battle their enemies, eventually finding a way to keep the Templars from ever finding them. Peace, at last.

Lord of Danger

ANNE STUART
HISTORICAL / 1997

> *"There were monsters who walked the land. Alys had never seen one in the flesh, but she had no doubt they existed."*

We love a good medieval romance—and this is one of the best!

✦ Stuart's first novel was *Barrett's Hill*, a gothic romance. Ballantine published it in 1974.
✦ According to Stuart, this is the first medieval romance she wrote, and still one of her personal favorites. Ours too!

The hero of this tale, the wizard Simon of Navarre, is not your average good guy hero. He practices the dark arts, is greatly feared by everyone who knows him, is thought to be a monster, not a man, and is otherwise the kind of person you'd not want to meet in a dark alley on a rainy night.

Richard the Fair (also a very bad man) wants Simon on his side and offers one of his sisters in marriage (this being the type of thing they did in the Middle Ages to cement alliances; now we'd sell some military hardware).

Alys, said sister, is more clever than beautiful. Though she's intelligent, she was raised in a convent and is not terribly worldly. Simon makes her afraid for her soul. On the other hand, he is very attractive, and he can be charming. And he is entranced by her.

Through danger and court intrigue (including the scheming of Richard), they are both tested, and must come to trust each other.

43

Lord of Scoundrels

LORETTA CHASE
HISTORICAL / 1995

> *"In the spring of 1792, Dominick Edward Guy de Ath Ballister, third Marquess of Dain, Earl of Blackmoor, Viscount Launcells, Baron Ballister and Launcells, lost his wife and four children to typhus."*

Some readers call this tale the perfect Regency romance. We won't go so far as to assert that, but we do love a bright, not-naïve heroine, delightful dialogue, and the reformation of a rogue!

- *Lord of Scoundrels* won a RITA for best short historical.
- Like many writers, Loretta Chase has held down various jobs on her way to success, including a six-month stint as a meter maid.

The Marquess of Dain, Sebastian Ballister, is a scoundrel. (You might even call him the lord of scoundrels.) In addition to his very many bad habits, he's arrogant, prideful, and occasionally sneering. He has no intention of redeeming himself; he enjoys his life of sin far too much. He has his reasons for being the way he is, but he has successfully managed to squelch any feelings of regret.

Jessica Trent has a plan to save her brother Bertie—"the greatest nitwit in the Northern Hemisphere." The plan requires extracting him from his friendship with the lord of scoundrels, which Jessica is fully prepared to do.

From their first meeting, Sebastian and Jessica butt heads—and the sparks fly. The sparks fly so much that they are caught in a compromising position and Sebastian is eventually forced to marry Jessica in order to protect her reputation.

When this rake is finally reformed, it's to the great satisfaction of everyone (including the reader).

44

Lord of the Night

SUSAN WIGGS
HISTORICAL / 1994

> *"Sandro Cavalli's day took a turn for the worse when he walked into the airy, sunlit studio and encountered a naked woman."*

Known for her contemporary romances and women's fiction, Wiggs also writes a compelling historical. This is her best.

✴. Wiggs has won the RITA award three times, including one for *Lord of the Night*.
✴. Wiggs finished her first novel when she was eight years old. Talk about precocious!

Set in sixteenth-century Venice, this novel follows the relationship between Sandro Cavalli (Lord of the Night) and the beautiful Laura Bandello.

Sandro is a nobleman who, as head of the sixteenth-century Venetian version of the police, brings criminals to justice. Laura is a commoner, training as a painter with the famed Titian with dreams of being admitted to the Academy (all male, of course).

When an important man is killed and Laura is assaulted, the two are thrown together—but they are separated not only by age (Sandro is nearly twice her age) but by social class. Yet in facing dangers together, they not only unravel the mystery but also find their common ground.

Love's Tender Fury

JENNIFER WILDE
HISTORICAL / 1976

> *"Pale, shaken, the girl descended the stairs clutching her pathetically battered bag and trying not to sob."*

This book never sits still and even contemporary readers will appreciate Marietta's Unsinkable Mollie Brown attitude.

- *Love's Tender Fury* was the first romance that romance writer Linda Francis Lee read after a friend gave it to her as comfort when her high school boyfriend invited someone else to the prom.
- Jennifer Wilde was the pen name for Tom E. Huff, who died in 1990. Tom Huff also wrote category romance novels as Beatrice Parker, Edwina Marlow, and Katherine St. Clair before finding fame in the historical romance category.
- Huff earned a Career Achievement Award from *Romantic Times*.

Marietta Danver was not exactly living a charmed life. Her employer raped her, a jealous mistress accused her of theft, and the feisty redhead found herself shipped to the Colonies to become a bond-servant for fourteen years to the highest bidder while she stood on the block.

Derek Hawke becomes her master in more ways than one, but sells her when he catches her helping two slaves escape his property. In her escape from the bondservant life, she makes her way to New Orleans, where she takes up with a man and together they run a gambling house. But Jeff tragically dies before he marries her, leaving Marietta penniless enough to be forced into marrying a rich German sadist who owns most of Natchez.

All the while, she pines for Derek and the chance to rekindle that spark they had.

It's only a matter of time before Marietta's German husband turns against her when she again pitches in to help someone—her sister-in-law this time—flee his evil grip. It's up to Derek to charge in and save her and their love, which continues across swashbuckling adventures in *Love Me, Marietta* and *When Love Commands*. The story continues to enjoy good reviews from modern-day readers who identify with the hero and heroine more sympathetically than with other classic pairings from the bodice-ripper days.

Lucky's Lady

Tami Hoag
Romantic suspense / 1991

> *"'You want to do what, chère?' Serena Sheridan took a deep breath and tried again. 'I need to hire a guide to take me to the swamp.'"*

Hoag's later novels are more suspense than romance, and her earlier novels are more romance than suspense; *Lucky's Lady* is a perfectly balanced blend of both—page turning, sexy, romantic.

✦. Hoag's first thriller, *Night Sins*, was made into a miniseries.
✦. Hoag competes in the equestrian sport of dressage.

Serena Sheridan returns to Louisiana to find her missing grandfather and enlists the help of Etienne Doucet (Lucky), who can guide her through the swamps and backwoods of the area. Serena's missing grandfather is just the beginning of her problems, though; her sister wants to sell their family home to an oil company, and Serena fears this will create an ecological disaster. Drama ensues and Serena's life is threatened.

Lucky is a madly attractive, rough-and-ready Cajun and Serena can't help falling into bed with him any more than she can help falling in love with him. But he has reasons for not wanting to settle down.

Hoag's evocative setting makes you feel like you're right there in the swamps with them.

Mackenzie's Mountain

LINDA HOWARD
CONTEMPORARY / 1989

"He needed a woman. Bad."

Mackenzie's Mountain is classic romance.

✦ This is the first in the Mackenzie family series.
✦ Linda Howard wrote for her own personal enjoyment for twenty-one years before deciding to submit a manuscript for publication.

Mary Elizabeth Potter is a spinster school teacher. Vietnam vet Wolf Mackenzie is a half-breed (the epitome of a romance hero!) who belongs in neither of the worlds he's part of. Mary goes toe-to-toe with him over sending his son to school, and the two of them develop an unlikely relationship. They are opposites in all ways (she wears her heart on her sleeve, he is deeply reserved; she is innocent, he is experienced) yet their attraction seems believable—and it crackles on the page.

While everyone else sees him as a dangerous criminal (he did not commit the crime), she is able to see the true person he is. When a string of crimes occurs in the small town where they live, Wolf is the main suspect. Will the true criminal be found, will Wolf be able to make peace with the townspeople who are so deeply suspicious of him, and can Mary and Wolf find their way to a happily ever after?

Married by Morning

LISA KLEYPAS
HISTORICAL / 2010

> *"Anyone who had ever read a novel knew that governesses were supposed to be meek and downtrodden. They were also supposed to be quiet, subservient, and obedient, not to mention deferential to the master of the house. Leo, Lord Ramsay, wondered in exasperation why they couldn't have gotten one of those."*

A delightful take on the classic romance theme of lord-of-the-manor-marries-the-governess.

✴ *Married by Morning* hit #3 on the *New York Times* bestseller list.
✴ *Married by Morning* is the fourth book in the Hathaways series.

Catherine Marks is the former governess of and now companion (the paid kind of companion) to the Hathaway sisters. Leo Hathaway (Lord Ramsay), the sisters' older brother, learns that to keep the family home he must immediately marry and produce an heir.

Cat and Leo have never gotten along, but their arguments hide a mutual attraction that blazes into full force the first time they kiss. So Leo proposes that Cat become his wife. A perfectly sensible solution.

But Cat and Leo both have pasts that keep them from being able to give themselves fully. Leo is tortured by the death of his former love, and his feelings of culpability in the death of one of his sisters; Cat comes from a horrific home, barely escaping being forced into prostitution by her evil aunt. Though Cat and Leo try to keep the past in the past, it doesn't want to stay there. Can they deal with their demons to get to their happily ever after?

Mistress

AMANDA QUICK
HISTORICAL / 1995

> *"'Your latest mistress is creating a sensation back in London, Masters. Society finds her vastly entertaining.' Charles Trescott, seated before the fireplace, downed a swallow of brandy and eyed his host with a sly expression."*

Amanda Quick, Jane Ann Krentz's pseudonym for her historical genre books, gives us a heroine who doesn't make virgin synonymous with naïve.

✳ Iphiginia (pronounced Eff en jeh NEE uh) was the daughter of Agamemnon and Clytemnestra in Greek mythology, with a name that means "born to strength."

Financially independent, twenty-seven-year-old Iphiginia Bright has a brilliant plan and her Aunt Zoe's best interests at heart: In order to find the blackguard blackmailing this sweet woman, Iphiginia decides to pose as Marcus Cloud, the Earl of Masters's, mistress. After all, he's dead, so what's to trip up this disguise that will lead her to uncover the villain's identity?

Well, the earl himself, for starters, who strolls into a ballroom as alive as any well-dressed noble in the room. Intrigued at what this newcomer, now infamously known as Lady Starlight, is trying to pull off, he backs her mistress story. After all, one of his friends is also being blackmailed, so he has something to gain from getting to the bottom of the mystery as well. He's bulletproof to emotional danger, thanks to his five guiding principles:

1. Never remarry.
2. Never discuss the past.
3. Never explain his actions to others.
4. Never retreat from an objective or alter a decision.
5. Never get involved with virgins or other men's wives.

Of course, you can't call off the hormones when a smart, beautiful woman declares herself a handsome, rich man's paramour, despite what isn't happening between the sheets. Marcus's seduction attempts lend the sexy to this story, which ends up as much about how he learns to let go of his rigid rules for living as it does catching a blackmailer.

And in a refreshing twist to the usual Regency novel to that date, the two are deceiving society, not each other.

Montana Sky

NORA ROBERTS
CONTEMPORARY / 1996

> *"Being dead didn't make Jack Mercy less of a son of a bitch. One week of dead didn't offset sixty-eight years of being mean. Plenty of people gathered by his grave would be happy to say so."*

One of Roberts's nonseries titles, *Montana Sky* showcases her at her storytelling best, as she juggles the demands of telling three romances—not to mention working in a suspenseful subplot and capturing the setting with vivid accuracy—all without dropping a ball.

- Nora Roberts is definitely the MVP of our favorite genre! When the Romance Writers of America Hall of Fame was established, Roberts was the first author to be inducted.
- According to *Publishers Weekly*, Roberts writes eight hours a day. Every. Single. Day.
- She's written more than 200 romance novels, and she shows no signs of stopping! She passed the 100-novel mark with *Montana Sky*.
- *Montana Sky* was made into a Lifetime movie.

When rancher Jack Mercy dies, he leaves his valuable ranch (worth millions) to his three daughters (all by different mothers) with one caveat—the three, who are basically strangers to one another, must live together on the ranch for a year or else lose it entirely.

Willa, Tess, and Lily are thrown together and must learn to get along. Willa, the bossy type, is the only one of them who knows anything about running a ranch. Hard-headed Ben is the only possible match for her.

Tess likes the idea of inheriting money but not of living with her sisters. A Hollywood type, she succumbs to the charms of the cowboy Nate.

Lily, a quiet woman suffering from her abusive marriage and subsequent divorce, is glad to have a place to go to. Adam, the calmest of the men in their lives, is the balm Lily needs to heal.

As each woman learns to get along with her sisters and overcome the obstacles in her love relationship, the stakes are upped when someone starts committing gruesome atrocities on the ranch. Who would commit such heinous acts—and why?

More than a Mistress

MARY BALOGH
HISTORICAL / 2000

> *"The two gentlemen who were in their shirt sleeves despite the brisk chill of a spring morning were about to blow each other's brains out. Or attempt to do so, at least."*

Balogh comes into her own with this novel, a charming Regency with a twist. The standard plot device is for the aristocrat's wife to feel threatened by his mistress and for him to give up his mistress and declare his love for his wife. Here, the aristocrat falls in love with his mistress. Unthinkable!

✴ *More than a Mistress* is one of two connected books (the other being *No Man's Mistress*), with a prequel called *The Secret Mistress* rounding out the Mistress series. It was Balogh's hardcover debut.

Jocelyn Dudley, the incorrigible Duke of Tresham, is shot during (yet another) duel. Jane Ingleby, who was trying to prevent it, rushes to his aid. Though Jocelyn finds her bold and impudent, he is deeply attracted to her and sets her up as his mistress.

Jane accepts the arrangement in order to keep a secret, telling herself it's just business. She is not, actually, a commoner, but in fact Lady Sara Illingsworth—and she believes she has killed a man.

The two are, naturally, stubborn, headstrong, and unwilling to admit that their mutual attraction has deepened into something more lasting. Jane doesn't dare reveal her secret, not even to Jocelyn. And Jocelyn, a confirmed bachelor, would never make the foolish mistake of falling in love with his mistress—would he?

Naked in Death

J. D. ROBB
FUTURISTIC / 2004

> *"She woke in the dark. Through the slats on the window shades, the first murky hint of dawn slipped, slanting shadowy bars over the bed. It was like waking in a cell."*

Here Robb (the pen name of Nora Roberts) shows she can deliver fast-paced suspense with emotional resonance—all the while building a world of the future.

✦ *Naked in Death* is the first in Robb's hugely popular In Death series. The other novels follow Dallas through other cases.

Set in a slightly future New York City, *Naked in Death* follows Lt. Eve Dallas as she tracks a murderer. A senator's granddaughter is killed with an old-fashioned gun, and Dallas is plunged into a violent case that brings her into contact with the wealthy and dangerous Roarke, a prime suspect.

Though Dallas wants to believe that the attractive and oh-so-sexy Roarke is what she believes he is (a man skating the edge between legal and illegal, but not a murderer), the evidence doesn't seem to back her up.

Robb creates a stunningly believable future world while delivering a page-turning mystery—and oh my, is that romance hot.

Natural Born Charmer

SUSAN ELIZABETH PHILLIPS
CONTEMPORARY / 2007

> *"It wasn't every day a guy saw a headless beaver marching down the side of a road, not even in Dean Robillard's larger-than-life world. 'Son of a. . . .' Dean slammed on the brakes of his brand-new Aston Martin Vanquish and pulled over in front of her."*

The witty, smart-alecky dialogue and ego smackdowns between everyone in this story keep you laughing and turning pages.

- ✦ This book, number seven and the last in the author's Chicago Stars series, has a strong male bent that attracted a few Y-chromosome fans, too.
- ✦ Phillips met her husband on a blind date, and now they have two grown sons.

Dean Robillard has it made in the shade as an NFL quarterback hotshot millionaire with an underwear advertising contract on the side that means his physique is plastered billboard-size across America. His problem? He's not sure this is the life for him, so he sets off on a Colorado backwoods trek for some alone time to think deep thoughts.

Unfortunately, he runs into Blue Bailey in this back of beyond, a spunky gal on a mission to murder her ex, if she could only get out of the advertising beaver suit she donned in one of her desperate schemes to earn money. He gives her a lift, and the two end up together for weeks that include returning to his Tennessee farm, where his contrite, former groupie mother shows up trying to make amends for giving her

son a lousy childhood, and the rock star father he never knew drops in when Dean's eleven-year-old stepsister runs away—to Dean's house.

The group manages to work out the kinks from their dysfunctional childhoods, and share a big group hug. Along the way, they also save the small town from extinction by outwitting the crabby old crone who is trying to choke off its livelihood. The characters are over the top, but never cartoonish in this fun story. And while down on her luck from a financial standpoint and freewheeling by nature, you never mistake Blue as either weak or unintelligent.

Top Five Romantic Scents

Men find these smells sexy!

1. **Cinnamon and vanilla**
   (or just make cookies!)

2. **Lavender**

3. **Sandalwood**

4. **Citrus—orange, grapefruit**
   (we're serious!)

5. **Baby powder**

North and South

ELIZABETH GASKELL

CONTEMPORARY AT THE TIME, NOW HISTORICAL / 1855

*"'Edith!' said Margaret, gently, 'Edith!'
But, as Margaret half suspected, Edith had fallen
asleep. She lay curled up on the sofa in the back
drawing room in Harley Street, looking very lovely in
her white muslin and blue ribbons. If Titania had ever
been dressed in white muslin and blue ribbons, and
had fallen asleep on a crimson damask sofa in a back
drawing room, Edith might have been taken for her.
Margaret was struck afresh by her cousin's beauty."*

Gaskell, a pioneer in using fiction to point out social problems, tells her story through the evolution of a romantic relationship between the two main characters. A seminal novel.

- *North and South* was turned into a television serial in 2004.
- Charlotte Brontë was a friend of Gaskell's.
- This is considered the second of Elizabeth Gaskell's novels to take place in the industrial city; the first was *Mary Barton*, published in 1848.

Gaskell explored tensions between workers and their industrialist employers in an earlier novel, *Mary Barton*, but *North and South* is a more balanced examination of what gives rise to those tensions.

In this novel, which was originally serialized in twenty installments (in *Household Words*, which was edited by Charles Dickens), Margaret

Hale moves from the south of England (still rural) to the north (undergoing industrialization) with her parents, and the difference in setting shocks her. She witnesses brutal strikes and develops a deep sympathy for the workers.

John Thornton is a manufacturer who treats his workers with scorn. Margaret confronts him about his attitude and behavior. It doesn't seem possible that a romance could result from this, but it does. John comes to appreciate Margaret's independent spirit; Margaret admires John's tenacity and ability to better himself. Both change and grow as they come to know each other.

A series of family secrets and outside events eventually culminate in John having to stop production at his mill and Margaret inheriting the means for them to go into business together—creating a future that is more balanced for themselves and the society they live in.

Nothing But Trouble

RACHEL GIBSON
CONTEMPORARY / 2010

> "Just because a man was lucky to be alive, didn't mean he had to be happy about it."

Gibson's edgy approach to romantic comedy has won fans worldwide—including us!

* *Nothing But Trouble* is the fifth novel in Gibson's Chinooks Hockey League series.
* Rachel Gibson's first novel, *Simply Irresistible*, launched her onto the *New York Times* and *USA Today* bestsellers lists.

Chelsea Ross is an actress who has never quite hit the big time. All right, her main claim to fame is playing a dead body. So when the Seattle Chinooks offer her a job as a personal assistant to one of their stars, she takes it.

Mark Bressler, an injured hockey player, knows his career is over, and he's a little bitter. Chelsea would dump the job in a second but she needs the money. And . . . he is hot. Very hot. Hot, hot, hot. A jerk, but hot. What's a girl to do?

In this delightful opposites attract, Mark's not able to push Chelsea away (she needs the money!) and discovers, to his surprise, that there is life after hockey.

Outlander

Diana Gabaldon
Paranormal (time travel) / 1991

> *"It wasn't a very likely place for disappearances, at least at first glance."*

We agree with Gabaldon, who is often asked to describe what kind of book this is: "'Pick it up, open it anywhere, and read three pages. If you can put it down again, I'll pay you a dollar.' I've never lost any money on that bet."

- ✦ The book is titled Cross Stitch in the U.K. release and contains six additional paragraphs scattered throughout where heroine Claire worries about the husband she left back in time. The publisher also made her remove the sex scene that ends the "Raiders in the Rocks" chapter.
- ✦ In 2010, an album consisting of fourteen songs that tell the story of *Outlander* was released under the title *Outlander the Musical*. It was so successful that several theaters are now considering staging a full-scale stage production of the musical.

In 1946, after World War II, a young Englishwoman named Claire Beauchamp Randall goes to the Scottish Highlands on a second honeymoon with her husband, Frank. As a combat nurse and an army grunt, the two have been separated for six years, and have set aside this time to restart their future. But one day Claire goes out walking by herself, and comes across a circle of standing stones, which are common across this part of the country, and is sucked through a time portal to 1743.

The first person she meets is Jack Randall, Frank's ancestor—a sadistic bisexual pervert. While trying to escape from him, Claire falls

into the hands of a gang of Highland Scots, who are also trying to avoid Black Jack Randall to escape political persecution.

To avoid being handed over to this common enemy, Claire is obliged to marry one of the young clansmen: Jamie Fraser, a loyal Jacobite who, in a romantic surprise twist, is a virgin. He's also a traditional kilt guy taught that the way to a great marriage is to keep his woman in line, a pronouncement that does not work at winning the love of a twentieth-century, independent woman.

Claire finds herself trying to escape from Castle Leoch and her Scottish captors, trying to avoid being recaptured by Captain Randall, needing to find the way back to Frank—and falling in love with Jamie, who is quickly proving he's got her back whenever she clashes with the culture, despite the fact he has no idea where she came from or who she really is. Does she really want to walk away from this love to go home? Gabaldon has spent twenty-one years and seven books providing hungry fans with the answer.

Over the Edge

Suzanne Brockmann
Romantic suspense / 2001

> *"The moon was hanging insolent and full in the sky just to the left of a billboard for a bankruptcy lawyer, and Stan knew. It was the full moon's fault. It had to be the goddamn full moon."*

This third book in the Troubleshooters series is where Brockmann hits her stride. You won't be able to put it down.

- ✦ *Over the Edge* can be read as a standalone, but you may as well go ahead and get all the books in the series. You're going to read them anyway.
- ✦ In her nonwriterly life, Brockmann is very active with several civil rights organizations.

Lieutenant Teri Howe is an excellent helicopter pilot who needs a little help. Fortunately, her friend, Senior Chief Stan Wolchonok, has got her back. He's a quiet kind of hero—not a flashy warrior but the man who keeps the mission under control. He's also a lot older than Teri, and he's determined to keep their relationship strictly platonic, going so far as to introduce Teri to the guy he thinks she should be with.

When a jet is hijacked, Teri and Stan must work together to save the day—and they push their relationship over the edge.

The subplot with Max Bhagat, the FBI hostage negotiator, and Gina, who bravely sacrifices herself as a hostage to prevent more deaths, is heart wrenching—and the relationship between Alyssa and Sam, which doesn't culminate for several books, is hot, hot, hot.

Persuasion

JANE AUSTEN
CONTEMPORARY AT THE TIME, NOW HISTORICAL. / 1818

"Sir Walter Elliot, of Kellynch Hall, in Somersetshire, was a man who, for his own amusement, never took up any book but the Baronetage; there he found occupation for an idle hour, and consolation in a distressed one; there his faculties were roused into admiration and respect, by contemplating the limited remnant of the earliest patents; there any unwelcome sensations, arising from domestic affairs changed naturally into pity and contempt as he turned over the almost endless creations of the last century; and there, if every other leaf were powerless, he could read his own history with an interest which never failed."

Though not as popular as *Pride and Prejudice* or *Sense and Sensibility*, the story of *Persuasion* just as easily sweeps readers into its timeless love story. The theme of lost love and regret is one that so many people can identify with, and Austen brings those feelings so brilliantly to life on the page—complete with, of course, an incredibly moving happy ending!

✦ *Persuasion* is Jane Austen's last completed novel—she finished it in August 1816 and it was published five months after her death in 1817.

✴. *Persuasion* is linked to Jane Austen's novel *Northanger Abbey* for two reasons: The two works were originally bound and published together, and both stories are set partly in Bath, the city where Austen herself lived from 1801 to 1805.

Eight years before the start of the novel, nineteen-year-old Anne Elliot, a lovely, happy young woman, accepts a marriage proposal from the handsome and smart yet poor Frederick Wentworth. Anne's friends and family, unhappy with Wentworth's position in society, persuade her to break off the engagement.

Now twenty-seven, Anne is unhappy and alone. She still loves Frederick Wentworth, even though she hasn't seen him in many years, and regrets her decision to turn down his proposal. Dire financial circumstances force Anne's father to rent out their home—and the tenant turns out to be Wentworth's sister and her husband! Thus, Wentworth, an extremely wealthy man now, re-enters Anne's life. He is cold and standoffish to Anne, but flirts openly with every other young woman he meets, including Henrietta and Louisa Musgrove, the younger sisters of Anne's sister Mary's husband Charles.

Unable to watch Wentworth around these flirty young women, Anne directs her attentions elsewhere and soon becomes the object of affection for several new men, including two military officers and her father's cousin and heir, William Elliot. As Anne's relationship with Elliot progresses, Wentworth starts hanging around more and more. Could he be jealous? And even if he were, is it too late? Has Anne finally moved on?

The Pirate Lord

Sabrina Jeffries

Historical / 1998

> "Miss Sara Willis had known a great many awkward moments in her twenty-three years. There was the time as a seven-year-old when her mother had caught her filching biscuits from the grand kitchen at Blackmore Hall, or the time shortly afterward when she'd fallen into the fountain at her mother's wedding to her stepfather, the late Earl of Blackmore. Then there was the ball last year when she'd unwittingly introduced the Duchess of Merrington to the duke's mistress. But none of those compared to this—being physically accosted by her stepbrother as she departed from Newgate Prison in the company of the Ladies' Committee."

A swashbuckling adventure—think Jack Sparrow getting his comeuppance.

- Jeffries was born in New Orleans and raised in Thailand—where her missionary parents moved when she was seven.
- Jeffries has also written under the names Deborah Martin and Deborah Nichols.

The Pirate Lord is the first of the Lord series. Gideon Horn, a pirate captain, and his men are ready to retire from the high seas. But they need wives if they're going to settle down. The pirates target a ship of

convict women (because, they reason, the women will surely rather be with them!) and get more than they bargained for.

Sara Willis is not a convict. She's a reformer, determined to learn how women convicts are treated when transported for their crimes. She knows exactly what Gideon wants, and she casts herself in the role of the protector of the other women. She knows she can't really stop the pirates from doing what they please, but she can negotiate certain demands.

Gideon is willing to negotiate with her—and the two of them find their sparring leads to attraction. But Sara's stepbrother is trying to find her, and when he does, he may destroy the happiness they've discovered.

Playing with Fire

GENA SHOWALTER
PARANORMAL / 2006

> *"Isn't it amazing how one seemingly innocent decision can change your entire life? For me, that decision came in the form of a grande mocha latte."*

With over-the-top plotting, bigger-than-life characters, lots of action, suspense, and laughs, you'll fall in love with this book.

- ✦ This is the first book in Showalter's Tales of an Extraordinary Girl series.
- ✦ Showalter often writes using the first-person perspective, a bit unusual in romance.

Belle Jamison spends a lot of her life unemployed or underemployed, which is why she's working at a coffee shop when her life turns upside down. A mad scientist type slips her a mickey, but not the usual kind—this one gives her the power to control the four elements (earth, wind, fire, water).

Rome Masters, a government agent, is supposed to kill her, but that would make for a short book, so instead he falls for her—which means the two of them end up on the run.

Belle just wants to get her life back and go back to being her normal self . . . or does she?

Neither of these characters is sugar and spice, but they both have hearts of gold—and it's a roller-coaster ride to see them reach their happily ever after.

61

Possession

DEVYN QUINN

PARANORMAL / 2009

> *"In a library crammed wall to floor with a collection of books unmatched by any public collection in the world, a specially constructed steel lectern stood by itself."*

A compelling, dark, erotic romance that will keep you riveted.

✦ Quinn got started writing paranormal romance and erotic romance under the pen names Caitlyn McKenna and Jaya Jenson.

Deeply scarred (emotionally and physically) Kendra Carter returns to her brother's home from a mental hospital. She opens an occult book—and unknowingly unleashes a demon. He's a very sexy demon, and he enthralls Kendra in the bedroom—but he may also steal her soul.

Remi understands her. He knows why she suffers and what she wants. But she thinks she may be losing her mind. She has memory lapses, people think she tried to kill herself, and now she's got a demon lover. That can't be good.

The paranormal suspense becomes a taut psychological thriller as Kendra discovers who is behind her mental instability. In the end, she and Remi must unite to save themselves and find a way to be together.

Pride and Prejudice

JANE AUSTEN
CONTEMPORARY AT THE TIME, NOW HISTORICAL / 1813

> *"It is a truth universally acknowledged that a single man in possession of a good fortune must be in want of a wife."*

Pride and Prejudice is the original love-spawned-from-hate romance story! Though first published nearly 200 years ago, the novel remains beloved among readers and literary scholars alike, and the story has spawned many dramatic adaptations, imitations, and modern-day retellings.

- Originally titled *First Impressions*, *Pride and Prejudice* received its new name after Austen's publishers encouraged her to choose a title that would play off the alliterative name of her previous, already successful novel *Sense and Sensibility*. It is widely believed that Austen got the title *Pride and Prejudice* from a passage in Fanny Burney's 1782 novel *Cecilia*, which is a book Austen is known to have loved.
- The opening line of *Pride and Prejudice* is considered to be one of the most famous in all of literature (see quote!).
- If you prefer a bit more gore with your Regency romance, check out *Pride and Prejudice and Zombies* by Jane Austen and Seth Grahame-Smith—it's basically the same story, but with a few fun twists. But, of course, only read it after you've read and appreciated the original in its pure, unaltered form!

Elizabeth Bennet is the second daughter in a family of five unwed girls. Her family's home is entailed, which means it will go to her father's

clergyman cousin Mr. Collins upon Mr. Bennet's death—therefore, it is of the utmost importance, especially to Elizabeth's mother, that the Bennet girls marry as soon as possible in order to ensure security for the family.

Two eligible, rich men, Mr. Bingley and Mr. Darcy, arrive in town. Mr. Darcy and Elizabeth clash immediately—Elizabeth believes Mr. Darcy is too proud and Mr. Darcy believes Elizabeth, and her family, to be beneath him. Mr. Bingley, on the other hand, takes an immediate liking to Elizabeth's elder sister Jane, and it looks as if the family is saved. But Mr. Bingley leaves suddenly and inexplicably, without proposing to Jane.

Meanwhile, Mr. Collins comes to visit and proposes marriage to Elizabeth—an offer that she quickly refuses even though it would mean her home would remain in the family. Her friend Charlotte marries Mr. Collins instead. Months later, Elizabeth goes to visit Charlotte and runs into Mr. Darcy. To her surprise, Mr. Darcy proposes to her—but, despite her attraction to him, she refuses, angrily citing her suspicion that he was responsible for the separation of Jane and Mr. Bingley, and also recounting the story she heard that Mr. Darcy cruelly refused to pay his old friend Mr. Wickham the money left to him in Mr. Darcy's father's will.

Only after Mr. Darcy writes Elizabeth a letter explaining everything does she realize how wrong she was about him, and that she loves him. But is it too late? Or is there a way for Mr. Darcy and Elizabeth to find their way to each other one more time?

63

The Proposition

JUDITH IVORY
HISTORICAL / 1999

*"The most highborn lady Mick had ever been with—
the wife of a sitting member of the House of Lords, as
it turned out—told him that the French had a name
for what she felt for him, a name that put words to her
wanting his 'lionhearted virility'; he liked the phrase
and remembered it."*

The action in this book is minimal, with much of it taking place in one setting—Winnie's house—so the book hinges strongly on the characters' personalities and chemistry to keep you turning the pages.

* The author's inspiration for this story was Cinderella, but with a gender swap in the roles.
* Ivory's father once bought all of the copies of her latest book from a bookstore and demanded that the owner reorder it. Now that's love!

Lady Edwina "Winnie" Bollash's unsavory cousin threw her out of her estate when he inherited the Duke of Aries title at her father's death. Not one to let life's disasters get the best of her, she offers elocution and deportment lessons to country folk and foreigners.

Two lords approach her on a gamble to see if this blueblood can turn an uncouth Cornish rat catcher, Mick Tremore, into a viscount that can attend her cousin's annual ball undetected in a mere six weeks' time. Recognizing both the challenge and the way to get some personal revenge on the current Duke of Aries, she takes Mick under her wing.

Mick is willing to go along with this bet because the reward will help support his large family of siblings, and he'd like to get to know Winnie better. He's pure Cockney from Cornwall, but he's not a big enough fool to turn down a big break. Still, he's more into flirting and trying to talk his teacher into risqué behavior than practicing his homework. While the two fall in love, she manages to transform her pupil into the suave, handsome Michael, Viscount Bartonreed—a stranger Winnie doesn't like nearly as well as the happy-go-lucky commoner.

True love lies ahead, but only after they complete this ruse (which eventually gives Winnie morality pangs) and learn the truth behind both the wager and Mick's background.

64

The Raven Prince

ELIZABETH HOYT
HISTORICAL / 2006

> *"The combination of a horse galloping far too fast, a muddy lane with a curve, and a lady pedestrian is never a good one. Even in the best of circumstances, the odds of a positive outcome are depressingly low. But add a dog—a very big dog—and, Anna Wren reflected, disaster becomes inescapable."*

You might call it a true-to-life fairy tale—a retelling of Beauty and the Beast. This one is a fan favorite—and we're definitely fans!

* *The Raven Prince* is the first in Hoyt's Princes trilogy.
* *The Raven Prince* was Hoyt's debut historical.

Anna Wren, a widow, finds herself in financial straits, forcing her to seek employment. Edward de Raaf, the Earl of Swartingham, needs a secretary—someone who can put up with him (not an easy task). They settle into an uneasy alliance.

But Edward has needs . . . you know, *needs*. And Anna has needs of the same variety. Still, it's unthinkable that they could even admit such a thing to one another, let alone assuage their needs together. So Edward decides to visit a brothel, and Anna conceives a plan that will satisfy them both.

But Edward is also intent on forming a betrothal with someone who isn't Anna, and it'll take some doing to convince him that love really can conquer all.

River of Fire

MARY JO PUTNEY
HISTORICAL / 1996

"The situation was even worse than he'd feared."

Deeply emotional, this one will stay with you long after you read the last page.

* Putney is not afraid to tackle tough subject matters. She's written about alcoholism, domestic violence, and other social ills but always leaves her readers with a feeling that hope can triumph.
* *River of Fire* is the sixth title in Putney's The Fallen Angels series.

Kenneth Wilding returns home from fighting the Napoleonic Wars and discovers that his estate is ruined and his sister dowry-less. In order to repair his fortunes, he accepts a paid commission to uncover a murderer. Doing so requires that he get a job as a secretary to an artist (Sir Anthony Seaton), which he is able to do because of his knowledge of art. When he was younger, Kenneth had been interested in artistic pursuits, but his father, Viscount Kimball, dismissed such hobbies as unsuitable.

While in Sir Anthony's employ, Kenneth realizes he has never lost his own desire to paint—and discovers a desire to possess the artist's daughter.

Rebecca Seaton is something of an outcast in society—at seventeen, she foolishly eloped, and in their eyes is "ruined." She now spends her time painting, despite the fact that society does not believe that women can create true art. She and Kenneth come to care for each other, but can their love survive Kenneth's unmasking?

The Rogue Hunter

LYNSAY SANDS
PARANORMAL / 2008

> *"Warm summer air swam over Tanya as she stepped out into the night."*

Sands knows the meaning of escapism, and she delivers! This one is lighthearted and fun.

✳ *The Rogue Hunter* is the tenth in Sands's hugely popular Argeneau series.

Garret Mortimer has spent 800 years as a bachelor. (And you thought your last boyfriend was commitment shy.) He's a rogue hunter who keeps vampires from behaving badly, which is a task made both easier and harder by the fact that he, too, is a vampire. Right now, he's been sent to stop a vampire who has been committing a bunch of no-nos.

Samantha Willan is a lawyer of the workaholic type, and she needs a break. Some fun in the sun with her sisters is just the ticket. Still smarting from her last romantic entanglement, she's not about to put her heart on the line again. But that neighbor sure is sexy. . . .

Can their attraction really be true love? Forever is a long time to a vampire.

Top Five
Sexy Cars

These babies will make you (and him!) drool.

1. Anything Porsche

2. Bentley Continental

3. Alfa Romeo Competizione

4. Aston Martin Vanquish (or the Virage. Either way.)

5. Corvette Stingray

The Runaway McBride

ELIZABETH THORNTON
HISTORICAL / 2009

> *"It was February, the coldest, most miserable February in Scottish memory."*

An historical with a paranormal touch—what's not to love? At turns charming, passionate, and poignant, this book shows why Thornton's a master.

✦ Thornton fell in love with the genre by reading Georgette Heyer (who can blame her?). She's also a Harry Potter fan. (So are we!)

Widower James Burnett isn't sure he appreciates his grandmother's gift—the gift of clairvoyance. On her deathbed, she tells James that his bride is in danger. James doesn't *have* a bride. He does have memories of Faith McBride—the one he calls *Faithless*. And if she's the one in danger, James isn't sure he cares.

Until the visions start.

Faith McBride waited for James. Waited and waited, and then she learned that he married someone else. So she can be forgiven her cynicism about love. Instead of looking for love, she's looking into her mother's death—but someone doesn't want her to.

James can save her from the murderer, but can Faith trust him with her heart again?

Saving Grace

JULIE GARWOOD
HISTORICAL / 1994

> *"'Holy Bishop Hallwick, will you explain to us the hierarchy in heaven and on earth? Who is the most esteemed in God's eyes?' the student asked."*

Fans clamor for Garwood's medieval Scottish romances, and for good reason! *Saving Grace* has realistic characters, a fine sense of humor, a well-drawn (but not overdrawn) romantic setting—and a tender love story.

✦ More than 35 million copies of Garwood's books are in print.

Happily widowed at sixteen, wealthy and beautiful Lady Johanna vows never to marry again—but King John (you may remember that he was a very bad man) intends to force her to marry the man he has chosen. Johanna's foster brother talks his friend Gabriel MacBain, a Scottish warrior, into marrying her instead, knowing that John can't have anyone good planned for her.

Gabriel is suspicious of all things English, including Johanna, and she has to learn to understand the new culture she's thrust into—and how to stand up to Gabriel and his clan.

Just when they seem ready to love one another, court scheming threatens to tear them apart.

A Season of Angels

DEBBIE MACOMBER
CONTEMPORARY / 1993

> *"The manger was empty. Leah Lundberg walked past the nativity scene Providence Hospital put out every year, stopped, and stared. The north wind cut through her like a boning knife as Leah studied the ramshackle stable, her heart heavy, her life more so."*

Macomber's heartwarming tale is sweet, sentimental, and hopeful.

✦ Macomber was one of the first romance authors who published Christian romances that did not have to fit a standard, predictable formula and that included a variety of real-life problems and issues. Breaking the rules certainly paid off for Macomber and her readers!
✦ In 2009, Macomber published a cookbook, a children's book, an inspirational nonfiction title, and a handful of novels!

A Season of Angels is the first in Macomber's Angelic Intervention series. Shirley, Goodness, and Mercy are each given a prayer to answer. Shirley must find young Timmy Potter a father, despite the fact that his mother Jody never wants to risk her heart again. Goodness must help Monica Fischer find a home of her own and a husband to love, although Monica has just about given up hope. Mercy has to help Leah Lundberg, who wants a child with her husband Andrew.

But answering prayers isn't as simple as granting a wish.

Seductive as Flame

SUSAN JOHNSON
HISTORICAL / 2011

> "The Duke and Duchess of Groveland were entertaining at their hunting lodge in the West Riding."

Did someone turn up the heat in here?

✳ *Seductive as Flame* is the most recent title in Johnson's Bruton Street Bookstore series.

Johnson is known as a writer who writes hot. And she doesn't disappoint with this title.

Alec Monro, Earl of Daigliesh, can have any woman he wants—and any woman would want him to want her. Wealthy, gorgeous, seductive—he's every woman's fantasy.

Enchanting and beautiful Zelda MacKenzie has an adventurous side. It's 1894, and she's just returned from a trip to the rain forest. But adventurous or not, she has no interest in rakes—and Alec is a married man. Her lack of interest in him makes her a challenge Alec is most delighted to take on. . . .

But what he doesn't realize is that he'll fall in love.

You'll wonder how they'll ever reach their happily ever after right up to the end.

Sense and Sensibility

JANE AUSTEN

CONTEMPORARY AT THE TIME, NOW HISTORICAL / 1811

> *"The family of Dashwood had long been settled in Sussex. Their estate was large, and their residence was at Norland Park, in the centre of their property, where, for many generations, they had lived in so respectable a manner as to engage the general good opinion of their surrounding acquaintance."*

Sense and Sensibility was the first published work by the world's most seminal and beloved romantic fiction author, Jane Austen. Without this novel, which sparked Austen's success, the romance world would be much different today. Austen first began writing *Sense and Sensibility* in 1795 when she was nineteen years old. The first draft of the novel was written in the form of letters, and called *Elinor and Marianne*. In 1811, the book, complete with a new title and new narrative form, was finally published—though Austen published it under the simple pseudonym of "A Lady."

* After *Sense and Sensibility* was accepted by the Military Library publishing house in London, Jane Austen had to pay out of her own pocket to have it published. The cost of publication was more than a third of Austen's annual household income.
* In 1995, a major Hollywood adaptation of *Sense and Sensibility*, written by Emma Thompson and directed by Ang Lee, was made. The film starred Thompson, Kate Winslet, Hugh Grant, and Alan Rickman, and won Thompson the Academy Award for Best Adapted Screenplay.

Elinor, Marianne, and Margaret Dashwood's lives are upturned when their father dies and their estate goes to their half-brother John, Mr. Dashwood's son from his first marriage. John and his wife Fanny move in and reduce the Dashwood women to the status of unwelcome guests.

Then Fanny's brother, Edward Ferrars, comes to town and develops feelings for Elinor, a connection that Fanny fervently objects to. When Fanny suggests to Mrs. Dashwood that Elinor is just after her brother's money, Mrs. Dashwood moves her family to the smaller, less luxurious Barton Cottage in Devonshire. It is there that they meet Colonel Brandon, a quiet man who falls in love with Marianne. But Marianne considers Colonel Brandon, at thirty-five, to be too old for her.

One day, while out for a walk in the rain, Marianne slips and hurts her ankle, only to be rescued by the handsome, desirable John Willoughby. She falls head over heels for him and the two begin spending a lot of time together, despite the fact that Willoughby has not yet proposed marriage. Then, out of the blue, Willoughby tells Marianne that he is leaving for business in London and won't be back. When the two finally meet again, Marianne is devastated to learn that he is engaged to someone else.

Meanwhile, Elinor still has feelings for Edward Ferrars, but learns that he's been secretly engaged to a vulgar woman named Lucy Steele for four years.

The Dashwood women are distraught and lovelorn, but they soon realize that things may not always be what they seem.

Seven Tears for Apollo

PHYLLIS A. WHITNEY
ROMANTIC SUSPENSE / 1963

> *"The museum's statue of Apollo was a copy. The original held a place of honor in Olympia in the faraway Peloponnese. On his pedestal, the god stood unclothed in the full magnificence of male youth."*

Whitney is a true grandmaster of the genre—and was awarded Grand Master status by the Mystery Writers of America. *Seven Tears for Apollo* is Whitney at her suspenseful best.

✦ Whitney's writing career spanned more than eighty years.

Dorcas Brandt suspects her husband Gino had some unsavory dealings in the art world, and after his death, her suspicions are confirmed when she is threatened by people who think she knows more than she does.

She and her young daughter escape to the Greek island of Rhodes, where she hopes they will be safe—but danger follows them, placing both Dorcas and her daughter in grave peril. Yet those around her fail to see the threats, leading Dorcas to wonder if she is slowly losing her mind.

Dorcas turns to Johnny Orion, a teacher who is traveling in Rhodes, for help, and as their relationship deepens, he comes to see that the threats to her are real. But ultimately, Dorcas must learn to stand up for herself to confront that evil that dogs her.

Shadow Dance

JULIE GARWOOD

CONTEMPORARY / 2006

> *"The wedding was no small affair. There were seven bridesmaids, seven groomsmen, three ushers, two altar boys, three lectors, and enough firepower inside the church to wipe out half the congregation. All but two of the groomsmen were armed."*

The way Garwood handles the taming of the bad boy by the unlikely heroine makes this one a must-read!

- ✦ Garwood has also written a young adult novel called *A Girl Named Summer*.
- ✦ Garwood is known for her historicals, but don't miss her contemporaries—especially her stories of the Buchanans, like this one!
- ✦ Eager readers of Garwood's contemporaries waited for Noah Clayborne to get his story, and Garwood delivered!

Jordan Buchanan's brother Dylan is getting married to her best friend, Kate MacKenna, but an unlikely wedding crasher in the form of a medieval history professor spoils the affair, leaving a warning about an ancient clash between the two families.

Jordan doesn't know what to think, but when an encounter with family friend Noah Clayborne prompts her to do something spontaneous, she sets out to discover what the professor was talking about—only to find herself threatened. When she's set up as a murderer, she calls in Noah and her brother Nick for backup. Dusty research was never so perilous—or so sexy!

Skye O'Malley

Bertrice Small
Historical / 1984

"It was a perfect early summer day in the year 1555."

Small is A Name in romance writing, and this is arguably her best work.

✦ Small's O'Malley series has six books and the Skye Legacy series also has six. *Skye O'Malley* is the start.

Skye O'Malley is one of those romance sagas that many of us grew up reading. She's the epitome of the bold romance heroine we love: In the end, she dares to stand up to Elizabeth I, the queen of England.

Skye swashbuckles (there's no other way to put it) her way through sixteenth-century England and Algiers, becoming a woman of great wealth and power, taking on the occasional lover and spurning countless advances. Through it all, she never forgets Niall Burke, her first love (and her first lover). Time and again they are forced to turn away from each other—will they ever have their chance to be together?

Slightly Scandalous

Mary Balogh
Historical / 2003

> *"By the time she went to bed, Lady Freyja Bedwyn was in about as bad a mood as it was possible to be in."*

Slightly hard to put down, *Slightly Scandalous* is a delightful they're-made-for-each-other-and-when-will-they-figure-it-out? romp. If you're a fan of smart historicals, this goes on your nightstand.

✦ Not surprisingly, Balogh's two main influences as a writer were Jane Austen and Georgette Heyer.

✦ This is the third novel in Balogh's Bedwyn series about the six Bedwyn siblings. They make their first appearance in *A Summer to Remember*.

Freyja Bedwyn is no shrinking violet: Having four brothers has taught her how to hold her own. So when Joshua Moore, the Marquess of Hallmere, steals a kiss, she punches him. And that is the start of their beautiful relationship.

This is no opposites attract story. Both Freyja and Joshua are reckless, restless, and unwilling to settle down. That's why Joshua's plan seems so perfect: He wants to stop his aunt's matchmaking scheme. What if Freyja pretends to be his fiancée? He'll thwart his aunt's ambitions.

Freyja agrees to the plan, because what could possibly go wrong? Neither one of them expects to fall in love. . . .

79

Smoke and Mirrors

BARBARA MICHAELS
ROMANTIC SUSPENSE / 1989

> *"They came to him every night. They never moved; they never spoke. They just stood there, by the side of his bed, their grave dark eyes fixed on his face."*

Even though the book is over twenty years old and the technology is outdated, Erin's thrill at becoming privy to the inner workings of a political campaign still ignites the imagination and makes you want to sign up as a volunteer. This is one of the few romances where the heroine's work plays such a prominent role in the storyline.

* Michaels (under her real name, of course!) studied Egyptology at the Oriental Institute at the University of Chicago, earning her doctorate at age twenty-three!
* Be sure not to confuse Barbara Michaels's *Smoke and Mirrors* with Jayne Ann Krentz's (also great) *Smoke in Mirrors*!

Erin Hartsock moves to Washington, D.C., and takes a job with a friend of the family, Rosemary White Marshall, who is running for Senate. Erin gets a bracing look at how politics works and how campaigns are run, and instead of leaving her squeamish, she realizes she has finally found her life's calling—politics, for her, is a great adventure.

Nick, a member of the campaign staff, helps Erin learn the ropes, and the two of them begin a friendship that deepens into something more.

But a secret from Rosemary's past threatens them all—including Erin, who thinks she may be the murderer's next victim, and who, as the outsider, must convince the others that she's not the criminal.

Something Wicked

Jo Beverley
Historical / 2005

> "'I'm going to miss you.' Lady Elfled Malloren went into her twin brother's arms, determined not to cry."

A young lady raised among a bevy of brothers gives us a strong heroine we can identify with and cheer—no one takes advantage of this savvy miss.

✦ The Malloren series eventually climbed to total twelve books, as the author brought the family friends' romances into the circle as well.

The third in the series of five books about the Malloren family, *Something Wicked* focuses on the sister of the brood, Lady Elfled. Elf visits a friend in London and ends up alone in the big city—the perfect opportunity for a boxed-in twenty-four-year-old to rebel a little and kick up her heels. A disguise, of course, will protect her reputation. Her night out on the town, however, puts her in the right spot in Vauxhall Gardens to overhear the family's enemy, Fortitude Ware, Earl of Walgrave, embroiled in a Jacobean plot.

And as nature would have it, the bad blood between the Wares and the Mallorens has only helped heighten Fort's sex appeal for Elf. He, of course, is not a Jacobite out to betray the king, but a spy determined to save His Majesty. And when it comes crashing down on his head, who else but the Mallorens would charge in to save his hide?

The action in *Something Wicked* takes a back seat to the character development, as Elf has to build her self-confidence and decision-making skills away from her brothers' overprotective ways. The result

is a mature woman who understands she can't choke the life out of a love if it's truly love. Fort wrestles with a history that tortures him, and has to learn that a woman—previously a gender he considered playthings—can hold the key to redemption.

Son of the Morning

Linda Howard
Romantic suspense/time travel / 1997

"The stone walls of the secret underground chamber were cold and dank, the chill penetrating wool and linen and leather, going straight to the bone."

While the suspense level is commendable, readers respect and remember Grace for honoring her dead husband's love throughout the book without shortchanging her emotional ties to Niall. The balance is truly heartwarming.

✴ As wildly popular as *Son of the Morning* turned out to be, this remains Howard's only time-travel story.

✴ Howard's husband is a bass tournament fisherman and she often travels with him to remote locations—but she always makes sure to bring her laptop with her. Yet another perk of being an author—you can do it from anywhere!

Grace St. John merely stepped next door for some computer help from her geeky neighbor, and returns to witness her boss killing her husband and brother. Now on the run herself from both the murderer's long reach and law enforcement who have pinned the deaths on Grace, she finally pieces together that the bad guys are after a document regarding the Knights Templar that she unearthed.

Determined to find the key to why her life turned upside down, Grace races to finish translating the writings of Black Niall, written 700 years earlier to explain why this half-brother of Robert the Bruce became a Templar—and then rejected the brotherhood.

Niall and Grace eventually connect by mind meld in a parallel dimension (yes, this includes a physical relationship with the hunky Scot) until he is able to shoot through time to arrive in this century and help Grace find her justice and freedom. In between, the story is filled with rich details of a hunted woman (she breaks into houses by day to shower and steal clothes, and is almost caught while merely stocking up on necessities at a discount store) and the complicated intrigues of the fourteenth-century church. It's a rich read that deftly leaves no unanswered questions.

Sweet Savage Love

Rosemary Rogers
Historical / 1974

"Virginia Brandon was sixteen, that spring of 1862, and the thought of her first ball, now only two weeks away, was much more exciting than the letter that had arrived that morning from her father in America. She had not seen her father, after all, since she was still a baby—perhaps three or four years old; and although he sent money for her care every month through his bankers in San Francisco, his letters were infrequent."

Before Christian Grey and his Fifty Shades, there was Union soldier, gunslinger, crusader cowboy Steve Morgan dominating women with his bad boy ways. Masochistic, horny heroes everywhere owe Morgan a tip of the hat.

- The book's dedication to C. E. refers to Clint Eastwood, one of the masculine models Rogers built her hero Steve on.
- Rosemary Rogers is a romance pioneer—she was only the second author to have her books published in the now mainstream trade paperback format!
- Rogers lived in Ceylon (now Sri Lanka) until the age of twenty-seven. Since then, she has lived in London, Missouri, California, and Connecticut.

Virginia "Ginny" Brandon is the daughter of a U.S. Senator raised in Paris who finds herself trekking across the west with her stepmother as part of her father's business, which is a front for running a wagon-load of gold into Mexico to help the French military. Like most bored, pretty young women, she has an eye for their guide, Steve Morgan.

Steve is in this spot because he fought a duel with a high-ranking Union army officer over a prostitute during the Civil War, and won. His punishment was execution, until he took a sweet deal as an 1860s version of a U.S. undercover agent. Now sent to stop this financial windfall from reaching his enemies, he fakes an Indian raid. But when his lady love Ginny recognizes him, he kidnaps her as his human shield.

The pair fight and love through the wilderness, giving us the yardstick for the term "bodice-ripper" as they hide in whorehouses, pretend to be married when they drop in on friends, and eventually find a relationship strong enough for Ginny to trade sex with the enemy to save Steve's life.

They admit their love and marry in the end, but do not manage to live happily ever after until enduring more international intrigue and wild children in *Dark Fires* and *Sweet Love, Last Love*.

Thief of Dreams

MARY BALOGH
HISTORICAL / 1998

> *"The day was going to be an extraordinarily busy one.
> A birthday was to be celebrated—the one and twentieth
> of Lady Cassandra Havelock, Countess of Worthing."*

Balogh is upfront in telling the reader that Nigel's motivations aren't pure, so everyone keeps reading to find out how a bad guy is actually a victim.

✴ For years, Mary Balogh was published in every country but her homeland, the United Kingdom, which is reluctant to publish books from America, despite the fact the author is Welsh/Canadian.

Cassandra Havelock reaches her majority at age twenty-one blissfully happy. She is free of her guardians, free from the year of mourning for her father, and free to assume the title Countess of Worthington. Although the family wants to see her wed, she intends to hang on to her independence and enjoy this sweet setup alone.

Then Nigel Wetherby, Viscount Wroxley, arrives on the Kedelston doorstep to pay his respects to the daughter of a man he claims was a good friend. Cassandra welcomes this man and his stories of her father, and the attraction builds so fast, Nigel proposes within days and they are married within a fortnight.

They can't begin their happily ever after, however, until Cassandra unearths a myriad of distressing secrets, including the ones that involve her father, her position, and her new husband's nightmares and scarred back. Along the journey, she discovers a man who has learned to reject all emotional feeling as a survival mechanism and thus, can't admit he loves the countess he married. Then she must swallow her own betrayal to see if their relationship has a chance at healing. Overall, it's a meaty historical with a dark and unpredictable side that belies its Georgian time frame stereotypes.

84

This Is All I Ask

LYNN KURLAND
HISTORICAL / 1997

> *"The twigs snapped and popped in the hearth, sending a spray of sparks across the stone. One of the three girls huddled there stamped out the live embers, then leaned into the circle again, her eyes wide with unease. 'Is it true he's the Devil's own?' "Tis the rumor,' the second whispered with a furtive nod."*

An early Kurland, we dare you to try to finish this one without a hanky in hand.

✦ Kurland is a trained classical musician. She plays the cello and the piano, and she sings.
✦ *This Is All I Ask* is the seventh title in Kurland's De Piaget series.
✦ Almost all of the main characters in Lynn Kurland's books belong to one of three families: the Macleods, the McKinnons, and the de Piagets.

Gillian of Warewick has been terribly abused by her father, so when he arranges her marriage to Christopher of Blackmour, she expects the worst. She has heard the rumors that Christopher practices black magic, but once they're married, she finds he is a much different man than she expected. He was, in fact, a friend of her brother's (the brother died young) and has made a promise to care for her, knowing how brutal her father was.

Christopher has suffered as much in his own way as she has in hers; his first wife betrayed him, resulting in his blindness; he is wary of love and of the way it can cloud one's thinking. Both of them must grow to trust themselves and each other before love can blossom.

It's no wonder this is a fan favorite.

Top Five Love Songs

Put these on your playlist, and you'll be in the mood for love!

1. "Wonderful Tonight" by Eric Clapton

2. "I Will Always Love You" by Whitney Houston

3. "Love Me Tender" by Elvis Presley

4. "I Don't Want to Miss a Thing" by Aerosmith

5. "Be Without You" by Mary J. Blige

This Rough Magic

MARY STEWART
ROMANTIC SUSPENSE / 1964

> *"'And if it's a boy,' said Phyllida cheerfully, 'we'll call him Prospero.'"*

Exotic scene-setting and lyrical prose make for a captivating read.

- ✦ The title comes from the Shakespeare play *The Tempest*, in which the wizard Prospero gives up his magic with the announcement, "This rough magic I here abjure."
- ✦ In 1964, the same year *This Rough Magic* was published, Mary Stewart's novel *The Moon-Spinners* was adapted into a Hollywood film starring Hayley Mills, Eli Wallach, and Peter McEnery.

When London actress Lucy Waring has a show fold under her and nothing on the table to follow it, she heads to her pregnant sister's summer home in Corfu, where she finds herself almost immediately ensnared in an intrigue.

Talented musician Max Gale is doing his best to protect his father, the famous actor Julian Gale, who has taken to drinking too much since the death of his wife and daughter. Julian has sought solace at Corfu, a place with some history for him—his godchildren, Spiro and Miranda live here and work for Lucy's sister. The island has the added attraction of being, he argues to anyone who will listen, the setting for Shakespeare's *The Tempest*.

Max strikes Lucy as suspicious and arrogant, but finds herself charmed by his father (think Laurence Olivier), with whom she, of course, shares a career path (if not similar success!).

Photojournalist Godfrey Manning is also on Corfu, completing a book project, and he hires Spiro to do some work for him. When Spiro

is apparently killed off the coast of Albania during a boating accident, Godfrey seems devastated and of course, Miranda, Spiro's sister, is inconsolable.

But the tragedy isn't just a tragedy—something is going on under the surface. Lucy befriends a dolphin in the waters near her sister's home—and someone tries to kill it. Why? Even more frightening, Lucy stumbles on a dead smuggler in the cove. Who killed him—and why?

Lucy isn't an amateur sleuth trying to dig up answers. She's a young British woman with a strong sense of responsibility and duty, and it is those characteristics that wind up putting her smack in the middle of the danger. She doesn't know whom to trust—but one of the men she cares about is a murderer.

Top Five Romantic Destinations

Bon voyage!

1. Rome, Italy

2. Paris, France

3. Santa Fe, New Mexico

4. Barcelona, Spain

5. Wichita, Kansas—okay, okay, just kidding! How about Maui, Hawaii?

86

To Have and to Hold

PATRICIA GAFFNEY
HISTORICAL / 1995

> *"But it is too rude of you, Bastian! How can you send me away like this? Don't you like Lili anymore?"*

Darker than Gaffney's other novels, with a morally ambiguous hero, this is a fan favorite.

✦ Patricia Gaffney worked as a high school English teacher and a court reporter before becoming a writer. It wasn't until she was diagnosed with breast cancer in 1984 that she decided to give her dream of being an author a try.

✦ After getting her start in romance, Gaffney began writing women's fiction, including her first bestseller, *The Saving Graces*.

✦ *To Have and to Hold* is the second book in the Wyckerley trilogy.

Rachel Wade is wrongfully convicted of killing her husband and sent to prison. Released ten years later, she has nothing left and no one to turn to. She's arrested for vagrancy, and the Viscount D'Aubrey, Sebastian Verlaine, cynically and selfishly offers to employ her as his "housekeeper," an obvious, in this case, euphemism for "mistress."

There is nothing remotely endearing or loveable about Sebastian at the beginning, and he torments Rachel in cruel ways. Their relationship is ugly and sad. Sebastian is debauched, Rachel beaten down.

But this is a story of transformation, and that is why readers keep coming back to it. How Sebastian learns to become kinder and how Rachel learns to stand on her own two feet again make for riveting reading. The characters are realistic, their trials are difficult to endure, but they are both able to find a way to connect, first as friends, and then as people who love each other with their whole hearts.

Touch Not the Cat

Mary Stewart
Romantic suspense / 1976

"My lover came to me on the last night in April, with a message and warning that sent me home to him. Put like that, it sounds strange, though it is exactly what happened."

Touch Not the Cat shows Stewart at the height of her suspenseful powers. Later novels are quieter and less thrilling, though still lyrical and well worth reading. This, though, is a superb balance of suspense and romance.

✦ Mary Stewart is best known for her Merlin series, a series of historicals with fantasy elements based on Arthurian legend.

Bryony Ashley's father dies under mysterious circumstances, and she returns home to Ashley Court, and the Ashley cousins. Significant to the story is the psychic link Bryony has to one of her cousins—she's not sure which one, for he isn't willing to tell her just yet. By the time the story concludes, it's clear why her psychic lover didn't reveal himself earlier, but throughout, his unwillingness to share this one vital thing chafes on her.

Eventually she decides she knows which of her cousins she shares this connection with, and since she loves and trusts her psychic partner, she loves and trusts the man she thinks he is. That sets her off on a path that ends in mortal jeopardy.

In the end, it's the man she has loved and trusted all along who turns out to be her psychic connection—and they become lovers physically as well as psychically.

True Confessions

RACHEL GIBSON
CONTEMPORARY / 2001

> *"There were two universal truths in Gospel, Idaho. First, God had done His best work when He'd created the Sawtooth Wilderness Area. And except for the unfortunate incident of '95, Gospel had always been heaven on earth."*

Romantic comedy meets sexy romance. Yum.

✦ *True Confessions* won a coveted RITA award from the Romance Writers of America.

The townspeople in Gospel, Idaho, have a tendency to blame all earthly ills on California, so when Hope Spencer, an LA-based tabloid reporter shows up, they're a little skeptical. "They" include sheriff Dylan Taber who doesn't think she'll stay more than a week in their little town.

Hope is looking for something to write about—she's been dealing with writer's block for months. And she definitely finds it in Gospel.

Dylan's living down a wild past. He's mature now. Got a son to be a role model for. He is not going to do anything foolish with Hope. Nope. No way, no how.

These two opposites become unlikely friends, but they both have secrets. And the only way they'll ever be able to live happily ever after is if they both make some true confessions.

Twilight

STEPHENIE MEYER
PARANORMAL / 2005

> *"My mother drove me to the airport with the windows rolled down. It was seventy-five degrees in Phoenix, the sky a perfect, cloudless blue. I was wearing my favorite shirt—sleeveless, white eyelet lace; I was wearing it as a farewell gesture. My carry-on item was a parka."*

Though Crimson doesn't publish young adult novels, we'd make an exception for *Twilight*. It's impossible to discuss the top romance books without including the phenomenon that is The Twilight Saga. Not only has the series earned billions of dollars in sales, been translated into thirty-seven languages, and been adapted into five blockbuster films, it is largely responsible for the recent boom in the young adult genre, and even inspired another international literary sensation—E. L. James's erotic novel *Fifty Shades of Grey*, which originally began as *Twilight* fan fiction!

- Author Stephenie Meyer had never written a book before *Twilight*, and says that the idea for the story came to her in a dream. Upon awaking, she immediately began writing the scene she'd seen (which is now Chapter 13 in the book). Less than three months later, the manuscript was completed.
- The four-book Twilight Saga has been adapted into five feature films, the first four of which have grossed more than $2 billion—so far!
- Stephenie Meyer is also the author of *The Host*, an adult science fiction novel about body-snatching aliens.

The first book in Stephenie Meyer's wildly successful Twilight Saga, *Twilight* tells the story of Bella Swan, a seventeen-year-old high school

outcast who moves from Arizona to a small, rainy town in Washington state to live with her father. But soon after starting at her new school, she meets the mysterious Cullen family and realizes that life in Forks is going to be anything but dull.

The pale, quiet, gorgeous Edward Cullen takes an interest in Bella immediately, and when he saves her, using what can only be described as super speed and super strength, from an oncoming out-of-control van, their lives become dangerously intertwined. Bella learns Edward—and his entire family—are vampires. He can read minds—everyone's except hers—and lusts after her blood, even though he and his entire family have sworn off human blood, instead subsisting only on the blood of animals. Still, the love between them is too strong to fight. They begin a relationship, even though he could kill her at any moment.

But when Bella goes to a baseball game with the Cullen family and catches the interest of a sadistic tracker vampire named James, Bella—and her family—are in a whole new kind of danger.

Until You

JUDITH MCNAUGHT
HISTORICAL / 1994

> *"Propped upon a mountain of satin pillows amid rumpled bed linens, Helene Devernay surveyed his bronzed, muscular torso with an appreciative smile as Stephen David Elliott Westmoreland, Earl of Langford, Baron of Ellingwood, Fifth Viscount Hargrove, Viscount Ashbourne, shrugged into the frilled shirt he'd tossed over the foot of the bed last night."*

A mistaken identity and amnesia story all rolled into one—no one but McNaught could have pulled this off.

✦ McNaught has been called the inventor of the modern Regency.

This sequel to *Whitney, My Love* tells the story of Stephen Westmoreland, the brother of that novel's hero. American Sheridan Bromleigh, a paid companion, is escorting Charise Lancaster to London for her wedding to the man her father has arranged for her to marry. But Charise elopes, leaving Sheridan in a bind. Stephen comes to meet the ship to explain that Charise's fiancé has died, and he mistakes Sheridan for Charise.

She is injured on the pier and suffers amnesia as a result. She awakens in Westmoreland's home, with everyone thinking she's Charise. The doctor tells Stephen to pretend to be Charise's fiancé so that the shock of learning her fiancé is dead does not do further damage to her health.

Sheridan and Stephen come to care for each other, but then Charise shows up, demanding to know why Sheridan is pretending to be her, and Stephen believes that Sheridan has misled him all along. Sheridan isn't all that happy about being duped either, and it takes some intervention by Stephen's family to make sure all ends well.

The Viscount Who Loved Me

JULIA QUINN
HISTORICAL / 2006

> *"Anthony Bridgerton had always known he would die young. Oh, not as a child. Young Anthony had never had cause to ponder his own mortality. His early years had been a young boy's perfection, right from the very day of his birth."*

Families in a Julia Quinn novel are wonderful things, full of supportive, loving people who ensure a plot won't lean on dastardly lies from wicked, jealous mothers and other romance clichés.

✦ Fans of the Bridgerton series know that the parents named their children in alphabetical order: Anthony, Benedict, Colin, Daphne, Eloise, Francesca, Gregory, and Hyacinth.

✦ Julia Quinn once considered becoming a doctor. Just as she was trying to decide which medical school to go to (she got into both Columbia and Yale . . . smarty pants) she got a call from her agent and found out her first two novels were in hot demand by some pretty big publishing houses. That should be the end of the story, right? Wrong. It took her several months of actually going to medical school for her to realize that she was meant to be a writer, after all. We could have told you that, Julia!

Kate Sheffield shares her first London season with her younger half-sister—platinum blond Edwina, considered the family beauty—and finds herself concentrating more zealously on protecting her sibling's reputation than her own. After all, if Edwina makes the right match,

the Sheffields can hope to end their cash flow problems and take their proper place in Society. Kate's idea of Mr. Right for herself is as vague as "a kind-hearted man."

Certainly, affirmed rake Anthony Bridgerton doesn't fit the bill for either one of them despite his viscount title, but sure as gun's iron, he shows up to call on Edwina, sending Kate into a flurry of sharp-tongued barbs to barricade her innocent sister. This sets Kate and Anthony at deep odds with one another, complete with bickering, from the minute she opens the door.

What the infamous *Lady Whistledown's Society Papers* gossip rag can't know to spill about Bridgerton's wifely pursuit is the young man figures he'll die at a young age—his father, after all, cocked up his toes at age thirty-eight—so he wants to get this heir affair behind him before he departs for clouds and harps. He needs someone attractive, pleasant, and smart, but who leaves him with no special feelings beyond the lust he needs to reproduce.

So his mother, hoping to help her eldest son's cause, invites the Sheffield sisters to their country home, where Kate relents to let him marry little sister. But before she can relay the happy news, the two are innocently caught in a compromising situation, thanks to a bee sting, and Society's rules and reputation threats force Kate to stand at the altar as the Bridgerton bride. As she falls in love with her accidental husband, she must convince him theirs is a relationship worth living for.

What Happens in London

JULIA QUINN
HISTORICAL / 2009

> *"By the age of twelve, Harry Valentine possessed two bits of knowledge that made him rather unlike other boys of his class in England of the early nineteenth century."*

Quinn's trademark wit is on full display here.

* In 2001, Quinn appeared on the game show *The Weakest Link* and won a $79,000 jackpot.
* Quinn is the youngest member of the Romance Writers of America Hall of Fame.
* *What Happens in London* is the second book in Quinn's Bevelstroke series.

Olivia Bevelstroke is told that her new neighbor, Sir Harry Valentine, killed his fiancée. She doesn't really believe it, but she does do a little spying—and discovers that whatever the truth about the dead fiancée, he is indeed up to something covert.

Harry works for the War Office, but only in the most boring of ways. He's a translator, not a spy, but he knows when someone's spying on him. And then he's enlisted to spy back, because Olivia's Russian friend may not have the country's best interests at heart.

Though they don't like each other at first, they soon discover that a mutual attraction can lead to love.

This lighthearted, fun romp ends with satisfaction all around.

Where Roses Grow Wild

PATRICIA CABOT
HISTORICAL / 1998

> *"Lord Edward Rawlings, second and only surviving son of the late duke of Rawlings, was unhappy."*

Warm and witty, this charming Victorian-era historical (Cabot's debut) is a treasure.

* Patricia Cabot gained fame later as herself, Meg Cabot, the author of the young adult Princess Diaries series.
* After Patricia's first manuscript was rejected, her grandmother gave her some sage advice: "You're not a hundred-dollar bill, not everyone is going to like you." Based on that advice, Patricia kept trying, and *Where Roses Grow Wild* was published five years later. Ironically, she published it under a pen name so her grandmother wouldn't find out she was writing "smutty" novels!

Edward, Lord Rawlings, learns that his dead brother has a son, a ten-year-old who is the rightful Duke of Rawlings. Edward goes off to find the boy and discovers him in the care of Pegeen MacDougal, the boy's aunt, whom he has to persuade to let the boy take up his inheritance.

Pegeen is not afraid of voicing her opinion, and she's something of a surprise to Edward, who can't fit her into a convenient category. He's a bit of a rake and accustomed to women of dubious morality, not women who have a social conscience and aren't that interested in letting him kiss them.

But eventually Pegeen decides that kissing Edward isn't that bad. . . .

Top Five Romantic Date Destinations

Tired of the same old dinner-and-a-movie? Try changing it up a bit.

1. The beach, any beach. Well, almost any beach.

2. A park, garden, or other natural environment.

3. A theme park, amusement park, or arcade.

4. A sporting event—or play a sport of your own. You get the idea.

5. Couple's spa day! You're welcome.

White Hot

SANDRA BROWN
ROMANTIC SUSPENSE / 2004

> *"Some say that if he was going to kill himself, he couldn't have picked a better day for it."*

Like the title says, this one is white hot—suspenseful and sexy.

* Sandra Brown started her writing career on her husband's dare! With more than 80 million copies of her books in print today, we bet she's glad she did!
* As if she isn't already busy enough, Sandra Brown is also a TV presenter, having guest-hosted episodes of truTV's *Murder By the Book* and Investigation Discovery's *Hardcover Mysteries*.

Sayre Lynch escaped from her terrible father and swore to herself she'd never return to Destiny, Louisiana, where her family owns an iron foundry and controls the town's fate. But after her younger brother kills himself, she finds herself back in Destiny for his funeral—and asking questions about his last days. Her corrupt family doesn't want her looking too closely into anything—and they've hired Beck Merchant, a handsome lawyer, to keep trouble off their backs.

Sayre is attracted to Beck even as he gets in the way of her finding answers about her brother's death.

When Sayre discovers that her brother's death might not be suicide but murder, and that her family might well be involved in his murder as well as its cover-up, the stakes get even higher—and her relationship with Beck gets even hotter.

Can they work together to discover what happened to her brother? Or is Beck just trying to keep her from the truth?

Whitney, My Love

JUDITH MCNAUGHT
HISTORICAL / 1985

> *"As their elegant travelling chaise rocked and swayed along the rutted country road, Lady Anne Gilbert leaned her cheek against her husband's shoulder and heaved a long, impatient sigh. 'Another whole house until we arrive, and already the suspense is positively gnawing at me. I keep wondering what Whitney will be like now that she's grown up.'"*

As a debut novel for McNaught, *Whitney, My Love* was an emotionally elevated bodice-ripper that eschewed the usual pirates and outlaws in favor of a duke.

- ✦ *Whitney, My Love* received the *Romantic Times* award for Best New Historical in 1985, which propelled sales and made it an instant classic.
- ✦ McNaught rereleased the book in 2000 with a longer ending and a few changed scenes—the hero stops short of beating and raping the heroine in the do-over.

Whitney Stone puts the wild in wild child, living out her impulsive tomboy ways and embarrassing herself repeatedly in attempts to get the object of her fifteen-year-old crush, Paul Sevarin, to notice her. Eventually, her widowed father packs his rebellious daughter off to relatives in France, hoping someone can apply a coat of social polish on his daughter.

Whitney does blossom under her aunt's instructions to become the toast of French society and a perfect matrimony match for Clayton Westmoreland, the family's new neighbor back home, who, behind the scenes, makes all the arrangements for a trip down the aisle. But Whitney, unaware she is betrothed, still harbors fantasies of charming the elegant Paul, despite the Duke of Claymore's flattering and steady courtship, Regency style. When she finally gets her chance to elope with the man of her dreams, she realizes Paul's intentions aren't exactly pure, and puts an end to their relationship. Ah, her heart is free to give to the man who appreciates her.

But misunderstandings and overheard rumors pull Whitney and Clayton apart three heartbreaking times before they finally leave the reader with satisfied sighs as Whitney (and their son) survive a premature delivery and the two star-crossed lovers finally get this trust thing right.

Wildfire at Midnight

MARY STEWART
ROMANTIC SUSPENSE / 1956

> *"In the first place, I suppose, it was my parents' fault for giving me a silly name like Gianetta. It is a pretty enough name in itself, but it conjures up pictures of delectable and slightly overblown ladies in Titian's less respectable canvases, and, though I admit I have the sort of coloring that might have interested that Venetian master, I happen to be the rather inhibited product of an English country rectory."*

Although an early novel, this one showcases Stewart's incomparable style, and features a divorced couple as the main protagonists, a very unusual approach.

✱ Stewart herself called this a "closed-room" mystery—only a small group of people (who know each other) could have done the murder—and the process of solving the mystery serves to illuminate the characters as their romantic relationship develops. That sets this novel apart from any ordinary mystery.

Gianetta Brook needs a vacation—from her work, from England, from her family, and from her ex-husband. Gianetta, a model, is not and never was the sophisticate her husband Nicholas Drury believed her to be, and Gianetta was, at a decade younger than her husband, too young to understand Nicholas's wartime scars. Thus, their brief marriage has ended.

A trip to the remote Isle of Skye is just the place to help Gianetta escape her troubles. But Skye is not remote enough: Gianetta's ex-husband just happens to be there, too (a coincidence explained at the end with the author's usual charm).

Having to share the same hotel with Nicholas would be bad enough, but someone has killed a girl, and the evidence points to Nicholas.

Gianetta must decide if she believes Nicholas is capable of such a thing, and they must both set aside their masks in order to love again.

The Windflower

LAURA LONDON
HISTORICAL / 1984

"Merry Patricia Wilding was sitting on a cobblestone wall, sketching three rutabagas and daydreaming about the unicorn."

Though London had only a brief career, *The Windflower* is a much-loved fan favorite.

✦ Laura London is the pen name of the author team of Sharon and Tom Curtis.

When Merry Wilding is accidentally abducted by pirates, the roller-coaster ride starts. How is one accidentally abducted? The pirate Devon Crandall thinks she knows something about the people who killed his sister, and he's out for revenge. But Merry doesn't know anything about it.

For many thousands of words, Merry tries to escape the pirate ship while trying not to fall madly in love with the devilishly handsome Devon.

The vivid characters (including secondary characters) and the beautiful prose style make this one stand head and shoulders above other romances of its time.

Winterwood

DOROTHY EDEN
ROMANTIC SUSPENSE / 1967

"From the moment of leaving the hotel the enchantment of the night had grown."

Writing around the same time as Mary Stewart, Eden also was a master of taut psychological suspense—but sadly, her novels are not nearly as well-known now. A forgotten master.

✦ Dorothy Eden also wrote novels under the name Mary Paradise.

Lavinia Hurst goes to Venice to escape the publicity following a trial she's been involved in. She becomes involved with the Meryon family, who are there to bring an elderly relation back to their home, Winterwood.

They hire Lavinia as a paid companion to their crippled daughter, Flora. Daniel, the father, is deeply attractive to Lavinia, but his wife (Charlotte) is cruel and conniving. When Flora inherits a fortune, the intrigue heats up.

Is that enough plot twists to keep you guessing how this will wrap up?

The Wives of Bowie Stone

MAGGIE OSBORNE
HISTORICAL / 1994

> *"Sheriff Gaine squinted up at the gallows and thumbed back his hat. 'Well boys, this is your lucky day.'"*

Only Osborne could redeem two such unredeemable characters—in the same book!

✷ Osborne also wrote romances under the name Margaret St. George.

Rosie Mulvehey suffered horrifically at the hands of her stepfather. She's become an alcoholic and is not at all interested in marriage. She doesn't need love; what she needs is a ranch hand.

Bowie Stone is a former Army captain (dishonorably discharged) and a convicted murderer.

According to local custom, a man can escape the death penalty by marrying a local woman. Rosie agrees to save Bowie from hanging, thereby getting a husband and a ranch hand. She's more interested in the ranch hand. Bowie works to clear his name and to get his wife to trust him.

But Bowie doesn't happen to mention that he already has a wife. . . .

You won't be able to put this down without first finding out how all three of them get their happily ever after.

The Wrong Hostage

ELIZABETH LOWELL

ROMANTIC SUSPENSE / 2006

> *"The phone rang four times before Judge Grace Silva pulled her head out of the legal documents she was reviewing. 'Maybe it's Ted. Finally.'"*

Action, danger, romance—Lowell later in her career is just as riveting as she was in the beginning.

✦ Lowell has also published several successful science fiction and nonromantic suspense novels. She often collaborates with her husband of more than forty years, Evan Maxwell, and together they have published several suspense novels under the name Ann Maxwell (Lowell's real name).

Judge Grace Silva pulled herself up out of poverty through hard work and determination, never once losing sight of the brass ring. If that didn't leave much room for love or laughter, so be it. She's an upholder of the law, period. She upholds the law with the same determination that pulled her out of her nightmarish beginnings.

Joe Faroe has paid the price for believing in the law. Now he knows it's just a thing made by humans, too often corrupt, and that sometimes it needs to be bent. After a friend tries to kill him, he retires from everything.

Until Grace comes to him for help. Her son has been kidnapped and Joe is the only one who can get him back. If only Joe didn't hate her. . . .

Top Five Romantic Movies

With a happily ever after, of course!

1. *An Officer and a Gentleman*

2. *Bull Durham*

3. *His Girl Friday*

4. *When Harry Met Sally . . .*

5. *While You Were Sleeping*

The Authors Who Make Us Swoon

CRIMSON
ROMANCE

Crimson Romance is the romance eBook imprint of F+W Media, Inc. Crimson Romance is the place to find heartwarming, smart romances in your favorite genres—including contemporary romance, historical romance, paranormal romance, romantic suspense, and spicy romance! You'll find fresh takes on classic themes, new themes that will delight and excite you, heroes you'll fall in love with, and heroines you'd want to meet in real life.

Visit us at *www.crimsonromance.com*.

CPSIA information can be obtained
at www.ICGtesting.com
Printed in the USA
BVOW09s1803060817
491242BV00001B/1/P